Gerti's War

A Journal of Life Inside the Wehrmacht

By
Lois Buchter

Gerti's War is a true story taken from Gerti's journal and stories relayed to her cousin. For the writing of this story however, some minor creative license was taken in its telling. This story relays the stories of how civilians suffered and the manner in which lives were affected by difficult times, which happened to coincide during a difficult period in history. All references to events, organizations, governments, persons, or locals are intended only to relay the experiences and feelings of Gerti during her life as they affect her story.

Copyright © 2017 by Lois Buchter

Library of Congress Control Number: 2020935264

All rights are reserved. No part of this book may be reproduced in whole or in part by any means without prior written permission, except by a reviewer who may quote brief passages in a review to be printed in a newspaper, magazine, or journal. These rights also pertain to any form of electronic transmission, copying or uploading to free download sites. Please discourage piracy.

Published by Evershine Press, Inc.
1971 W Lumsden Rd #209
Brandon, FL 33511

ISBN: 978-0-9975108-4-3
eBook ISBN: 978-0-9975108-5-0

First edition: 2020

Printed in the United States of America

Table of Contents

Dedication i

GERTI'S WAR 1

Chapter 2 – March 1938 19

Chapter 3 – September 1938 29

Chapter 4 – June 1940 47

Chapter 5 – February 1941 55

Chapter 6 – May 1941 65

Chapter 7 – November 1941 87

Chapter 8 – December 1941 95

Chapter 9 – February 1942 105

Chapter 10 – September 1942 131

Chapter 11 – July 1943 147

Chapter 12 – May 1945 179

Chapter 13 – September 1945 193

Chapter 14 – April 1948 209

Chapter 15 – PART TWO – JULY 1992 221

Chapter 16 – December 1992 235

Chapter 17 – February 1993 251

About the Author 265

Dedication

Gerti's War wouldn't have happened without the urging and support of Jack R. Tarvin, Jr., and Mark Murphy, past editor with the Fort Worth Star-Telegram. Both of these incredible men kept urging me on as I started my literary journey. I was blessed to have time with both of them.

You truly grow when you accomplish something you thought only a dream.

I humbly bow to those team members of the writing groups I attended. I thank you all.

Thank you to my children, Eric and Jill, as well. They had to put up with me during the weeks where my head was in Berlin, and rationing and food shortages filled my dialogue.

And, finally, thank you to Gerti and Sigi, who taught me the real meaning of love.

GERTI'S WAR

September 1937 – Near Arnbach, Black Forest, Germany

"Tag, you're it," said Rolf as he hits me on the shoulder and disappears into the shadowed canopy in front of me. Ahead, the darkened floor of the forest lightens as the meadow comes into view. Sunbeams streak through intertwined Linden branches illuminating a hidden footpath. Thick caramel-colored trunks guard the majestic grove in front of me.

"Rolf!" I call out, but the words melt into the air. Long braids flying behind me, I take off running in Rolf's direction.

We know these woods with our eyes closed. We have played the same game for years.

Papa called out, "Don't go far." I heard him but doubted Rolf did. At fourteen, I adore my older brother and want to do everything he did.

Once, just once, I must beat him to the Madonna shrine. My muscles pump faster and faster as I dive under branches and leap over bushes. Holding my blue jumper up over my knees gives my legs the room they need. To win, I must take a short cut. My chest burns, and I feel scratches on my calves as I blaze a new trail through the brush. A broken branch slices cleanly into my arm. I don't even feel it. Dashing through, I spy a raspberry bush loaded with fruit. In the glade ahead, I can see the small roof of the chapel covering the shrine. It is clear.

I focus on the hallowed enclave at the back of the meadow.

Out of the corner of my eye, I catch movement to my left. Rolf runs like a panther—swift and with purpose. His long legs have ample room to move in his loose shorts. Knee socks keep his legs free of scratches. He moves in a blur.

My legs and chest burn with exertion, reaching my arms out, I lean toward the shrine willing my arms to grow.

"I will win, Gerti," he calls out and then laughs easily.

Lois Buchter

His feet barely touch the ground as he sprints. I can hear muffled giggles as he begins to taste victory.

I don't respond to him. I ache to get enough air into my lungs. It will be close—closer than it ever has been before.

Blinking back tears, I reach out further, fingers spread wide. I can hear my heart pounding in my ears. One more jump and I will be there, but Rolf has taken the clear path with no obstacles before him. Only inches ahead, he touches first.

He cheers out *"Hauptkerle!"* (I am what I am – King!) Bending to pick up a large stick off the path, he holds it up with one hand and carries it like a scepter. Sweat marks his white shirt with long streaks. Honoring me, he lowers his head and bows deeply before me. He raises his head and smiles. I catch a twinkle in his eye as he says, "Next time, Gerti, maybe next time. You are getting faster." Skipping, he takes off back down the path.

Falling back against the carpet of pine needles around me, I slump down, and pull my knees toward my chest. I mutter out loud, "I can't believe he didn't even look winded." Inhaling the heavy pine scent and closing my eyes for a few minutes, I listen to the canopy above sway in the breeze. I try to match my breathing to the melody the trees call out to me and don't hear Papa and Rolf approach.

"Gertie, Rolf tells me you almost won this time. *Das ist gut,*" says Papa. He drops his backpack on the floor next to me.

Rummaging through the contents of the bag, he pulls out a small carving Rolf made at a meeting and a bit of Mutti's blueberry cake, she has carefully wrapped in brown paper. Papa sighs as he kneels by the wooden altar at the shrine and closes his eyes. I watch his thick short mustache dip and rise with each breath as he says a prayer. He leaves the offering of cake and the carving in front of the worn Madonna statue before sitting down beside me.

Rolf doesn't waste any time digging through the bag. When he looks back at us his cheeks bulge with the rest of the blueberry cake. He had just eaten a huge meal and two helpings of cake at lunch. At sixteen, Rolf's appetite causes much laughter in my family. Humming a little song, he grabs one of my long braids to brush the crumbs off his face.

I try to get away from him by scooting over closer to Father.

With a loud "Harrumph", Rolf sits down next to me and uses my braid to make a mustache on his upper lip. Secretly I love his attention.

Papa ignores Rolf's foolishness. He leans back on his hands and begins to sing. His massive chest expands, and his song lifts to the horizon of pine above us. Papa's voice is a source of wonder for me. His tenor voice, always perfect in pitch and volume, reverberates into my being. He can hold a note forever.

As lead vocalist in the men's choir group, he constantly rehearses. Today's selection includes an Old Russian folk song- one of Grandmother Oma's favorites. The song starts out slowly.

The words drip off the ocean of green around us. As the volume of the song rises, so do Rolf and me.

We danced around the small shrine. Rolf grabs me around the waist and we spun. Faster and faster, we move as the song increases in tempo. Three times the song goes back to a slow and quiet melody before it returns to the electric pace. We muffle our laughter against Papa's chest as we collapse in a pile on top of him. He lets out a loud belly laugh and holds us in a strong embrace. His brown eyes pool with tears of happiness. I command time to stand still, right now, right here. My old Papa is still in there somewhere. I haven't heard him laugh in months.

He kisses my brow and murmurs "my Gertie," before he releases me.

Papa stirs me from my daydreaming. He hands me a jar to gather berries and asks Rolf to find mushrooms. After cleaning the bushes by the shrine, I head for the edge of the forest where the berry plants are more numerous. From this vantage point, I can see our small village of Achenbach in the valley below. A cluster of cream-colored houses with red tile roofs stands just past the round church. Long shadows cast by the late afternoon sun spread like fingers across the town center. Farming fields of golden wheat and rye circle the edge of our village. Apple and cherry orchards stretch across the southern end of the clearing.

It's a very neat and orderly town. "Just so," as Oma would say.

To my left and down the other side of the hill is the larger town of Nuremburg with the River Enz meandering through the valley. It is very pretty with tall steeples, narrow streets, and buildings with murals from the past. A round fountain stands in the middle of town close to Papa's office where he works as a tax accountant for the district. This city is many times larger than our small village.

Rolf and I attend the upper school together in Nuremburg.

He will be going to University soon, after he passes his exams.

He finished his mandatory two-week political Summer Camp last summer. Papa says all they try to do is force a single-minded point of view on the youth, and we were all glad to have him home again.

Shortly after coming back, Rolf made the mistake of quoting a slogan from the camp, "Never doubt the Fuhrer – the Fuhrer is always right." Papa went into a rage. He spits on the ground when he hears that political rubbish. Down in the cellar, he talked with Rolf when he came home from camp and re-educated him into our family values.

Papa doesn't trust Hitler. I don't either.

Rolf ran up behind me. "Boo!" He chuckles over the prank and kisses me on the cheek. I slap his hand as he tries to grab some of the raspberries I gathered.

Pulling away, I step over to Papa giving him the berries.

"Glad to see you filled your jar." He holds it up to the light inspecting the clusters before putting it into the backpack. Rolf shows off his basket filled with mushrooms.

"So, tell me about your week. He holds my hand and starts a slow walk out of the woods. How is school?" Papa asks in his deep no-nonsense voice. Rolf takes off chasing a wild rabbit through the brush.

"Fine, I guess."

"Fine? That's all you have to say? How are your studies of Goethe? Are you still studying Faust?"

"Yes, I made good marks on the last testing. Faust is one of my favorites."

"I had trouble with the memorization, and I could be easily distracted by the pretty girl on the first row--back in the olden days," he says.

"Papa! Are you teasing me?" I frowned, but I quickly smiled.

"I enjoy the memorizing, but Marta has trouble with some of the passages. I told her I'd help her."

He nods his approval and smiles. His eyes shine as he winks at me.

"Thank you for singing today," I said. "It is perfect."

He stops walking for a moment and turns toward me. "Next time let's make Mutti come with us. She doesn't relax enough."

His face lights up as he speaks about my mother. He leans close to me and lightly touches my nose. "Ta-tooch, you look a lot like your Mutti."

We resume our walk. Many minutes pass before I asked, "Papa, why do we have to march so much at the meetings?"

Required attendance at the BDM (*Bund Deutscher Mädel-The German Maiden Group*) meetings takes several hours on Wednesdays for *Heimatabend* and most of my Saturday afternoons for sports and crafts. What used to be our girl-scouting group is now something totally different. They fill our time with memorizing political songs, marches, and sports, rather than German history, theater, traditions and crafts. My best friend, Marta, and I have almost completed all the badges of achievement when everything changed.

Now our group marches at the beginning of the meetings at the school and through the town at the end of the meetings. I like the community services, such as helping the needy and the home improvement programs, but I still don't like politics. All our friends must be involved with the youth programs, as it is required.

"I don't know Gerti, I just don't know," he says as he squeezes my hand.

"Frau Launsmann says I can't get into university without my BDM membership."

5

Lois Buchter

"I haven't heard a directive regarding the girls' program, but I do know Rolf has to be a member in good standing with the Hitler Youth to be accepted into the architecture program." Rolf will be a great architect someday. Father sighs and puts his arm around my shoulder. He smells like the forest and Bay Rum cologne. I turn my head toward his shirt and inhale deeply.

Rolf and one of his friends walk with Marta and I to the meetings each Saturday. They do lots of marching as well, but Rolf enjoys the relay races. He usually wins. Almost every Saturday he boasts, "I can run like the wind!" and comes home sweaty and dirty after each meeting. They met in a Hitler Jugend clubhouse in an old bus on the edge of town, but Papa makes Rolf remove his armband before entering the house as a reminder of family loyalty.

Walking past the church, in the distance our home sits across from the elementary school. Happy noises of young children on their way to school fill the yard every morning.

Our two-story house has a large circular room off to one side on the main floor and that's where I do my homework. A huge garden fills most of the back yard. Red geraniums plants are scattered in containers outside. Standing in front of the house, the open windows in the kitchen make the lace curtains dance in the air, catching on the flowers in the planter. Looking like a big tongue saying "Ahhh," my feather bed lays on the windowsill on the upper floor beckoning me.

Turning the corner, Marta runs up to us and asks permission for me to join her at the cemetery. Papa agrees, and we skip across the street and through the park.

"Gerti, I've been waiting for you for hours" Her cheeks flush, and she speaks so fast I can hardly understand her. We finished our dinner. Papa said we can work on our homework together, but he wouldn't let me go alone in the woods to find you. I am so tired of him treating me like a child. Did you have a good walk? See any animals?"

"We had a grand time. I almost beat Rolf to the shrine!"

Sitting down at a wooden bench in the park near the cemetery, I bend over and look at the scratches on my calf. I

Gerti's War

brush off bits of skin from my lower leg, parts torn from the bushes earlier in the day.

Since my childhood, I go to the cemetery for the peacefulness and the perfect emerald green grass that always beckons to me. Posted signs forbid us to walk on the grass. Marta and I are forever wary of Herr Vossler, a pensioner who maintains the park. Fussy over this section of grass, he tends it wearing felt slippers. We are alone for the moment.

"We saw two hedgehogs and Rolf tried to catch one, but missed," I said.

Small groups of people mingle in a far corner of the cemetery as they visit with neighbors and tend to the plants decorating the small cemetery plots.

Marta's eyes light up with mischief as she leans close and whispers, "Olympics?" Marta has been obsessed with the Olympic Games on the radio. Her favorite swimmer, Gisela Arendt, is her cousin and looks like her. Marta goes to all her competitions.

With no one looking in our direction, we slither on our bellies toward the emerald field and enjoy the cool refreshment of "swimming in our green pool." As I lie on my side, Marta does a mock backstroke. I call out the last few seconds of a world record event: it is a close call against the Russian and French teams. Marta wins every meet. Sometimes we stop and have a race coming back from school if the park is empty. We've done the same routine for years rolling around on the grass before the risk of being caught becomes too great. Its sweet smell covers us.

Keeping below the hedge lining the park, we crawl back to the bench. Indentations of our bodies are visible on the pressed sod.

"Do you think we were seen?" Marta asks as we brush off our outfits. "I know we're getting too old for this, but it never gets old for me. I saw Otto looking at you during class yesterday. I think he may want to talk to you."

Lois Buchter

A family approaches and we both grab our books and begin to study. As they pass, a child asks, "Why does the grass look strange?"

Marta snorts through her fingers, "Snort!"

Marta can always make me laugh. Not just a giggle, but a hard belly laugh. Spontaneous bouts of giggles break out often as we try to do our homework. It is difficult to get through our memorizing and finish the assignments.

Working to help bring in the last of the fall harvest after school, I bend over pulling the last onion out of the garden. Our backyard nursery contains almost every vegetable that you can grow in Germany.

I learned that anything and everything could be canned. The cellar pantry shelves are always full. Mother is skilled at delivering babies, but she surpasses everyone when it comes to gardening. The flowers against the house have already lost their blooms for the season. Pulled bulbs and the last of the garlic lay scattered around the ground, like broken arrows. The compost heap is full nearby.

Mutti has her apron on and hair pulled back with a scarf. A bucket of trimmings sits beside her ready for the composting pile. She doesn't believe in wasting anything. Both of our hands are covered with dirt.

"Gerti, when you're finished there, gather the bulbs and hang them in the cellar for me. Okay, *Liebchen*?"

Before I can answer, a horribly off-key melody floats into the garden, from the direction of Frau Petter's next door. She has a big heart and we love her, but cringe whenever her operatic bug bites. Whenever Papa hears her, he joins us in the garden and starts singing, which always ends her mangled attempts at singing. Last year, he compared her vocal abilities to a duck slowly being strangled.

Mutti throws the last item into the compost pile and turns quickly making sure no one else other than me can see her. She bends her knees, bobs her head a few times, and starts to strut like a duck. She holds her neck at an odd angle and uses her hands to mimic someone being choked.

I have never seen this dramatic display before, and a loud burst of giggles comes up from the tips of my toes. I pull my hands up to cover my mouth and stop when I see how filthy they are. I quickly head for the cellar doors. Mutti comes in behind me. We both laugh and hold onto the walls for support. Our dark handprints stain the white plaster walls.

Our laughter travels up the ventilation shafts and before long before Rolf thunders down the stairs. His bedroom, on the opposite side of the house from Frau Petter's, shelters him from the concert.

He stands at the top of the cellar stairs and shouts down to us in an authoritative tone.

"What's going on down there?"

I walk over to the outside door and open it a crack. Frau Petter sings a particularly high note and I wince. Mutti tries her duck strut again and Rolf's face comes alive. Thankful not to be on the receiving end of Rolf's teasing tirades Rolf joins in our game. Tears streak down my cheek as his gesturing becomes more intense. Rolf keeps opening the door pretending to be an Opera star. By the time I make my way to the stairs, Rolf has a mop on his head and his body wrapped in a sheet hanging from the clothesline. My sides feel like they will split open.

Later that evening as I help Mutti clean the kitchen, I glimpse a pamphlet lying with her purse. Official looking documents appear bundled up next to them. A large black and red Swastika has prominent placement on the front cover and stamped beneath it the words, "Be fruitful, multiply, and replenish the earth with good Germans".

"What is this, Mutti?" I hold up the packet.

"Rubbish. More rubbish."

She grabs the packet from my hands and tucks it into the bag she uses for deliveries. "I now have to report and document all births with the government offices. No one gets the birthing stipend without completed documentation. And now, they want me to start teaching motherhood classes and proper nutrition."

Her fingers tuck a few strands of hair back into place, and her hands tremble.

"Herr Obermeyer said the party officials would attend the first few classes next month to make sure the content is correct.

If one of those men tries to tell me how to be a mother, I may lose my patience all together." Dropping the ladle into a bowl of batter sitting on the counter, she vigorously stirs it free of lumps. When Mutti gets upset, she cleans or cooks and it's best to stay out of her way.

With nothing left for me to do, I kiss her goodnight and head up the stairs. I can hear her muttering "permits…bureaucracy," as I close my door.

The next morning a confectionary masterpiece sits on the edge of the counter in the pantry above my book bag. I smile as I think about my favorite buttercream cake. More than anything, I want to grab just a bit of the icing on my out. Instead, I reach for my book bag and call out, "Mutti, can I take a slice of cake to school?"

"No, Gerti. Remember, we have dinner with Uncle Erwin this evening."

My heart sinks into my chest. *Uncle Erwin, the windbag, I hate being around him and his friends. I don't like crowds and all the commotion that goes with it. It's always the same with him. Perhaps I can blend into the wallpaper. Papa and Rolf can talk to anyone, at any time. I envy their abilities to make others feel so at ease.*

After a day of testing, I began to think about Uncle Erwin's party. I daydream as I dust the living room. *Maybe I wouldn't have to go to the party.* All day I tried to come up with a way to stay home, even if it meant missing out on the cake. Mutti catches my eye and raises an eyebrow. *How do mothers always know what you are thinking?* I dust with a frenzy.

She follows me down the hallway and comes up beside me.

She wraps her arm around my shoulder and whispers into my ear, "Gerti, why so quiet? Everything all right at school?"

Gerti's War

"We have a new teacher who makes us stand and say 'Heil Hitler' every time she enters or leaves the room. I don't like her." I try not to look in Mutti's direction as I bring up the real subject I want to address. "Mutti, do you think I could stay home and not go with you to Uncle Erwin's?" My voice has no power or punch to it. I sound like a wimpy little girl.

"Another new teacher? What did Herr Deist say about that?" She asks in a firm voice.

"Herr Deist hasn't been at school all week," I reply.

He is my favorite teacher, the kind of teacher the girls fight to sit next to in the break room. His movie-star good looks, dark wavy hair, and chiseled chin make many girls dream about him. He makes history fun. We act out historical events and put on plays reinforcing some of the more popular triumphs. He fought against the changes in the curriculum and remained firm with district officials, keeping our old textbooks in the classroom. Mutti knows him and his wife because she delivered their baby earlier this summer.

"Hmmmm, I have a potential delivery near his house any day now. I'll just stop by to see how they are doing with the new baby," she says.

"Mutti...couldn't I stay home this evening?" I ask again. My voice stronger this time.

"No, Gerti. We are all going." Her brow remains creased.

A cool evening breeze follows us as we arrive at Uncle Erwin's. Several cars I don't recognize line the driveway. The windows are closed, yet I could hear Uncle Erwin's booming voice all the way from the street. Sweat breaks out on my forehead and my stomach begins to hurt. I burp a few times trying to relieve the pressure.

As we walk into the room, several conversations are going on at once. An irate Uncle Erwin rants and raves about a lame horse he purchased years ago from a Jewish family. It was five years ago, but he talks about the event as if it happened yesterday.

11

Lois Buchter

It's a story I've heard many times.

Uncle Erwin loves to be the center of attention and jealousy overtakes him if anyone more accomplished is around. Uncle Erwin forever quotes the many injustices he has suffered in his life. Always on a short fuse, his temper fills the room.

"I tell you, they are a bunch of shysters - a bunch of crooks, all of them. When I took the horse back to him and demanded my money back, he laughed in my face." He thrusts his fist into the air and continues the tale. "I lost more than the cost of that horse – part of my crop was destroyed as well."

Aunt Eva says to the woman sitting next to her, "I heard the Jewish people are moving to be with relatives out of the country, leaving by the thousands." Heads nod in agreement around the room.

"Good riddance," says Uncle Erwin as he spits on the floor.

"I'm through with them and any other foreigner who wants to go."

He leans over the table and bits of spittle land on the tablecloth.

I try not to make eye contact with him and keep my eyes lowered, but I swallow wrong and started coughing. Everyone turns in my direction. The more I try to suppress the coughing, the stronger it becomes.

Uncle Erwin leans even closer and asks, "Do you have something to say on the subject Gerti?"

Suddenly my mouth goes dry and I try to hold back another round of coughing. The room seems to shrink as I look around.

Silence fills every inch of the space. I manage to say in a small voice, "I don't understand how you can hate so easily."

My mother's face blanches and my father rolls his eyes toward the ceiling. A chilling quiet fills the room for a few seconds before the steam engine of my uncle's voice encloses everything. I focus on the grandfather clock on the wall and watch the pendulum swung.

Uncle Erwin bellows for what seemed like hours before we can excuse ourselves and go home. His tirade includes wildly exaggerated postwar conditions and standards of morality and decency; all blamed on the Jewish Marxist programs after World War I and in the early twenties. Everything is someone else's fault and holds him back from his true potential. A big proponent of the National Socialism programs, especially the industrial plants, he likes to talk about how great Germany will be in the years ahead. The power and glory of Germany and our history dominates all his conversations.

Later, on the way home, Rolf lays his arm around my shoulder and asks me if I enjoyed the evening. I start to cry.

Mutti says, "Sometimes it is best not to say anything than to fuel his rage. I want both of you to remember, jealousy is a dangerous thing that can rot your soul. I've known Erwin for a long time. He is a bitter man with a scarred heart. He doesn't have the strength of character your father has." She moves her hand and caresses Papa's shoulder.

"Mutti, he looks scared to me, not jealous," I say.

"He is scared someone will point out his own inadequacies," she says.

Papa looks at us through the rearview mirror and raises one bushy eyebrow at us. "I had better never hear such intolerance coming out of your mouths. Erwin's soul has been twisted for years. There are good and bad people all over the world, but you must do better. A madman may be running Germany now, but I won't have a monster in my house. Understood?"

"Yes, Papa," we both reply.

My mouth is dry as I kiss my parent's good night and head up the stairway. While getting ready for bed, I can hear my parents talking in the kitchen.

Papa says he is proud of me for standing up to Erwin, but he doesn't know how to discuss the situation with me. As I close my door, I hear him say, "We must be careful with our children, Emma, they are all we have."

Lois Buchter

I love the few minutes I have alone with Rolf when we walk to school before our friends join us. Rolf talks about his dream to become the world's greatest architect. He has covered all the walls of his bedroom in pencil sketches of hotels and resorts.

Often, we play a game discussing all the fancy amenities and decorations his designs will have, with each spa more fantastic than the last. My lofty ambitions are much more subdued. I want to work in an office, have a loving husband, and have lots of children.

Rolf jingles the change in his pocket.

"Gerti, you will be making money like me this summer? What will you buy? Clothes, shoes…?"

"I will save half and maybe go to the cinema more often."

As his friend's approach, including Otto's older brother, Rolf jingles the change reinforcing his new wealth. I look for Otto, but he isn't there. I don't dare ask about him.

As Marta catches up with us, we talk about our big adventure next year, taking the train into Pforzheim twice a week for required business training. Riding the train by ourselves is something we have dreamed of doing. Already Mutti has altered a few of her skirts for me to wear, and Papa bought me a new hat and gloves and I am thinking of cutting off my braids.

Red Swastika flags stand outside our school and in front of the city offices. Political posters decorate the train station depicting Hitler as a lover of children.

Papa is upset over the Nazi Party reorganizing his Veterans Association into a division of the party. He's been a leader in the Veterans Association for a long time. Now the newspapers detail flowery stories of how great Germany has become under Hitler's leadership. Mutti doesn't like the syrupy-sweet news reports telling how wronged or threatened Germany has been by different countries and that we must rise and eliminate any threat to our way of life. The same story now repeats at school.

Mutti and I overheard a conversation at the grocers last week regarding a prominent family in Neuenburg. The district Socialist Democratic Party leader moved into their home one evening and no one knows where the family went. When our local priest made inquiries of the displaced family, he received no information. Papa talked to the priest and later received a warning by the Party to keep his opinions to himself or he too could end up at another place with the priest.

It is only through the filtered information of others that we know pieces of reality. Papa spends an hour every evening down at the men's club listening to the conversations. My parents urge me to focus on the positive and stay out of trouble. Only once did I try to make a stand for what was right, and that left me waking up at night with cold sweats. Marta and I tried to find out what happened to the Diest family, but I only heard the true story months later.

Mutti did her part by discreetly asking probing questions about the Deist family. His wife and child are now living in France. Herr Deist was sent to a work camp because of his stand over the classroom curriculum. His refusal to comply with the mandatory propaganda films and literature in the school has him digging ditches somewhere east of us. At least that's what they told some friends of Mutti's. The principal of our school commented at assembly that others would follow if we don't toe the mark.

The silence of my friends is my first lesson in fear. Those same girls who used to fight over who would sit next to Herr Deist at lunch, now look at us with blank eyes. Marta and I were called into the principal's office where we were threatened with expulsion from school for pacifist troublemaking. Expulsion from school, for any reason, automatically closes the doors to any advance schooling. No one wants to take any risks that might have such lasting consequences for our future, Rolf's schooling, or my parent's situation. I am so tired of hearing about politics.

For my birthday, Rolf hands me a journal to pursue my love of writing. Last night we had a small family dinner celebration by candlelight. Thankfully, Uncle Erwin and his wife didn't come.

Shortly thereafter, a great snowstorm hit our valley. I've never seen the snow so deep. Other than the trouble of walking to school in drifts, we have a great time. We build forts, have snowball fights, and Rolf rides his bike on the packed snow, slipping and skidding. Best of all, though, are the sled races on our street and the day that Otto invited me to sled down the hill with him. Everyone gets involved. Even a few of the Moms bundle up and wobble as they try to stay centered on the sleds.

Roads and schools close, and even most businesses. It's a winter paradise. You can hear the laughter of our friends and the sounds of the metal sled runners on the ice as soon as you walk outside. If you don't wrap up properly, ice crystals will bite into your face.

In the dim evening light, sometimes a Father or two will join us in the races. Mutti provides many cups of hot cocoa for us and our friends. We have a brief respite. No one talks politics, not even the parents.

As the temperatures start to warm in early March, I come home one day to find Papa sitting at the kitchen table with a pint of dark beer in his hand. Papa doesn't drink much at home, and only on very hot days did he drink this early. A few of his friends sit with him at the table. They are in high spirits.

"Gerti, the most wonderful news has come to us. Germany signed an *Anschluss* with Austria." The men clanked their beer mugs together with Papa's announcement. He always loved the Austrians and never really understood the need for a border between our countries. The old Germany is coming back together, truly a time to celebrate.

Papa told me they are heading down to the meetinghouse to rejoice with their friends. I watch them walk down the street, laughing and gesturing wildly with their hands. (Papa always talks with his hands). It must be a good thing.

Mutti asks me to go get him from the men's hall, as dinner was ready. When I open the door and look into the darkened chamber, Herr Ottmann, the leader of the men's choir, is standing on a stool. All the men in the room circle around him, including Papa. The heavy wood paneling, thick cigarette, and cigar smoke gives the room a cave-like feel. The men start clicking their heels and someone calls out a loud *"Prosit"* from the back of the room. Everyone raises their beer mugs. " *Eins,"* said Herr Ottmann, looking down the long table before him. *"Zwei, "* he announces as he waved his mug in the direction of the rest of the room. When he says *"Drei, "* all the mugs are lifted to drink. The mugs hit the table in a crash at the same time. I jump as the sound rings in my ears.

Papa stands in the center of the room and they ask him to sing. Holding his head high he sings the popular German song, *"Unkissed...is no way to go to sleep."* The men accompany him on the second chorus. Finally, my father spots me at the back of the room and calls out to his friends, "I must go home, and kiss my wife." Everyone laughs.

He wraps his arms around my shoulder, leads me outside into the cool, clean air. Singing and laughter resumes in the background as we walk away. It gives me a strange comfortable feeling to have his arm around me and to see him so happy. I feel older and more like the young lady father had called me during my birthday celebration.

"Papa, it's wonderful to see you so happy," I say as I look in his direction.

"Gerti, maybe now, things will get back to the way they used to be. We can hope for a strong united Germany in our future….in your future." He says as he kisses me lightly on the nose. "You two are all we have".

Chapter 2 – March 1938

In early spring, Rolf rides his bike down the hill towards the small town of Neuenburg. He enjoys the feeling of the warm spring sun on his face and stands on his pedals, pushing the bike faster. Splashes of color appear among the small dark piles of slush along the way. Daffodils are beginning to bloom in clusters beneath the trees. Bird songs float on the breeze as they celebrate the beginning of spring. Most of the snow has now melted and you can hear the rush of rapids in the swollen river at the bottom of the hill. The dirt roads change into cobblestone streets as he leans into the tight curve ahead.

    Rolf squints and shades his eyes briefly as something catches his attention in a brilliant flash of light reflecting off the river's edge. He slows his pace. Rolf stops his bike, runs a hand through his short blonde hair, and listens after a car passes. Taking off his backpack, he drops it into the large basket on his bike where he hears a faint "Help…Help!" The high-pitched voice is from the direction of the river.

    Rolf drops his bike and lands running in full stride towards the River Enz. The calls for help continue as he gets closer and Rolf can see two dark heads being carried along by the cold, swift current. Dripping arms lift free of the water trying to grab a hold of anything. Rolf unfastens his wool coat and uses it as an extension as he tries to reach the first boy.

    "I see you! Reach!" He calls out to the first boy.

    "Somebody, please help!" He calls to the houses a block away.

    "HELP!" The boy misses the jacket, and a second boy floating quickly by with his head face down in the water briefly distracts Rolf's attention. Rolf jumps in, and icy barbs shoot into his legs and torso as he hits the current and swims out to the nearest boy who clings to a small branch. Chunks of ice break and float by as he swims to the boy through a deep channel. Water splashes over his head, completely soaking him.

"Grab the jacket" he calls to the boy, whose hands are in a frozen position and unable to get a grasp it. Finally, he reaches the boy and grabs the back of his jacket, pulling the lad from the rushing current.

When he looks up, Rolf sees a man running toward them from a small repair shop nearby followed by a few others. "Help!" Rolf cries as he tries to pull the boy along with him into the shallows. Shouts arise coming from the residential area, as more people began to arrive.

As the first man approaches, Rolf calls out to him "Quick, another boy, d-down river," and the man takes off running in the direction, desperately scanning the water. The biggest man he has ever seen arrives and quickly pulls Rolf and the boy from the water as a small group of people cluster at the bank edge. Rolf pulls away as the man cradles the lethargic boy in his arms.

Someone calls for blankets and the next thing he knows, a large down comforter wraps around his shoulders. Trying to stand, Rolf's legs feel like putty and he collapses, tearing his pants and leaving a bloody mark on the gravel beneath him.

All attention diverts to the boy of about seven who has begun to breathe again as he lays quivering against the mechanic's barrel chest. The boy's skin has a transparent bluish tint to it. A woman rubs his hands between hers and tries to subside his uncontrollable shaking. More blankets arrive as they try to get his wet clothing off. The boy begins to cough, turns his head, and opens his eyes.

A well-dressed woman rushes up, calling out that she has called the authorities. Someone recognizes the boy and asks him if his name is Wilhelm Rommel. The boy nods. Another woman leans in and asks, "What happened?"

Rolf replies, "I was on my way to the tax office for deliveries and I heard someone shouting for help. There were two boys. Did anyone get the second boy?"

Wilhelm weakly says "Dieter".

Heads nod "no" and look downriver as the local police pull into the area.

Slowly rising on his injured leg and testing his ability to stand, Rolf shakes his knee a few times. Someone slaps him on the back in congratulations, but it pushes the cold wet fabric against him. Rolf groans.

Marta and I enjoy collecting spring flowers for our hair. The first spring blooms, snowdrops, daffodils, and yellow clusters of meadow saffron, appear in spots on the hillside.

I pick a small handful of daffodils and white snowdrops for Mutti to put on the kitchen table. I know they will make her smile. They are her favorite.

Arriving home, I find Rolf's leather satchel lying in a pool of water on the floor in the kitchen, and his wet shoes thrown over in a corner.

"Rolf," I call out. "Are you home?"

A muffled and low groan of "Gerti..." comes from the upstairs landing. I drop the daffodils and race up the stairs. I find Rolf lying on his bed, wrapped in a blanket, hair wet and plastered to his scalp. Shivering uncontrollably, his skin looks the same color as one of his ashen pencil sketches. I quickly grab the feather comforter from my bed and throw it over him.

"Rolf, what happened? Do you want me to fetch Mutti?" I tuck the comforter around him.

"Gerti-freezing...fell in the Enz...two boys...tried to reach ... them...both...Can't get warm." His teeth chatter in between the broken comments. His raspy voice chills me to the bone and for a moment, I am paralyzed.

I run to my room and look for any warm clothing that might help him. Nothing seems to be the right size. My old woolen hat and thick socks will have to do.

"Rolf, stay put. I'm going to find Mutti."

I push the socks onto his feet and take the stairs down three at a time. Rushing, I can't remember what Mutti said about her deliveries today. Not finding the regular note on the kitchen table, I glance out the window, and see Frau Petter next door carrying a bag of groceries. Before I know it, I pull her inside and ask her to stay with Rolf while I run to a telephone. She hands me some change and I fly down the street.

"Papa, come home quick! Rolf is sick. He really looks bad."

My voice shakes with urgency. Rolf is never sick, and he never complains.

"I'm on my way. Stay with him Gerti." The phone goes dead in my hand.

By the time I get back to the house, and upstairs I find Frau Petter trying to hold on to Rolf as she walks him towards the stairs to the tub in my parents' bathroom. She wants to put him in a warm bath. Several pots of hot water are on the floor by the tub waiting for him. Rolf's body feels cold and clammy to my touch, as we put him in the steaming water.

"Rolf, this will help you stay warm," I say as I put the woolen cap back on his head.

Frau Petter agrees and says, "You need it right now." The look on her face tells me she is worried too.

He keeps taking his hands out of the tub and she puts them back in for him. I fold a towel and put it behind his neck to make him more comfortable.

"Rolf, where is Mutti today?" I lean in close and press my hand to his forehead. He feels cold.

He keeps his eyes closed, but the chattering of his teeth finally stops as the warm water works its magic. "She's at the circus," he says in a deadpan voice.

"Gerti, I'm going to get more help. You stay with him," Frau Petter says. "I'll be right back." As she rises, her knees pop and she grabs both of them as she grimaces.

I had forgotten about her swollen joints. "Hurry, please hurry," I plead to Frau Petter. "I don't know what to do." Tears run down my cheeks.

Rolf tries to get out of the tub twice before Papa arrives home. By that time, Frau Petter and two other neighbors are standing in the hallway trying to help. Another friend stands by the stove, cooking some clear soup for him to drink. Everyone has a different diagnosis and treatment. Papa asks them to make some tea, and he will put some brandy in it for Rolf.

Gerti's War

A small group of people mill about the front yard by the time Mutti comes home. Word has spread to the next town regarding Rolf's heroics in trying to save the young boys who fell in the frozen river. Some of the men in the neighborhood of the accident talked to Rolf for quite a while before he rode his bike home, and Papa thought he had taken his chill there. As I heated the second batch of tea, I could hear the hushed tones of people talking in the courtyard. Looking around the kitchen while the water boiled, I notice the crushed daffodils still lying on the ground by the back door.

The days pass slowly, and I walk in a daze trying to go about my regular duties while Rolf is sick. Friends at school ask about Rolf's condition and talk about how he saved young Wilhelm Rommel. They never found the other boy, Joerg Detmeyer. The local newspaper has an article about Rolf with a school photograph. It talks more about Rolf's involvement with the Hitler Youth than what happened on the river. Rolf's condition hasn't improved. He now has a high fever and his coughing won't stop. Sometimes he doesn't know us.

Each day different groups of people fill the kitchen. However, I dread the nights. The piercing coughing spells echoing down the stairway drown out quiet hushed voices. I lie in bed staring at the ceiling, waiting for him to catch his next breath.

Sleep does come, but not often. Papa keeps a vigil sitting at the top of the stairs outside Rolf's bedroom. He is chewing on his unlit pipe when I say good night and is still sitting there when I open my door in the morning. Papa's back remains hunched over, even when he stands. He looks so tired.

When I go into Rolf's room, I wash my hands and we talk in quiet tones. Rolf lies on a rubber sheet with heavy flannel blankets tucked in around him. Mutti constantly changes the bedding because he sweats so much. Then she spreads goose grease on his chest and covers it with another flannel sheet. The windows are open to bring in fresh air. Nothing is working. His fever remains high.

We don't have a hospital or doctor in our town, but the visiting nursing nuns in Neuenburg do come to see Rolf. They suggest hot steaming towels be put on his chest and hot broth three times a day. Mutti also takes one of her good socks and fills it with warm mashed potatoes and onions and then she wraps the sock around his neck. You can hear my brother's strained breathing now, even with the door closed. He is becoming weaker by the day. Pneumonia has set in.

On the sixth day, one week before his seventeenth birthday, Mutti put her head on Papa's shoulder. "Ta-tooch....he's gone."

Sometime later, I found myself wrapped in Mutti's arms and sitting on the sofa in the living room. I don't remember much else. We are numb. The light in both my parents' eyes died. I feel a complete emptiness.

We have a small family service at the church for Rolf before going on to the cemetery. We bury Rolf next to Grandmother Oma.

The whole town came for the ceremony including the *Burgermeister* and *Blockleiter*. Rolf's friends from the Hitler Youth came wearing their uniforms and armbands. Several of his closest friends stand silently at attention, their bodies frozen and faces hardened. Only Gerhard, Otto's brother, has a single tear running down his cheek.

The men's choir group came to support Papa, and they sang a few songs. Papa remains quiet with his lips firmly set. Mutti shuffles her feet when she walks. Somehow, Papa seems shorter.

I sit by my window later that evening and watch the clearing fires burning near the edge of our woods. For me it seems the woods are mourning our loss.

Marta sleeps on the floor beside my bed. Sometimes she lies next to me and holds me as I cry myself to sleep. At least that's what she told me, days later. I have no memory for those first few days.

Father didn't sing again until the May Day parade, weeks later. The strength and vitality that had boomed in his voice before, is no longer there. People congratulate him on his performance, but they are just being polite. He won't let me out of his sight

Gerti's War

during the festival. Rolf has been gone one month and people are still talking about his bravery and courage. With every compliment new waves of anguish wash over me.

Returning home, I honor May Day with my regular planting of red geraniums in the flower boxes around the house. No one touches Rolf's duties of planting the colorful blooms by the driveway. It looks empty without them. Mutti putters about the garden wearing her good dress and an apron. Marta kneels beside me pushing fresh soil into the beds and tries to cheer me up, but it is a one-way conversation filled with endless questions.

"Gerti, do you think we should plant daffodil bulbs in the garden around the house? Maybe we can line the driveway with them? Frau Petter has some new pink poppies planted around her house. I bet she'll give me some seeds. Would you like to get some?"

I don't remember what I said, but she left to see what our neighbor would give her.

The windows in the cellar are open and I can hear the men talking politics in the cellar. Papa and some of his friends are sampling his homemade pear brandy and their voices keep increasing in volume the longer they are down there. Someone voices an opinion about not getting involved with things that don't concern them. I can't place the voice.

Yes, most adults are very self-absorbed, I think as I walk back to the garden. Mutti has her good copper pots stacked by the plant bench and scours them clean with a wire brush. Mutti has cleaned everything in the house during these last few weeks, except Rolf's room. She brings new meaning to the Swabian saying, "Nothing exceeds cleanliness!" Rolf's door is closed and off-limits. Many evenings I find her standing outside his door.

Sometimes she puts her hand on the door and leans against it, but it is still too soon to go inside. I can't open the door either.

Next month, Marta and I will graduate from the high school program and then we plan to go to the business school in

Pforzheim. The BDM has assigned me a summer work position sorting mail at the Post Office in town. Marta's father made some inquiries and now we will be working together. We held hands and hugged each other.

Today I saw Papa give the *Blockleiter*, with his Hitler-like mustache, a few bottles of his homemade wine. Papa is trying to stay in good graces with him, because he still won't go to the party meetings. *Blockleiter* attends the men's choir meetings and listens to all the conversations along the beer tables. Papa asks me not to tell Mutti about the wine. It will upset her. My stomach stays in knots so much lately. Is this from our loss or the political changes?

The big event of our summer is the annual charity concert at the castle in Hechingen. The choir group will sing this year and they will be accompanied by the Stuttgart Chamber Orchestra. Papa will have a small solo part. Everyone in town is talking about it. We will take the train and spend the night near Hechingen.

The members are all having new jackets sewn and Mutti has altered a soft blue woolen dirndl dress for me. I am finally able to wear Oma's embroidered apron. Marta and I have experimented with new shorter hairstyles. It is strange not to have my braids anymore and I keep feeling for them.

"Gerti, you look so grown up," says Papa as he hugs me for the tenth time. Mutti uses her new camera and we smile for photographs outside the kitchen window in our new outfits.

I desperately want Marta to go with us.

"Papa, isn't there any way Marta can come along? I'll promise to work extra hours the rest of the summer." I know he didn't have any pull in the postal office, but I really want Marta to go. She will be working my shift at the post, so I can go.

"I tried, Ta-tooch. Maybe she can go next year," he says as he kisses my forehead. "Why don't you take lots of notes about what you see and maybe Mutti would let you take a few photographs as well?"

Gerti's War

Running back into the house, I remembered the diary Rolf had given me for my birthday and put it with my small knapsack.

Prince Louis Ferdinand of Prussia, the handsome grandson of Kaiser Wilhelm II, opens the children's charity concert. His uniform is covered with medals and a colorful sash. The castle sparkles in the evening night air. Glass candles illuminate the trees outside in the courtyard. Colorful banners hang from the large family portraits and Swastika flags have prominent placement along the balcony. Young girls run through the courtyard wearing woven garlands of flowers and ribbons in their hair. The large foyer of the castle has huge murals on the walls, including the entire Hohenzollern family tree. The ancestry of Prince Louis goes back centuries. When I shake his hand, I feel as if I am touching history. I know my face turned red.

Dignitaries, party members, and people of substantial wealth mingle together on the upper levels of the foyer. Most of the women upstairs wear long formal gowns and gloves. Everyone looks like a movie star to me. Some of the men smile at me.

Tucking my diary in the pocket under my apron, I write little observations for Marta and Mutti. Deep into my writing, I stop when I hear some men behind me mention Papa's name. I discretely turn my head and find two party officials with their backs turned away from me. Papa has just finished singing. At first, I thought they were discussing the concert, but they were frowning and motioning towards Papa. An official-looking supervisor walks over to them and I jump when he slams his fist into his hand. I heard him say Fritz will join or he will learn first-hand the power of the Third Reich. My blood stops pumping in my chest as I take in the meaning of his statement. *What will happen to Papa?*

On the way home, I keep one hand on the diary in my pocket.

My hands shake slightly from the comments made earlier. I caress the cover of the book. It makes me remember something Rolf said months ago. He encouraged me to write down my thoughts, especially as I grew into a woman. He said when I was old and gray it would be a comfort to me to see how much I would change.

Would I realize my hopes and dreams? Rolf's dreams now would never become a reality.

By the time we pull into our driveway, I decide to start writing regularly. Rolf always gave me hope that things would be better – better tomorrow. For Rolf and myself, I will try to write.

Chapter 3 – September 1938

Finally, Marta and I can ride the train into Pfzorheim three days a week by ourselves. Marta has been assigned to work in a metals factory not far from my school and I'll be going to business school. I am glad we will be able to ride the train together, but Marta isn't happy about her assignment. She wants to work in a jewelry store. Now she won't be going home until after six o'clock. We won't be able to ride the train home together. I won't be nervous riding the train home by myself, at least that's what I keep saying to myself. Mutti keeps muttering about my clothes. I grew another two inches this summer and all my skirts must be re-hemmed.

Our first day started very early. The sun hadn't come up as I left the house. Mutti hugged me so tight before I left and handed me my favorite lunch of pancakes and dark cherries from our tree. She wanted Papa to walk with us to the train station, but Marta is already waiting for me at the end of her drive. I kiss both of Mutti's hands before I run down the street and on to my new adventure.

Marta's mother waved good-bye to us and we later saw her watching us as we boarded the train. I think both our mothers are more nervous than we are. Butterflies flutter in my stomach over walking into a new school. I must have checked for my train pass and work permit a hundred times. Marta and I thought we looked very grown up with our new hats and haircuts. We walked arm-in-arm to the station breathing in the cool morning air and are feeling grown-up. We had no problem meeting the 6 a.m. train.

Church steeples and smoke stacks are visible for miles surrounding the city of Pforzheim. The industrial district glitters in the morning light looking mystical. It's as if all the industrial factories of gold and silver have spotlights on them. Old half-timbered houses surround the pockets of industrialization. What a strange contrast to have the old and new so close together and so different from home. Everyone's in a hurry as they walk briskly by us with a sense of purpose.

Marta and I rehearsed the route we were to take, and we giggled over our Dad's notes on our city map. I have been to the business school with Father earlier this summer and knew where it was. Marta's assignment took us longer to find off a back street.

We looked for the address at the post office in Arnbach and found it listed under "Metal Manufacturing Company." We are surprised that her metal company is a small watch manufacturing company and only three blocks from my school.

So far, the business school is exciting. I have been enjoying my math and languages classes, but my homework load is heavy. Our teachers make us stand and "*Heil* Hitler" them when they enter the room. It makes me feel like a puppet going through the motions. We've heard many of our teachers are new to the school. My typing teacher stands by my desk and watches everyone in the room from there. She wears her union party membership pin prominently on her shirt.

Now on school days I don't get home until late afternoon and my homework can take up to four hours. I also have longer work hours at the post office for two days a week while Marta must work five days at the factory. At least we still have weekends together at the post office. On Fridays when I don't have business school classes, I still get up and walk with Marta to the train station. I don't want her to be lonely. Some of the girls at the school are nice, but no one is like Marta though, my best friend, my true sister.

This morning we saw a few SA men (Storm Troopers) standing outside a Jewish dry goods business. Four *Scharfuehrers (squad leaders)* with armbands stood leaning against the building. They only looked a few years older than Rolf. They shouted and told people not to shop at this store. One stood in the doorway making it difficult to enter. Black graffiti covered one large front cracked window. *"JUDE"* stood out on the cream-colored stonewall.

It is the first time we had ever seen a SA patrol. Marta and I are surprised at how young some of them looked. Their brown uniforms and dark leather boots are sharp and neat, but the red armbands on their arms hung loose and seemed too big on their arms.

The store they approached didn't have many customers. Where is that nice elderly clerk with a long white apron who smiles at us when we passed him in the mornings? He sweeps the front walk every morning as we walked by. What would happen to his family now? Why are they doing this to others? We will have to find a different route from the train station.

Today I heard more news about the SA patrol from some of the girls at school. A small jewelry business burned over the past weekend. People are saying it is a Jewish-owned business. You can still smell a faint odor of burned wood in the neighborhood this morning.

More news on the radio and now I listen to people around me, especially on the train, even the hushed whispers. I saw several more businesses that have been affected by vandalism. The smell of burning lingers in the air. The headlines in the paper read; "Night of the Broken Glass" with photographs of citizens smashing windows. Why? I bet those SA squads are involved. Maybe even Uncle Erwin.

Fall has come and gone, and Marta and I had snowfall on us today as we walked to the station. My *Abitur* exams will be tough in the spring and I must pass them to go to university. I have finished studying for the geometry, algebra, and biology sections of my exams. My race studies were easy to complete.

The teachers gave us the questions and answers prior to taking the test. They can't have any party members questioning their teaching or my test scores. My grades are good, but not as good as Rolf's. I wish he could help me with chemistry. I wonder if sleeping with my chemistry book under my pillow will help?

Papa thinks I may be able to work with him in the tax office in the future. I would like that. Marta thinks they may move her to a larger factory soon. Someone came into their office and she had to fill out a survey. I don't want her to go.

"Gedenktag der Entschlafenen" (Memorial Day) Today we all went to the cemetery. A brass band played somber music to honor the veterans in the park. I felt Rolf breathing on my neck and sometimes I can hear his voice when I am alone in the house. It is a sad day. Even Mutti's cake didn't cheer me up afterwards.

I lit one of the four candles in our Advent wreath, Rolf's job. I hung our Advent calendar in the hallway with its twenty-four little doors, and remember how excited I used to be hanging the calendar when I was younger. Today I feel much, much older.

I've met a nice girl at school. Her name is Magdalena. We are both tall and quiet. We listen to others in the class talk.

Her laugh always makes me smile. We sit beside each other in transcription and bookkeeping classes and stay out of trouble.

Today the headmaster of the school called Magdalena to the front of the class. She glanced at me quickly, but with knees shaking, she walked up there. He asked her in a loud voice if her grandmother is Jewish. She slowly nodded her head. He told her she was a *Mischling* 2nd Degree. Told her to collect her belongings and follow him to the office. She isn't Jewish, she's Lutheran. Where did they get this information?

Susanne and Magda made derogatory remarks as she walked out of the class. I tried to catch Magdalena's eye as she walked past, but she wouldn't look at me. What should I have done?

The headmaster pointed to the slogan on one of the posters at the front of the room. "You are nothing, your nation is everything!" It made me feel very empty and ashamed. Yes, today I am ashamed.

I stopped by the Christmas market before heading home today.

There are many booths filled with everything you can want for Christmas (foods of all kinds, hand-carved wooden nutcrackers, nativity scenes, and all types of arts and crafts). I could have stayed there shopping for hours. It is so much fun. I purchased some *Gluehwein* (spice wine) for Papa and a new tablecloth for Mutti. Wish I had more money to spend, but I still have no idea on what to get Marta this year.

Marta's family joined us for our Christmas goose dinner. I wore my new blue dress that Mutti embroidered all along the hemline. Papa gave me soft house slippers. I love them. I hope Marta likes the embossed diary and book of poetry that I gave her. We ate all the bonbons on the table after dinner. My stomach hurts because we ate too much. Marta and I had two glasses of wine with dinner and giggled all night.

Mutti is making a new party dress for me to wear to Erika's dance. It's a cut-down version of one of her old fancy dresses.

I don't get many new clothes, but I've outgrown just about everything in my closet. Papa said he would be my escort for the dance. There aren't enough boys around for partners. They've all gone for training or are already in service, even Otto. He likes to visit with Erika's father anyway. I wish they weren't so protective. I'm old enough to go to a dance by myself!

When I went to class this morning, I found my Christmas greeting card to Magdalena returned to me. When I inquired at the administrator's office to check on Magdalena's home address they wouldn't give it to me. Why hasn't she come back? This must be a big mistake! No one listens to me.

Saw more businesses with graffiti on them. What is happening to our clean and tidy city? The train is more crowded than before. There are many travelers with suitcases on the train now.

People don't look at you anymore. Families hold their children close to them and aren't as friendly. Yesterday I tried to give a sweet to a child on the train and the mother knocked it out of my hand.

I helped Mutti put the Christmas decorations away this weekend. We carefully wrapped all the ornaments in tissue paper and stored them in the cellar. The holidays are empty without Rolf. Mutti tried to set a place for him at the table, but it made me cry and she put it away.

I have noticed little changes in the way the government is responding to the small things around us. We are being told what to think and what to do more and more often. No one at school speaks up or questions the changes. It's as if we are a bunch of cows keeping in line. They have tightened admission standards at the business school too. Some of the new girls that have just started with the school now have to work at factories on their free days. Once I get certified and graduate, I will have to work in industry as well.

Marta is moving to a different, larger factory closer to the train station, but far from school. She will be working on an assembly line. Maybe we'll be able to work together someday.

Our time together is short. I miss her.

Today is the sixth-year anniversary of The Third Reich's power in Germany. We had many special programs and speeches at school today. I hated sitting through all those speeches and tried to keep my face attentive but have discovered I am good at escaping and daydreaming of skiing in Switzerland.

Now they have party propaganda songs playing on the streets by the train station every morning. The songs are beginning to play in my head when I'm away from them.

Today is my birthday, but I don't feel like celebrating. We will have a special dinner and butter cream cake this evening. Marta, Erika, Hanna, and Marie will join us for dinner. As I prepare for the party, Papa is all excited about the new Volkswagen plant in Wolfsburg producing a small reasonable-priced car. Papa said he would order one and, in a few years, we will share it. He has the paper work for the pre-order request lying on the kitchen table. I can't believe it. I wish they came in colors other than black!

Next week I begin working in an armament factory, which is three blocks from Marta's work. They want me to work three days a week and I will have to stand up all day long and Mutti wants me to change my shoes into something more durable. There are hundreds of people working in the factory. They remind me of a bunch of ants all clustered together going in the same direction.

Today I must go into an orientation class on how to assemble shell casings. The welding crew works right behind me. Sparks from their torches almost hit my legs. What if my dress catches on fire? When I asked the supervisor about it, he told me not to worry about it, but I do. It's very noisy in the factory from the clanking and screeching of metal being knocked together. I already long for some peace and quiet in my woods.

Yesterday I found Papa, yet again, talking out loud to himself down in the wine cellar. He likes to vent his frustrations down there where no one can hear him. Herr Koska pulled him aside after the Men's vocal concert yesterday and told him he would have to take a more active role in politics. He told this to father in confidence not as a party leader, but as a friend and suggested a role with the Red Cross would fit his needs. I hope Papa can control his temper. If he says the wrong thing, he could be labeled a Communist and lose his job and perhaps be imprisoned. He was president of the local branch of the WWI Veterans Association and had to resign years ago when the Third Reich took over the organization. I heard my parents talking long into the night about his job and what we would do if he lost it.

Papa went and talked to some friends and will run the Red Cross office for our district. At least the party won't be single him out anymore, and it will give him an outlet to put some of his energy into. Mutti has a good calming influence on him. He seems happy with this decision. He is doing some of his accounting books in addition to his work with the Red Cross.

Papa came home today holding the newspaper headlines for me to read. "The Polish City of Memel is now German again". It is an important port city that Germany lost with the border changes after the Great War. When I took the train home, the conductor on the train told the crowd around me about the reclaiming of Memel. Many people started singing. People relaxed and started conversations with strangers around them. Marta and I kept to the shadows and whispered among ourselves. Could this be an end to the conflict? My parents will be so happy.

Papa often sits on his bench out in the garden with his head in his hands. He rubs his baldhead and sometimes tears run down his cheeks. When this happens, I try not to let him see me. It is so hard to watch my strong, proud father sobbing. The triumph of the easy victory in Czechoslovakia last year brought a sense of relief – a hope Hitler would be content with the campaign and things would go back to the way it used to be. However, now

Gerti's War

Papa says that war is coming to Germany and our hope for a new Chancellor for Germany seems more remote. Hitler is here to stay. His promise of a changed Germany under his direction has no boundaries. A chill runs down my spine and today I am afraid.

My grandfather was killed in Russia during the Great War while guarding Russian prisoners with the Red Cross—he froze to death. Papa always felt it a senseless death—a waste. He says this will be a senseless war. The rebuilding campaign of the late twenties brought so many good changes to Germany. Hitler helped get elected by promising so many unemployed jobs and his *Freikorps* helped calm the trouble between the Communists and Nazis. Papa says that now it's all slipping away. He tells me often how horrible war will be for Germany. War – Germany – Future?

I now must spend every Saturday morning at the BDM meetings.

Membership in the BDM and attendance will help me get into the higher education programs and out of the factory. We have endless lectures on Nazi ideology. "Blah, blah, blah, blah." I hate having to march through town after our meetings. Now they want to me to take a two-week leadership summer camp program this summer and I don't think I can put it off another summer. Maybe they will forget about me. I remember how different Rolf was when he came home from his summer camp. The sports, games, crafts, hiking and enjoying nature would be fun, especially with a bunch of girls, but I don't like the instructional political sessions in the evenings.

Mutti tells me to stay out of trouble and not to say anything controversial. We have long talks at the kitchen table after meetings. I remember the look in Magdalena's eyes and I will never be one of them. Could Germany turn from our family as well?

Another Saturday, another BDM meeting and I long for the warm mornings when I used to awaken to the peaceful song of the birds or the kids on their way to kindergarten. Sometimes I lie in bed waiting to hear them. Now all I think of is another Saturday, another rubbish meeting. My weeks go by in a blur. My summer camp session has now been scheduled for July 15th. Six more weeks and then I must leave. At least I still get to work with Marta two evenings a week sorting mail.

Papa now leaves the newspaper lying on the kitchen table for our evening discussions. The army wants to draft German men who live in Poland. There is much tension and hatred of Germans throughout Poland. The propaganda machine of our newspapers has many stories about beatings and even murder. Whom do you believe?

What do you believe? The newspapers are full of many stories about how wonderful the Fuehrer was and how he has kept his promises to make Germany stronger.

Since I started working at the factory, school, and post office, my days melt together. Mutti is worried about the dark circles under my eyes. Often, I've missed the 7 o'clock train out of Pforzheim and don't get home until after 9 o'clock at night.

Before I know it, another week has gone by. Mutti's evening hugs last a little longer these days. She wants me to talk to Herr Buchter about quitting the post job, but it's the only time Marta and I have together. I have been losing weight and don't want to eat when I get home, just fall into bed exhausted. Papa has arranged for a family retreat before I go to camp. We will take the train down to the Tyrol where the fresh clean air will put the color back in my cheeks.

We hiked the mountains and ate picnic lunches in God's splendor. It felt as if God was watching us and smiling down as the sunbeams streaked through the sky to our feet. Papa wanted to take advantage of a longer spa vacation, but I couldn't get the time away from the factory and school. They wouldn't let me ride the train by myself, so we all came home early. It felt so good to get away from our routine.

While we were away, Russia signed a non-aggression pact with Germany. We are all thankful for a breath of relief and an answer to our prayers. No one wants to go to war with Russia

My two weeks at camp were not as bad as I thought it would be. We had lots of exercises and songs. Marta was able to go to camp with me. If she hadn't been there, I probably would have been very homesick.

Today I made a big mistake. At an empty store near the train station in Pforzheim, I saw some SA men handing out free radios.

They checked my paperwork and gave me a small radio. As I walked into the kitchen, my mother took one look at the radio and the look of joy on my face. How do mothers always know? She told me I would have to take the radio to Papa's office at the Red Cross. I could not benefit from the misery of others. Who knows where the radio came from – maybe it was Magdalena's? Mutti said they were taking radios from the Jews.

Today, Papa met me at the train station and whispered in my ear that Hitler had invaded Poland. The newspaper that Papa held said that we were attacked at the border town of Gliwice. Why would the people of Poland do this? I don't believe it.

KREIG! – France and Britain have *declared war on us. Kreig!*
It has finally come. My hands are shaking as I write. *Kreig*!

Hitler has expanded his dreams by invading Poland. Most of the people I know are silently stunned. The quiet on the trains in the morning speaks volumes to what is happening around us.

No one speaks out in public against the campaigns unless you are an idiot. If you did, you and your family could disappear in the night. Papa heard reports of relatives of some close friends evaporating without a trace. Two families came to him to see if the Red Cross could intervene with the government. I heard Papa talking to Mutti about it when they thought I couldn't hear.

Never here, in Arnbach, but in some of the larger cities the papers report strange murders and disappearances. They give very little comment to those matters or don't report them at all.

The Nuremburg Laws expand into many Jewish laws and decrees. I've noticed small changes are occurring little by little here and there. Political banners and posters are now in the small shops instead of just the larger businesses. German-Jews are forbidden to use public transportation or to buy books or newspapers. I must keep my papers with me always. Yesterday I heard a shop owner talking to a customer about possible rationing of goods. A woman sat next to me on the train and cried when she saw that her papers had accidentally been torn. I will never forget the large signs at the train station detailing the anti-Jew campaign. I hoped Magdalena and her family were no longer in Germany. How I wish I could have talked to her.

Mutti listens to the radio all the time. I've noticed there isn't much laughter in our home anymore. Some of Rolf's friends are being called into training service. She worries about the young strong men and their futures, many of them she delivered when she was younger. Her work delivering babies used to bring her joy. She doesn't talk about it much anymore either.

Last week the *Blockleiter* met Mutti outside one of her deliveries unexpectedly and asked her if she had heard any political dissension. He told her rumors have been spread she was not happy with the party. He said they have room for her at one of the work camps if she is unhappy in her current position.

Gerti's War

She has known him almost all her life. How could he speak to her this way? We had a long talk before Papa came home about the meeting. I don't want to be around when Papa finds out about this! He can swear like a grenade when he gets mad!

Mutti is stunned with this confrontation and can only think of one person who could have said anything, Frau Koenig. Mutti helped at the delivery recently when a niece of Frau Koenig's had a baby. She couldn't remember saying anything out of the ordinary in the hours surrounding the birthing, but something must have reached Frau Koenig. She always has been a meddling, malicious, and jealous woman. While Rolf had been an outstanding student, athlete, and liked by everyone, her son, Theodor, was a poor student and always in trouble. He was now a young officer, a rising Nazi in the SS. Yes, he truly is a Nazi, radical and extreme in his party views. They were the lowest of the low. It made us all shudder to think of Theodor in a position of power and this time fed by the information from his mother.

We are all so busy these days with Papa working two jobs, Mutti now with two jobs, and me working three. Mutti oversees keeping track of the *Mutterkreuz (Mother's Cross)* program, which is promoting motherhood and early childhood development. How many mothers can have the most fair-headed, blue-eyed babies? They get to wear a special medal according to the number of babies they have; bronze for four children, silver for six and gold for eight or more, and a Hero Mother if you have more than ten. They are awarded every August. Mutti calls this the rabbit award. Another one of Hitler's brilliant campaigns. She hates smiling and being part of handing out these awards. I can tell her smile is forced, but I don't think others can.

I do the market shopping on days I come home from school. We are all going in different directions. Where is my family?

A campaign worker looked tired as he asked me again this morning for donations to the war campaign at the train station.

Hitler wants us to fix a simple soup the first Sunday of the month and donate the money we save for a regular meal to the poor. Maybe this is a good program?

Conquering Poland didn't take long, and they are calling it a sit down war. Now, the part of Germany lost in the past has been returned to us, but the war continues to escalate. So many staunch supporters of Hitler are surprised by the recent declaration of war from France and Britain. It has fueled his campaign now that we are being attacked. The victory in Poland has brought the addition of many factories and armament industries into the fold of Germany. Young men are being trained and more young women sent to work in the factories. Many girls in the factory where I work are being sent to Poland. I missed being sent because I wasn't 16. What will happen to them? My birthday will be soon, and I will be old enough.

My hours have increased at the factory and physically they are having me do more as well. I felt dirty and tired on the train ride home today, just like many days. Marta has been moved to a vehicle plant, where she pushes heavy parts around on a cart all day long. We are so exhausted most evenings we don't even talk on our way home when we do get off at the same time.

Christmas is coming. The Christmas market is set up not far from the factory. I remember how much fun it was last year. This year it doesn't excite me at all. There is too much uncertainty about our future, but I purchased some slippers for Mutti and new gloves for Papa.

Mutti now must teach a weekly class on early childhood development and baby care in addition to getting the curriculum together for other districts. The *Blockleiter* asked her to let him know if there are any women who don't participate or do not follow a healthy pre-natal routine. She has paperwork to fill out on each participant. When I got home this evening, she was still shaking over the meeting, and it had been hours since her class met. The mayor sat through her orientation and took lots of notes. It doesn't feel like Christmas is days away.

We went through the motions of the holidays, but it passed without comment. Thinking about it now, doesn't even make me smile. I felt the heavy loss of Rolf all around me. Mutti made me a beautiful linen *dirndl* outfit for special occasions and gave me Oma's embroidered apron to go with it. I keep it hanging on a special spot in my room, so I can look at it often. We had Christmas dinner with Marta's family this year. It was good, but not as good as Mutti's special goose dinner. New Year's Day was bright and sunny. We all went ice-skating in Neuenburg off the square. Crowds are light on the ice. Even there, I don't remember much laughter.

The war continues, and my updates come from different sources. Marta and I can hear men discussing the newest conquests on the train and from the headlines, we see in the newspapers.

The boisterous noise coming from the bar near the train station gives us a measurement of how the war is going. The men in the beer hall have so much pride and enthusiasm over each conquest.

Every night we hear them as we walk by.

My birthday came and went. I turned sixteen and I can still hear Rolf teasing me that I wouldn't have a boyfriend until I was old and gray. I think a part of him will always be with me.

I keep his photograph by my bed and two of his framed drawings are on the wall over my bed. Will I ever be kissed by a boy?

Will anyone ever look in my direction?

Mutti has noticed my clothes are a little loose despite my height and decides to start a new campaign to have me gain weight. I'm already taller than her and still growing. My appetite has been non-existent lately. More canning supplies are showing up in our pantry. Mutti has been busy or she's been paid in canned goods. Some blood sausages are sitting on the counter this week. They were Rolf's favorite.

Some people are giving Mutti gifts of food with the birth of babies. Last week she got lard and an extra dozen eggs from a farmer's family. She fixes heavy cream soups and lots of *Spaetzle* ("spetz-la" homemade German egg noodles fried in butter) and on special occasions, my favorite *Maultaschen* (fried pockets of sausage). She keeps telling me to EAT! Papa is happy with the rich diet and her cooking. My Papa isn't fat – he's solid!

Cherry cake with chocolate shavings and whipped cream continue to show up. I know it's her way of telling me again how much she loves me. When does she have time to cook?

Papa has resisted hanging a Swastika flag over the front door of our house, but it now hangs down low enough to catch in the door. Every house on the street must have one. I don't like it at all. Neither does Papa. We had put up a small flag, but were told we had to put up the larger one they provided. Party officials gave us the center part and we had to provide the red background. Mutti tried to stall finishing the stitching, but she finally finished it.

Our coal supply at home is running low. My parents have moved into Rolf's room for sleeping. The first couple of nights I could hear Mutti crying as Papa comforted her. We close off the main floor at night to conserve heat, even with a heavy down comforter; it's freezing when we wake up.

The *Arbeitsbuch* (an employment record book) has given me an identification card and I must keep it with me always. There was a long process I had to go through to get it. They asked all sorts of questions about my parents, place of birth, dates, and history of relatives in the past. All my past work history and education is listed on it.

Gerti's War

Mutti and I are planning a surprise outing for Marta on her birthday next week. We are going to take her to the cinema in Pforzheim and then out for dinner afterwards. She's been talking about the movie *Camille* for weeks. I'm excited too. I can't wait to see the expression on her face when she realizes what we have planned for her.

On Sunday, we headed for the city with high hopes for a day of escape. Not telling Marta about the surprise has been killing me. We told her we had to do some shopping and would eat somewhere along the way. Marta is a world-class shopper. She takes a long time to decide on purchasing, every item gets a detailed inspection. I don't like to shop very much and usually try to get it done as quickly as possible. With Marta, it is an Olympic event.

Marta picked up some new shoes with her coupons. She was in great spirits even though the shoes are a little tight.

Before she knew it, we stopped in front of the cinema and pulled out our tickets. She couldn't believe the surprise! The look on her face was worth the wait.

Before the show started, they showed a newsreel on the war and the push of troops into Belgium. A series of refugee images were shown. Specifically, Polish refugees marching past lines of German troops. There was something in the faces of those families of refugees, which stood out in my memory, a resistance. They are a mass of humanity in gray, moving North into Germany and will work in factories and farms to help keep Germany productive.

Some of the people in eastern Poland will be sent with the Red Army. What would happen to them was never discussed in the newsreels. Mutti and I talked about the refugees before but seeing faces large on the screen is very unsettling. Unpleasant rumors are rampant about the history of Russian-made refugees, many families separated, fathers killed, and mothers and young girls raped and beaten are familiar stories of the past. Would the new Russia treat these people with respect? Would we?

The movie *Camille* was beautiful and we all cried together when the heroine died at the end. Our light mood crashed again with the ending of the movie as we held our handkerchiefs to our noses. Once the tears started, I had trouble getting them to stop.

We were all still sniffling a little by the time we dropped Marta off at home. Not quite the big happy celebration I had planned for Marta's special day.

Mutti put her arm around my shoulders and told me she will never forget the looks on the faces of those refugees. "Gerti, what if it were us? What if they were shooting at us and we were trying to run away? War is nothing to celebrate." I can still hear her words. They made an impact on me.

Chapter 4 – June 1940

The Midsummer's Eve Celebration begins at sunset, with the suns decent into winter, and my favorite time of the year. Our family walked passed Father Rommel while he made the final adjustments to the procession altar for the Feast of St. John.

Adorned with flowers and fruit, a small statue of St. John peeked out from the piles of fresh flowers the young children placed beside it. So long ago, I remember doing the same when I was little. Happy children lead the procession to the edge of the forest bank. I could see their ribbons catching on the wind as they danced and tried to stay together. Many of the adults marked the field with lit ground torches. Our St. John's fire was ready to be lit.

The young girls wore long black skirts with beautifully embroidered white aprons. You couldn't help but smile over the excitement of the children. They ran like ants on the lawn of the church. Several boys practiced jumping with a stick they found near an aged fir tree. They were getting ready for the real jumping contest later. A group of other boys wrestled in another corner of the lawn and many had dirty faces already. How many times have I seen Rolf do the same thing?

We arrived at the festival early and helped Father Rommel set up many of the smaller details for the celebration. Papa enjoyed greasing the pole, but had trouble placing the handkerchief on top. I remember watching the men discuss how they should secure the pole deep into the ground. Everyone suggested new ways for securing the pole. We could hear their loud voices across the meadow, and from the tables it was funny to watch them talk with their hands. *Why do men do this?*

Mutti and I set up the tables with colorful tablecloths and a large assortment of baked goods. Thick blankets are spread on the ground, as parents get ready for the celebration. We could hear the ringing of the bells at the church signaling the start of the procession.

Father Rommel, wearing his long dark coat and hat, carried a vessel of holy water in one hand. He sprinkled the ground as he walked past us. Behind him, the boys carried the altar.

Some of the older children wore papier-mâché dragon masks to scare away the evil spirits. Even some of the adults wore masks.

A few of the masks are very old; their faded colors blending together. I remembered when Rolf smashed our mask accidentally several years ago. Finally, at the end of the procession, the rest of the villagers' march, carrying wooden torches up the hill to the clearing.

It was such a happy, peaceful moment. A warm breeze pulled at my skirt. It was a needed respite from the talks of war and made me feel normal again. I am comforted to be a part of this town, but a part of me feels a conflict over those absent. Where are all the friends of Rolf? Please God, keep them safe. I am thankful Herr Buchter closed the post early today, so we could attend.

There were many activities planned for the celebration, but the most popular is climbing the greased pole. It was very funny to watch. Soon all the men were participating. Papa participated in the men's wrestling and lost, but it took a while for him to lose. His face was very red, but then he started laughing too hard to keep his composure and he was finally pinned.

The cake-eating contest is always my favorite. Children make a circle around a huge cherry cake, but they must keep their knees on the ground. They can't sit still they are so excited.

They must find the silver coin hidden somewhere in the cake.

Most of them kneel on the ground with their hands behind their backs and lean forward so their faces are right over the cake to maintain their balance. Many just fall into the confection. The first one to find the coin keeps it. What a mess!

We have a small religious ceremony before the jumping contest starts. It is so popular; I think the priest keeps it for last so everyone will stay. The men stand on one side and the women on the other. I am surprised to see Mutti in the women's line. She won a carafe of oil. I held babies for friends all day.

What a good day! Papa's arm comforts me as they light the bonfire at dusk. My hair smells of his cologne and the smoke from the fires.

The Red Cross has started a new voluntary program offering rooms in private homes for soldiers who are in training. Papa's in charge in our district, so we must set an example for others. Mutti isn't happy to have company in Rolf's room and told me to stay away from the lodgers. It is easy for me to keep to my quiet activities as they leave early in the morning and don't return until evening. I try not to talk to them, but Heinrich, our current soldier, will be with us until the end of the week. We will have a new soldier every two-weeks. Their grey uniforms are already familiar in town and at the train station.

Marta and I can hear talk of war everywhere. Hitler's radio machine spits out massive amounts of flowery talks about how much progress Germany is making, after conquering the Netherlands and pushing into France. The business school radio addresses are turned on loud during our break time and we can't leave the room while the broadcast is playing. Some of the girls listen intently as many have fathers and brothers fighting for the Fatherland. My teachers watch all of us to be sure we are listening.

I am thankful war hasn't touched my immediate family, but everyone around us is affected in some way. Mutti comes home muttering over the helplessness of sending our only children to an uncertain future. Mutti reminds me every night as she says goodnight to hold on to hope. We pray the war would be over soon. I pray for all families -- on both sides.

This evening I received special gift from Mutti. We sat on my bed as we do most nights. In her hand is a beautifully embroidered blue linen handkerchief with a large H in the center.

She whispers to me to keep it with me always as it represents her hopes and dreams for my future. I can't stop the flow of tears that run down my cheeks. Mutti doesn't like to see me cry and keeps telling me that everything will be fine. I carefully inspect Oma's stitching on the handkerchief. It's the first blue handkerchief that I've seen.

Oma made it when she was young, and she gave it to Mutti during the Great War. Now it is my time to keep it close to me.

Mutti said the H stands for Hope and the blue color for blue skies, a clear future. She planned to give it to me on my wedding day, but wants me to have it now. I will cherish it always. Will I have a daughter to pass it to someday?

I showed the handkerchief to Marta when we got off the train. She thought it very beautiful. Now she often whispers to me if I have hope. I've decided to make a handkerchief for her birthday this year. I enjoy doing needlework and the crocheted edging will be fun to do. The nuns taught us well. Our house is full of doilies and tablecloths I have done.

My wedding chest is already complete with towels, linens, and sleepwear for my own home. Needlework is a comforting activity worked in the evenings as we listen to the radio. Mutti worries about straining my eyes when I'm working and makes me sit near the lamp.

We've watched Rolf's friends sent off for compulsory training one by one. There are too many goodbyes these days, but today I hold the handkerchief tightly in my hand as we wave goodbye to them at the train station. This isn't training it is war.

The train station is full of new propaganda posters that show the purity of the Aryan race, "The New Germany" or Hitler embraced by a group of children; another of Hitler dressed up like Sir Galahad – complete with white horse, lance and silver armor—leading us to victory.

Mutti laughed out loud when she saw that poster.

Ridiculous! I am worried someone will report her. The changing of the posters at the train station marks the passage of time for me. I remember the good-byes by the poster on display. Months have flown by – only the posters have been changed.

Our tiny city has blackout orders for the evenings. Now we have Air raid wardens assigned to make sure all windows are covered with black paper and a strict no light policy has gone into effect at dusk. I try to do my needlework by candlelight in my room now.

I've advanced in my coursework at school. The headmaster has been more visible to the girls in this program.

He listens to our lectures and slowly walks around the classroom.

His heavy heels click on the floor as he walks past, always wanting to know who had the lowest marks on exams. When he finds someone who does poorly, he calls them to the front of the class to discuss their marks in front of everyone. I am too nervous to type when he is present.

Today the headmaster told us a "fairy-tale" story; his term, not mine. He talks about the work camps where bad boys and girls go who can't handle the tasks the Fatherland needs. He went into vivid detail over what the camps would be like and said we were lucky to be useful citizens for the Fatherland. He makes my skin crawl. Now whenever I see him, my skin turns to gooseflesh.

All the students try to stay away from him as much as possible.

My parents raised me to believe adults are always right. For the first time I believe real evil can exist. Adults aren't always right.

We've had early heavy snows and time to go sledding with my friends. Marta and I spent our only free afternoon flying down the hill by the cemetery. We are the oldest on the slope. Hot chocolate and Mutti's *Lebkuchen* (cake) make it a perfect day.

There is no talk of war out on the hill, just laughter and lots of exercise. I'm getting too big for my sled. Papa put a wooden extension on it to make room for my long legs.

Germany has signed an agreement with Italy and Japan. Papa is very upset over this news. I heard him talking about another world war. We sat around our radio in the kitchen and listened to the radio announcements about the Luftwaffe bombing raids in London. I feel so powerless. Papa warns me to watch what I say and sometimes it feels as though it is going to bubble out of me.

Mutti and I kneel and pray for all the families. We spend more time going to church lately.

We joined our neighbors in celebrating Christmas Eve with many families brining a favorite dish. I think I wore four layers of clothes today against the bitter cold. Mutti, Papa, and I walked to the woods to see the beautiful Christmas tree lit with candles and sang carols. I didn't sing much this year, just wanted to take it all in. I held little Karen as she slept in my arms. Maybe I should have fifteen children? I think all the neighbors know how much I like children. They seem to pass them along to me as if I am a member of their family.

We stopped at Rolf's grave on the way home and sang "Silent Night" to him. My favorite day of the year has changed so much without Rolf. I miss him terribly.

Mutti and I held each other the whole way back to the house. Our exchange of gifts seemed so empty.

Yesterday we went back to the cemetery and decorated Rolf's grave for the New Year. There are many other families putting decorations up as well. Papa shoveled the pathways clear of

Gerti's War

snow and replaced some gravel around the park. Ulrich and Katharina Schmidt laid flowers on Jurgen's new grave. He was only 18 and a childhood friend of Rolf's. I remember his silly laugh. They are such a nice family. Herr Schmidt cursed Hitler in his grief. No one, but us heard him. Papa walked home with them and stayed for a while.

Later we huddled in the room and listened to the radio communiqué of the High Command reports. Mutti can get foreign stations to come in on our radio. We can't let others know we sometimes listen to French stations. Every time there is a victorious campaign to report, the announcer gets louder and louder, our voices get quieter and quieter. I'm glad we don't have a boarder right now.

Chapter 5 – February 1941

Today a well-dressed woman asked Herr Buchter about me at the post office. I overhead her say she is an officer's wife.
She wants a Nanny to help with her children and thought I looked strong and healthy. When she called me over, she asked if I had completed my year of mandatory service training. Normally this is done after I complete my schooling, but I hoped my business school would delay my service. Sometimes I think there are too many different programs, the BDM and RAD (Reichsarbeitdienst *der weiblichen Jugend*). I know I don't need any additional motherhood training. I want to work with Mutti delivering babies.

I do love children and look forward to this program, but I hope they pick someone else to work with her. I do not want to do the mandatory agricultural service with the BDM.

I hope that I'm too old for this program. They send many young girls to agricultural service, so the men can fight and train.

A women's advisor contacted the RAD and my school about my service record. They are giving me my exams early and sending notification to the factory as next week I start working as a Nanny. I tried to talk to the advisor about working with Mutti, but she didn't respond to my request. I can't believe that my time with Marta at the Post office will be finished as well.

I now have a new identification card and paperwork that I must keep with me. I have a special pouch I keep them in with a letter of introduction for Frau Weber. The slogan on the top of the letter says, "Before one can command, one must have learned to obey." The advisor made me sign my name and gave me no choice in the matter. After I signed, I asked again if I could train with my mother in mid-wife duties. She dismissed me as if I wasn't there. When do I get to decide?

Mutti is pleased I will be in a home environment, instead of taking the train into the large crowds of Pforzheim, but I know she wants me to train with her. Over the years, I have asked her every possible question about babies and children. I'm trying to look forward to the new assignment, but I am failing. Today I received my graduation certificate from school. There wasn't a big ceremony and I will be glad to get away from the headmaster.

Happy Birthday to me! Sunday, I spent the day with Marta and a few friends and we all went to the cinema in Pforzheim. We saw Gone with the Wind – Clark Gable is so handsome.

Frau Weber and her children live in Calw—the painted city.

It is over an hour to get there by train and bus. The town has beautiful, colorful murals on the front of some of the larger buildings. A large medieval bridge sits in the center of town as if a large troll sleeps underneath it.

Narrow streets, whitewashed walls, empty geranium planters, and red tiled roofs take me to *Lederstrasse*. My heart pounds in my chest as I approach the three-story house with a huge pointed gable. My hands shake slightly as I knock on the door.

Today I took more care in my appearance for my first day as Nanny Gertrud. I wear Papa's Christmas present to me, my new wool skirt. Mutti gave me a pair of her imitation silk stockings to wear. I've never had a new pair of my own. A small round woman with warm eyes answered the door and ushered me inside. She is the cook, Rosa. I can hear a commotion from the upper landing and slowly walk upstairs.

Two three-year old girls are rolling on top of each other at the top of the landing. They stop when they see me. They are Katharina and Christina—identical twins. Their hair is white blonde. One is shy and the other very outgoing. Another older child, Petra leans inside a nearby doorway. Her dark hair and dark eyes are such a contrast to her sisters. I think she is eight. The twins run down the hall toward their mother's room, with each trying to reach the doorway first. The noise level increases with my arrival.

Petra never smiles. She calls to her mother that I am here.

Three children shouldn't be too difficult, but I knew Petra would be a handful by the stern glare she sent my way. Petra smiled so sweetly to her mother as she approached and then stood behind her and locked her eyes onto mine.

Frau Weber is very small in stature and about thirty-five.

I felt very tall next to her. She has noticeably small wrists and ankles. After introducing the children, she called for Johann and Kaspar. I held on to the railing as my mind flew at the thought of five children. Two tall thin boys came running up the stairs, eleven-year old twins! The boys resembled each other but were not identical (thank goodness!). They smiled at me and I quietly asked Frau Weber if she had more children. She laughed and said, "No."

Petra lingered inside the doorway as her mother showed me around. I had a small room for studies with the children and a small bed in the corner if I stayed the night. That child's bed would never fit me! My feet will still out!

My work schedule will be Mondays-Saturdays and I am to check in with Frau Weber first thing every morning and receive the list of duties for the day. I must still attend Saturday morning BDM meetings in Neuenburg, take the train and bus back to Calw, and then I can go home after 3 pm. I must spend time with the younger children, and take them on outings and work on their reading and mathematics. "Keep the children presentable" is what Frau Weber told me as she leaves the room. I am responsible for house cleaning in the children's areas and must occasionally help Rosa in the kitchen or serve dinner at parties they may have.

I have no idea on what to do with the boys. Frau Weber said she would help guide me on this. I remember taking a deep breath and smiling again at Petra. There is a hard shell on that child.

Lois Buchter

This may be harder than I thought.

Captain *Hauptmann* Weber is very tall, thin, and handsome. I try not to stare at him. He is full of smiles for his children, and they adore him. Petra (or the monster child as I quickly refer to her) will do anything to get her fathers' attention.

Her tears never fail to get her lap time with either of her parents. The children have never had a nanny in the house before and Petra has decided I am now her maid and attendant. She is very demanding and likes to run to her mother and tell her I did or didn't do something. I have never met a more disagreeable child in my life. No wonder she doesn't seem to have any friends.

The girl twins are very loving and active, and I am enjoying my time with them. We like to curl up together on the small bed in my room and read. Many afternoons they fall asleep leaning up against me with their blankets tucked in snug around their small bodies. Will I do this with my own children someday?

I don't know what Frau Weber does to fill her days, as I never see her after my duty assignment. Rosa is teaching me some of her specialty cooking. We get along well. Maybe I can surprise Mutti with a special meal.

The boys are interested in the war. They are also interested in what their father is doing. They practice their running skills on our outings and I'm having trouble keeping their clothes clean and presentable.

Thank goodness, the boys are in school during the day. Sometimes I help with their homework, especially as they struggle with math.

I've stayed late several times these last few weeks and almost missed the train again last night. I must remember to bring a change of clothes to keep here just in case. Will I ever have free time with Marta again?

The monster child knocked over a beautiful vase today and told her mother I did it. I honestly don't know what to do with her.

Gerti's War

Last week she broke one of her porcelain dolls and said I dropped it.

This is the first time I spend the night. I made a pallet with the feather comforter on the floor and slept between the girls' beds. Petra wouldn't join us for a story even when I go out of my way to include her. Maybe she's jealous. When I woke the next morning, both little ones were on the floor sleeping beside me, but there was no Petra. She barely lets me braid her hair or touch her. Rosa told me not to let her get away with her tricks. She's always a problem.

We don't see their Papa very often. The officer is having a large dinner party next week and they asked me to help with it.

I took the girls grocery shopping today. Petra boasted to others in the store that her father is a Captain. She said how strong and fit the German army is ... "just like Papa." We stopped at a *baekerei* and picked up some sweet breads and cookies and Petra spilled jelly on her shirt on purpose. I watched her do it and then she denied it right to my face! That child needs a good spanking!

The dinner party is very lavish, with silver and china everywhere. I can tell that everyone likes Captain Weber. Many of the young officers and members of the high command complimented Frau Weber on the excellent meal. She blushes in their praises.

They bow and give her hand-kisses. A few of the men look at me and inquire over my situation. I am glad to go home this evening, but I am still tired just thinking about all the preparations and clean up. What a day.

Captain Weber's regiment is heading East. Petra screamed and rolled around on the floor when he tried to say good-bye. He looked at me and told me to take care of this situation. Why won't he reprimand her directly? She kicked me in the shin.

Frau Weber spanked Petra today when she caught her digging in the flowerbeds with a good silver spoon. Of course, I was also reprimanded for letting her get to the silver. These last two weeks of hell have been unbearable with Petra. Frau Weber stays in her room most of the time during the day and the children aren't allowed in there anymore. If my husband were off to war, I would want my children closer to me not further away. I've noticed she doesn't hug or touch her children often.

I tried to get Petra to play with some girls her age in the park today. She won't talk about her school friends but does very well in school studies. She walks alone outside the schoolyard at dismissal. I guess she has pushed all of them away too. She spends her time on her scooter outside in the side yard. I am glad when she is away from me. I want to pull her braids, hard the little tattletale!

Today a telegram arrived saying Captain Weber received a bad leg wound. He's had surgery, and will be sent to another hospital by train in a few weeks. The tantrums with Petra have increased and sometimes her mother holds her until the crying stops. I tried to comfort her, but she gave me a cold stare. Even Mutti doesn't know what to do with this child. Now I keep my comments and hands to myself.

Today Frau Weber asked me to accompany the family to see the Captain at hospital where they transferred him. We took the train to Stuttgart and walked several blocks there. This has been our first clear hot day in a while. I'm glad I had my straw hat with me.

Gerti's War

The Captain is in good spirits and he has compliments for all, including me. He said I looked lovely, I always blush easily, and I know I turned several shades of red. It was an innocent comment, but now Frau Weber won't look in my direction any more or talk to me. She did not like him looking at me or even noticing my existence. The ride home was very quiet and uncomfortable.

Papa's assignment is to transport wounded soldiers from Russia into Poland with the Red Cross. The radio updates on the war are not going well and we've had our first loss in Russia.

He will take the train back and forth. Mutti says he will be required to bury the dead along the way. He leaves today. Be safe, Papa. Be careful. I don't know how long he will be gone.

He told me he is excited over seeing some new parts of Germany. I think he told me that to make it sound better for me. His work sounds disgusting. I tried to put on a good strong face for him as he left.

Mutti acts differently since Papa left. She is convinced that Frau Koenig is watching her and others in town and reporting strange activities to her son. Mutti has a radio hidden in the spare room behind the bookcase and listens to the BBC late at night when we don't have a boarder to worry about. She wants to know what is really happening in the war. We could be shot if they find us listening to the BBC! This makes me nervous. I am forbidden to tell Marta about the radio, or what we learn. It is my first secret from Marta.

The Captain has arrived home for recuperation. He now walks with a cane, has a bad limp, and hopes to rejoin his regiment in two weeks. Petra has been constantly at his side trying to help him. Thank goodness, she's not around me. Her behavior has been better since he arrived home. Let's hope it lasts.

Frau Weber has increased her tirade against me. I can't do anything right anymore. She constantly tells me how ineffective

I am and looks to put me down as much as possible. That little monster stands behind her mother loving my belittlement. At least I have the twins and we are very close, but they won't go to their mother anymore. It seems strange to see Frau Weber out of her room during the day and the tension in the house is high.

Captain Weber is now getting around better. I complimented his quick healing and the attention Petra was giving him and told him it must be her good attentions fir his mending so well. He returned the compliment and told me how pleased he is with the girls' reading skills. Frau Weber overheard his compliment and saw the blush on my cheeks. She told me to go home early.

Marta's father came to our house this evening and told me he saw new paperwork regarding my work status. The RAD is reassigning me to a *Landjahr* work camp not allowing me to return to the Weber's. They would send me my things. I feel crushed.

I want desperately to say good-bye to the twins. Frau Weber has filed a complaint regarding my home service and I am not allowed an appeal. I will have to leave for the camp in three days. What a mean and vindictive woman! She knows I don't want to go into the agriculture service.

My handkerchief of hope is completely soaked now. How can I say good-bye to everyone? How I wish Papa were here. We haven't had word from him in weeks. Mutti, Marta, her father, and a few neighbors came to the train station to see me off.

I can't believe my future is so uncertain. How long will I be there? I know the work will be hard, but I am strong. Many people tell me it will only be for a few months. I try to be strong for Mutti.

Her good-bye hug hurt, but at least I can still feel it.

Gerti's War

This is too much for my emotional shield. My eyes pool just thinking about it. Marta and I pressed our hands on either side of the train window as it left the station. I can still see her hand print on the train window as I write this.

Chapter 6 – May 1941

I made it. After many stops and a three-hour train ride. I am only allowed one suitcase and I join the line of girls standing on the platform. They herd us into the back of a flatbed trailer for the short ride to HilgerLene.

"Master Sergeant" Frau Ruffin is in charge. She tells us in her stern, no-nonsense way, that her responsibility is to see that, "We work hard like steel and are quick like the dog."

Her shrill voice makes the hair on the back of my neck stand up.

There are twenty girls in my orientation group, all about my age. Everyone is glued to their places outside one of the barrack areas waiting for assignments. There are a few younger girls in one of the groups, some 12 years old.

Our new home is one of four long barracks stretched across the embankment. A large workhouse with an underground shelter encompassed the back yard. A scattering of small houses in the distance dot the countryside. The HilgerLene work camp is perched on the side of a hill with no comforting Black Forest woods in view.

I have been trying to take it all in. We are divided into groups of six girls. Our daily activities include 6:15 a.m. gymnastics followed by breakfast, farm work, and then back for dinner and showers in the evening. Lunches are served by the farmer's family at their discretion. The main barracks displays a chart showing rotating shifts for food preparation and laundry duty by squad. A large poster of the German Ten Commandments covers the wall in the front of the room.

The German Ten Commandments

- Remember that you are a German.

- If you are of healthy stock, you should not remain unmarried.
- Keep your body pure.
- Keep mind and spirit pure.
- As a German, choose only a partner of German or other Nordic strain.
- In the choice of your partner, consider ancestry.
- Health is the prerequisite of outward beauty.
- Marry only with love.
- Seek no playmate but a marriage comrade.
- Desire as many children as possible.

They issue me a dress uniform complete with skirt, jacket, white blouse, and hat. I brought with me two pairs of sturdy lace-up shoes along with my sport shoes. They also gave me a thin woolen blanket for my bed, three used blue work smocks, and stripped sleeping wear.

We change into our work clothes immediately and Frau Ruffin makes each of us stand on a chair and with a tape measure as she checks the hemline. Some girls must alter their smocks with pins.

Needles and thread are not available.

The girls who have dresses that are too short, or who don't complete their work assignments to the farmer's satisfaction receive severe punishments. Laziness is not tolerated in any form and is considered the worst offense. I know it will be hard work, but after working with the Weber's I think I can do it.

My new roommates are Louise, Margret, Cornelia, Jeanette, and Annemarie, we make up Squad H. Annemarie and Jeanette are from districts close to France. None of us has ever been away from home before. We have kinship in our loss of family.

Our room is small with three sets of wooden bunk beds, one tall Schrank (armoire) with shelves and drawers, and a small desk and chair in the corner. Some girls must use the lockers outside in the hallways. Louise, the shortest in our group, asks if it would be all right if she took the lower bunk beneath me. I

Gerti's War

threw my suitcase on the top bunk. At the sound of a sharp whistle we all go outside and then into the main lodge. We go to work immediately. Some sweep the area outside the lodge. Others help prepare dinner. I set the tables. Marta, how I wish you were here with me.

After 6 o'clock, the girls from the camp began to arrive.

Dinner is at 7p.m. They were filthy and ran for the shower area.

Each barracks holds six sleeping rooms. The center of our building encompasses a large bathroom with showers. I can't imagine the noise of thirty-six girls hitting the showers at one time, but it's very noisy and I was shocked to see girls walking around barely covering themselves. Goodness! I could never do that!

We squeezed onto the benches and they filled the room. The girls who prepared dinner didn't eat with us; they had plates in the kitchen. Frau Ruffin stood in the front of the room and gave the news of the day, the same old propaganda. I noticed all the girls watched her carefully as she addressed the group. She tells us to hold hands for a blessing and wishes us good appetite. I tried to stay small. All the new girls are quiet. I think the reality of our new situation is beginning to settle on us.

After dinner, Frau Ruffin distributed the mail and left the room. The atmosphere in the room changed dramatically without her. Everyone was more relaxed. Some girls write to their families or to any soldier. There is a box for miscellaneous writing in the corner. To one side, four girls sing songs. They are good.

In the back room, a small group clusters around a wooden carving of a chandelier on a center table. It feels as though I am in a dream, as I walk over to them. Their skill is incredible.

Small fairytale creatures cascaded down the sides and front.

Snow White and the Seven Dwarfs, the Three Bears, Red Riding Hood, and the wolf, all came to life under the knife. They are working to dedicate it to the girls who have been here before. These girls must be from the southern regions. I am spellbound as I watch the tiny chips litter the table.

Lois Buchter

I've written two long letters home and told Mutti about my roommates. Marta's letter is even longer. They haven't assigned me to a farm yet. This week I've spent learning the routine, mostly laundry, kitchen and clean up duty.

I am slowly getting to know my roommates. Louise is the most outgoing of our bunch. Cornelia and Margret look as if they are going to cry all the time. Jeanette sings with other girls in the camp, and has made friends easily. Annemarie disappears a lot. Not sure where or what she does, and I still don't know her well.

This evening one girl started crying after the post distribution. She received word that her father died. Again, war is in my mind. So many families seem torn apart and hurting.

I hope Marta would be able to offer a little comfort to my mother. I worry about her being alone. Papa should return soon.

They assigned Marta to service duty by helping Mutti in her parenting classes two nights a week in addition to working at the factory. That is the position I was to get. I try not to picture Marta taking the train by herself. I know how lonely she gets.

What a miserable bunch we are. If one of us starts crying late at night, the whole crowd starts. We are anxious over our situation, and have much to learn about the heavy work we will be called to do. At least I am strong. Some of the petite girls don't look strong. How would we manage tomorrow?

Why in the world do we need early exercising, when we are exercising all day long! The alarm sounds at 5:30, and we must be lined up for the flag raising at 6 o'clock. We get our assignments and are picked up by truck, or some must walk to their farm. Most of us are distributed in lots of three to eight girls. At the end of the day, we don't look like a work crew with puffy eyes and bent backs. I am sore all over and won't be able to write much these days.

Fritz runs my assignment. He lives adjacent to the property with his elderly father and crippled sister. She has arthritis; her

Gerti's War

hands are swollen and twisted at an odd angle. I wonder if she has had a stroke. Her face stays contorted as if in a constant state of pain. Fritz has a bad shoulder. He leans to one side when he walks. These people need help!

Their main farm was a beautiful small vineyard with a small family garden area to one side of the house. Fritz shows us how to clear the paths through the vineyards and to bind the young branches to the stock. I think they looked like rows of neckties when we finish the binding.

A relative of Fritz's brought us homemade bread two days this week for our noontime meal. It tastes like home again. Usually we have only a light clear barley soup, day after day. Fritz is not a tolerable man. He likes to criticize our abilities and boasts that the previous work crew was exceptional, good hard workers. He says we are lazy.

My back aches, and I must pop and stretch it often. I also have large blisters on my feet from my shoes. We are all trying to make the best out of our situations. I almost dropped my towel after the shower, and part of me didn't care. Frau Weber may you forever stay in a deep depression! I would never have wished this existence on my worst enemy.

The noise of the barracks still bothers me, especially in the common room. I miss the quiet of my room back home. My favorite time of the day is the evening sitting together on the bottom bunk talking about our homes and families. Cornelia has a boyfriend who is now an infantryman fighting on the Russian border. She is worried about his safety.

Annemarie's family runs a small bakery shop. She saw the German troops march through her town after the victory in Poland.

She is teaching us how to make pastries as she weaves wonderful stories about her kitchen. She practices with a towel for us.

Mouths water as she discusses the chocolate delicacies.

Margret is from Baden Baden and her family has a small spa and rooming house. She is a bit of an actress and now we act out funny stories about their guests on a wooden suitcase we nicknamed the stage.

Petite Jeanette comes from a large farm near Heidelberg at the edge of the Rhine Valley. We can't understand why she is here when she is needed on her own family farm. She's a talented artist and draws sketches of castles and the landscapes around us. Jeanette has three brothers in the war.

Louise is from the Southern Alps, near Garmisch Partenkirchen. Her extended family runs a restaurant. She has many cousins and two older married sisters expecting babies in the next few months. Louise is the easiest to cry at night.

Today on the farm, a refugee girl from Russia brought out soup to us in the field. Usually one of us goes inside to help prepare the meal. She's a very small girl, perhaps thirteen. Her long dark braids are held back by a very colorful scarf. She has a nice smile with perfect straight white teeth. Elsa doesn't understand much German. One of the girls understood a little Russian and we found out she was an orphan sent here to help on Fritz's farm. I try to give her small kindnesses when I can. Today, I helped her carry water to the field workers. This work is hard. My hands are rough like a mans.

Today I received a letter from Mutti. Marta's father found out Papa has been injured and is in a field hospital in Southern Germany. He has a stomach bullet wound. While loading some dead soldiers into an area for burial, a rifle accidentally discharged and shot him on his left side.

Oh, Papa, how I wish I could be there with you. Mutti is very upset. He will be sent home in a few weeks when he is well enough to travel. All my prayers Papa! Please don't be hurting too much. I wish desperately to be home giving Mutti a hug. I love them so much.

It's another very hot day that goes on forever. On the farm, a neighbor woman brought over smoked ham and two loaves of bread and we were each given a thick slice. I took mine over to a shady spot and started cutting up the ham with my small pocketknife.

Some girls shoved huge pieces of the bread into their mouths.

Elsa and I laughed together over their antics. Movement caught my eye as I held the ham and I stopped cutting it and looked closely. There are maggots in the meat! Ugh!

I was unable to stop Elsa before she took a bite. We quietly piled the uneaten meat back on the plate. By this time, all the workers had discovered the "prize inside." We tried to make it look as if we hadn't eaten yet when Fritz came into the clearing and told us to get back to work. Maybe if he gave us something more substantial, we could work harder. It was very satisfying to see Fritz bite into the ham! On the way home, they told us they assigned us to another farm.

This is a nice farm with a clean household and good kitchen. The farmer's daughter is in her early thirties and due to deliver any minute. The grandmother is a very hard-working Swabian woman, but I think her husband likes to supervise rather than sweat.

They have a young man on the farm helping them, a Polish POW, "Leo". His mind is sick. His eyes tell you a story of pain and suffering. How has he gotten here? What happened to him and his family? He doesn't speak German. We communicate through hand gestures and body language, but I long to find out his story.

I work with Leo side-by-side in the fields. The Grandmother on the farm handles Leo with indifference and doesn't talk to him or call him by name. She stands close to Leo and shows him what he needs to do.

Lois Buchter

We spend our days working in the hay fields. The fields are hard to clear with so few workers. The farmer demands me to lift heavy loads of hay with the pitchfork, the same loads Leo strains to lift! I can see the muscles bulging in his back through his thin shirt. I'm not strong enough to do it. Leo helps me when he can. I work with tears running down my face. Leo sees my tears and I think understands I am just as much a prisoner as he is.

I am so tired; but I could hardly make it to dinner. The food is abundant at this farm and they feed us good noontime meals. We all have good appetites. The girls in my squad feel my pain and try to lift my spirits as I moan on my cot. Jeannette gives me some of the chocolate her mother sent. Louise sings some of my favorite songs when the lights are out. We all take turns giving each other back massages. We all have hands that are rough and calloused.

Margret used me to demonstrate the fine skills of massage she learned from her mother at the spa. I am a welcome bag of flesh to be pounded and kneaded like a lump of flour dough.

Hopefully, we will finish the hay fields tomorrow.

Now that the hay is finished, we are up on ladders pruning cherry trees and binding branches. Today Grandmother interrupted our work with frantic calls to come in a hurry. Her daughter is in labor and having difficulty. I told the Grandmother when I arrived that my mother is a midwife and I have helped deliver a few babies.

I cleaned up and inspected the mother-to-be. She screamed loudly. After massaging her abdomen, I could tell the baby is upside-down. I had watched my mother turn a baby once before, but I was not sure how to do it myself. The Grandmother coated my hands with sweet oil in the kitchen. My hands looked large and rough even with the oil. Sweat poured off me, and as gently as I could, I turned the baby. I prayed the cord would not get twisted or looped around the baby's neck.

The Grandmother was helpful, listening to my suggestions.

Gerti's War

It felt strange to be the one giving orders. After two hours of labor, a healthy baby girl arrived. I am exhausted and overjoyed.

I have brought a new life into the world. Mutti you would be proud of me today.

We were all surprised to find the main yard empty when we arrived back at camp. A large crowd assembled in the back by our garden area. Frau Ruffin held a large fire hose in her hand that is turned on high. One of the new girls laid on the ground with the jet spray hitting her hard, turning her over and over in the mud. Her screams were unheeded.

When she stopped moving Frau Ruffin gave us a little speech.

We were not to have anything to do with "the louse." Until further notice, she would be given the hardest assignments available. What is her horrible crime? She fell asleep in the field on her assignment--unacceptable behavior.

To remind us of her guilt, they cut her hair very short.

She must wear the scarf of shame until she can prove herself worthy to join us again. It was a humiliating experience to watch and I ran for the showers. For the first time since arriving at the camp, I had a hot shower. I caught my reflection in the mirror as I left the washroom; an older, suntanned Gerti looked back at me. I feel older too. What a day!

I received another post from home. Mutti is very worried about Papa's wound. He has arrived home, but the wound looks and smells bad. The nurses say he needs another operation and right now, the Red Cross has put him on disability. Papa, I am so worried about you. I know Mutti will do everything she can. Will it be enough? She now must provide for both of them. Rations and tempers are short everywhere, maybe even at home. Please, let me go home!

They scheduled our squad for laundry and kitchen duty this next week. I much prefer to work the laundry than work in the fields. We are a singing laundry. It makes the time go by. I talked about my family to my group, more talking than I have ever done before, but did not discuss politics. We all concentrate on the people who matter in our lives.

I told them about Rolf and stories about my sweet Oma. She was widowed at 40, raised three children during the Great War, and kept food on the table by renting rooms in her home.

Her small bent frame hid the strongest person I have ever met.

She always thought of others before herself. When I close my eyes, I can still see her sitting off the kitchen, surrounded by flowers and potted plants, smiling at me. Those last few years she lived with us when her sugars took her leg.

All of us talked about the war and their hometowns. Many have gruesome stories about missing and murdered people before the war. That startled and surprised me. Some leaders in Anne Marie's community, who voiced an opposition or resistance to the Social Democratic Party, just seemed to disappear from their community.

Cornelia told us about a childhood friend of hers. The family left everything they owned in the middle of the night to escape to Palestine. Their home had been ransacked by the SA's shortly afterwards. Their beautiful furniture and goods are now in the homes of officers and district officials. She took a small painting of theirs when no one was looking. It had always been a favorite. She wrote to her friend that it was safe and would send it to her when it was safe.

Marlene joined us for work detail in the kitchen today.

She is from Dresden in the East and very popular among the girls in camp. She told us stories of bombing raids and Storm Troopers killing Jews, gypsies on the street and she had seen people killed and beaten. Her brother was wounded in a bombing raid.

Now he's a guard at a prison for the insane.

She saw one work camp and told us the horrors of the walking dead. Her family has had much sorrow in the past and she told us about her Aunt being brutally raped by a wandering group of Russian soldiers at the end of the Great War. Everyone here fears being captured by the Russians. We know they keep no prisoners.

It seemed everyone but I, had a story about the Russian rampages.

"Ivan" is someone I'm told to worry about, each story is more fantastic than the next. What will I do if I come face-to-face with Ivan?

Louise and I were canning cherry preserves yesterday in the kitchen and talking too much. While holding a large pot of hot wax, I stumbled, and the pot turned over on top of my left hand.

The pain is intense and searing. Louise put large amounts of butter over the forming red blister. The supervisor reprimanded us for talking and not paying attention to what we were doing and put us on gruel rations for a week. They will make me pay for the butter I used. I found myself squeezing my handkerchief of hope several times as the pain increased, especially last night. It looks horrible.

I've had three days of gruel and my stomach has been complaining loudly. Louise has always had a healthy appetite and food is a comfort for her. She is having a harder time with the diet restrictions. We find her normal gentle manner replaced with a rough impatience as her temper flairs in short bursts throughout the day.

The large blister on my hand burst this evening, finally giving me some relief. I was caught by the supervisor tending my wound and she insisted I let her take care of it. She cut away the dead skin around it and I wondered how scarred I would be as she cut away those last pieces of skin. Then, she told me to follow her into the cellar. She swept my oozing hand through as many spider webs as she could find, wrapped my hand with gauze, and told me if I were lucky, there wouldn't be a scar.

Surprisingly, it seems to be working.

After several spider web treatments, I finally went back to the farm today. I was met by the farmer's daughter and her new little girl wrapped up in a light blanket. Their attitudes have changed towards me. The farmer is letting me help in the kitchen until my hand heals and I learned how to make several new dishes from the daughter. It has been my diet salvation! They have some good cold cuts for our noontime meal. I managed to smuggle some back to Louise at the camp this evening. I didn't tell them about my meal punishment and Louise loved my gift. She had a beautiful smile for me today.

The cherry harvest has begun, and we must help at a neighbor's farm to help get in the crop. This much larger orchard and dairy covered most of the surrounding area. Fifteen girls are assigned to this farm. It reminds me of home and all the cherry trees around us. While working in the orchard, I could smell home.

I received a post today. Papa has had surgery and doctors say he did well. I must have read it a hundred times!!! He will go home in a few days. Marta comes by the house often to check on Papa for me. What a great friend. How I wish I were home.

It has been hot and humid for about a week with heavy thunderstorms around us. Taking deep breaths while working feels like we are breathing through thick fabric and I have trouble getting enough oxygen into my lungs. When the clouds burst, we all took shelter in the cow barn. The sweat poured off us.

Klara, the farmers' 5-year-old daughter, was delighted to have lots of "friends" in the barn to play with. She is a pest.

We all tried to stay out of her way. She came into the room where we were and showed us an opened bottle of Coca-Cola found on her father's workbench. Boastfully she announced she wasn't going to share it with us since we wouldn't play with her. Our mouths were watering over the sight of that bottle. One of the girls whispered, if we were quick they could grab it from her without a problem. Before they could get it and dash into the rain, Klara took a few large gulps. She dropped the bottle and began to scream. Repeatedly the screams echoed through the barn as the lightning struck.

We didn't know what to do for her. Marlene noticed the spilled drink bubbling on the floor and eating through the wooden planks at the base of the barn. Soda would not do that! Marlene told us it probably wasn't soda; she picked up the child and took her over to the area where the milking cows were penned. We put her under the cow, with several girls holding onto each leg of the cow. It was difficult to control the cow, as she was not pleased to have a howling child underneath it. We began milking the cow directly into Klara's mouth, as much as we could get into her. After a few minutes, she started to vomit. We continued to force the milk down her.

Her father heard her screams and the commotion in the barn and couldn't believe the sight of his daughter underneath the cow. He grabbed a pitchfork and came at us full steam telling us to let his daughter go but stopped when he saw the empty soda bottle lying on the ground. Marlene plead with him that we were only trying to help her. Dropping the pitchfork, he cradled his daughter and told us he had put some prussic acid into the bottle after cleaning up some farm equipment.

Now he pleads with us to help his little girl. He doesn't know what to do either. Thank goodness, Marlene remembered milk was good for poisoning. There are no doctors in our remote area.

Marlene and her father went into the house and his voice shook as they were leaving the barn. I could hear him say, "…it's all my fault. Don't worry little Kara, Papa will make it all better."

Marlene's quick thinking probably saved that little girl.

Everybody has been talking about it. Word even arrived back at the camp. Frau Ruffin called Marlene to the front of the room after dinner and had her tell the story to all the girls present.

For being such an outstanding "good German," they told Marlene her service requirements at the camp were now completed. She would be able to go home in the morning. We all stood and gave her applause. She thanked us and wished us to "Be true to each other. I hope you all die laughing." I am happy for Marlene. Inside I longed to be in her shoes and going home. Tonight, home feels very far away.

The work schedule has varied as we are shuttled to farm after farm. We are now harvesting another hay crop, saffron fields, and another orchard needs attention. Will it ever end?

Many new girls have arrived at the camp this week.

We like to sing while we work. I try to remember my favorite
-- My Quiet Valley,
"In the valley of the nicest meadow
My homeland where I like to walk, my quiet valley A thousand greetings to you now
And when I have to go –
My pleasure is everywhere and oh such sweet sounds
That's my regret you hear – the last path to go
And when I die and am placed in the valley ground Sing for me at my grave – in the last hour – my golden sunset
Peace in my quiet valley"

Party propaganda material is the only literature allowed in camp. I long to read something that doesn't make my mind go quiet. I am so happy to hear that my parents are coming next weekend. Mutti says she will bring some fabric and embroidery thread. I can hardly wait. My four months here seems like a long time ago. Father can finally travel by train and I can meet with them for two hours on Sunday afternoon. The days seem to go by so slowly now.

These last few days seemed very long waiting for my Papas' hug. It has been worse than when I first arrived at the camp. I am worried something will happen to Papa, or I will mess up the arranged free time. Time inches by as I wait for them on a bench outside the meetinghouse. My hands look so awful, I know they will notice. I can still smell Papa as we all hold onto each other for the first few moments. He has lost weight and there are dark rings under Mutti's eyes. Both couldn't get over the changes in my appearance and think I am much too thin. I put on my best work smock, but it is very worn. My clean hair stands at attention, frizzy and dull. The soap we use can be harsh on your skin and hair. I'm glad I don't look into the mirror too often.

Mutti is in tears most of the time we are together. She told me she had talked to Marta's father about trying to get me reassigned to a farm closer to home. He didn't hold out much hope, and has been doing what he can. One of his supervisors found out he is looking into things not in his department and his supervisor showed up at our home a few weeks ago and said if we had any more complaints, Mutti can be sent to a work camp as well. She had some choice words for the supervisor when he left.

I hoped none of the girls overheard her today.

My parents brought canned goods; some light blue linen Mutti dyed herself, and some dark blue embroidery thread with some sharp needles. She brought her small sewing kit and a few books as well. How I hated to return those books, but I knew they were forbidden in camp. I want to make handkerchiefs of hope for the girls in my squad. Needlework has been an encouraged evening activity even though supplies are limited. Just about everything I own needs repairing.

I feel so much better after my parents visit. How long before we'll be together again? Mutti said she would try to get some decent shoes for me and took a tracing of my foot with her for sizing. I shared the canned items they gave me with my bunkmates. Louise has some white crocheting thread. I gave her one of the crochet needles that was in Mutti's sewing kit. She is going to stitch up the edging for each handkerchief. The needles were put to good use as we repair our smocks and underclothes, but word quickly spread we had needles amongst the girls in our compound. Soon a line of girls stood outside the door waiting for a chance to repair a hem or fix a hole here or there.

Lois Buchter

I finished my assignment with the "good kitchen" farm and my duties are a little lighter these days. A few girls from my camp received the best assignment, teaching at an elementary school in a small town. All the former teachers are gone. How I hoped my turn at a school would come next, but they've assigned me another farm.

A kind-hearted elderly couple who are barely able to get around owns this old broken farm. Their four sons are off fighting, even their youngest seventeen-year-old. He's almost my age! The Mother worries about them constantly.

Whenever she sits, she rubs her hands together nervously, and she must sit a lot because of poor circulation in her legs.

Her ankles are the size of melons. It pains me to even look at her feet. The farm Father looks older than his years yet has incredible strength in his arms. Today I saw him lift a very heavy bit of machinery by himself.

They have a stand for butchering cows in one area of the barn and a herd of milking cows fills up the rest of the barn.

Their small house covers a tiny patch of space in the yard, and covered with a lovely thick spray of vine flowers that spreads across the patchwork roofing. I expect Hansel and Gretel to come out the door anytime. One side of the barn has rotted away, and it leans at an angle. Chickens scatter across the back lawn they share with the two large oxen behind the house.

I spend most of my time in the barn cleaning up after the cows and feeding the chickens. It's a peaceful farm. I'm surprised to find myself smiling as I work and sometimes laughing out loud. I've never worked around cows before. Herr Maier has been patient in his endless explanations. He has a good sense of humor despite the war and announces new nicknames for the animals every day. I wonder what my nickname is?

Frau Maier showed me how to churn butter and we made our own Pot cheese. I took a little more than my share when it came to eating the cheese. It is delicious! My appetite has returned with a vengeance. I now check my food carefully after I found some moldy bread in the cellar. Their eyesight must be bad, as the Mother's eyes are cloudy.

Helma was sent to the farm to work with me. This new helper works slowly and doesn't like getting dirty. She didn't complain when I told her to put on some rubber boots while we were in the barn. She can't work any slower and I am frustrated at her work pace. She never stops talking. She repeats words and hums to herself all day long. I've decided she has something wrong in her head. Now I will try to stay away from her as much as possible. It makes me shudder to think about her survival if Frau Ruffin observes her work habits. Will she survive on another farm?

We must get ready for winter and butchering the cows. I watched the life go out of those beautiful big brown eyes and cried for each cow as it died. The butcher came to the farm, and hacked, and cut all over the wooden table in the barn. Blood soaked into the dirt and the flies are now everywhere. The wooden cart for transporting milk has been transformed into a butcher's cart. I lined the cart with a few bales of hay and burlap. We laid the huge quarters on top of each other. The Butcher took a handful of the best cows on lead behind the cart for transportation to the troops. I took a deep breath when the cart finally left the yard. At least they didn't ask me to kill any of the animals. I would be able to do it.

Helma spends her early afternoons in the woods gathering kindling for winter. I helped secure large woven baskets to either side of the two cows carrying the bundles for her. Her task is to fill the baskets and the one she carries on her back every day. She always returns complaining she can't find enough wood and only a few baskets are filled. I wonder what she is really doing all afternoon.

Lois Buchter

I received a package from home today with boots, a warm jacket, and extra socks!

Today I took bread dough to the communal baking oven at the edge of town. It is an opportunity to meet some local people and see a little more of the town. Many large wooden carts overflowed with sugar beets passed us by. The small children sitting on top of the piles laughed and waved at us. They look so gay. All the local women know the children, and a few of them blew kisses back and forth. What a happy sight to see.

Two days at this new farm, and I've had enough. When I arrived, a two-year old in soiled clothes stood alone in the kitchen crying his eyes out. The kitchen is a mess and there were no adults anywhere. I found a glass, rinsed it out, and poured some milk for the child. He calmed down and sat on the floor with his milk. His diaper hadn't been cleaned in a while.

I found an elderly man sitting on a bench in the barn. He mumbled to himself as he put together a very intricate model of the Hindenburg made entirely of matches. He didn't acknowledge my repeated requests for help. A screaming baby and mumbling mad man in the barn, what type of a farm is this?!!

The owner, Herr Schuller, is a very disagreeable old man.

He walks stiffly and holds one of his arms at an unusual angle.

When I approach him, he just points to the right and tells me to join the others in the cabbage field at the far end of his property. On the way, I pass a young woman leaning up against a tree. Her eyes are closed, and she cries. As I walked by, I ask her if she was all right and if she knew anything about the baby in the kitchen. Her blank eyes opened, she turned and walked back toward the house, not saying a word.

I join the six girls in the field picking white cabbage.

The cold wind cut through our clothes. We used a short knife to cut the stalks and put them in wooden crates. It is very quiet in the field. At the brief afternoon break, I found out the details of this farm. Mala, the farmer's daughter and mother of the child is deeply depressed over the recent death of the baby's father and is having trouble taking care of the child. Her mother died last year.

Herr Schuller has rheumatism in his joints and it is painful for him to get around. They have a boy, Zurek, a POW from the Ukraine, on the farm who at fifteen has a problem with alcohol.

This is a depressing place to be.

A loud roar filled the skies above us this afternoon.

Hundreds of planes passed over us traveling toward the east. I have never seen so many planes before. It is an impressive sight.

Many of the girls talk about it on the way back to camp. We find our duties cut short in the afternoons. We've been told to gather an armful of kindling each day for the camp. What will it be like working in the camp this winter? Will we have enough to keep us warm? The mornings have already turned murky and cool.

I'm glad for my shoes and jacket. All our work clothes are threadbare.

My hands look awful with scratches and rough spots all over them. Have I been digging up potatoes for an eternity? My knees have flat fronts on them from kneeling all day. Sometimes the old man comes out to watch us work in the fields. One of the girls said he had been gassed in the Great War and hasn't been right since then. He yells nonsense at us in between gesturing wildly with his stoic stance. Sometimes he salutes us when we walk by.

I've worried about that little baby in the kitchen. I can hear his screams all the way out into the fields.

Lois Buchter

The cold cuts into our clothing and radiates from the ground, keeping us in a cocoon of cold. Our faces are chapped from working outside. Heat and food are becoming more important and I have been dreaming of my old warm bed at home almost every night. I'm wearing three pairs of socks to bed and I can't seem to get warm.

Herr Schuller does not feed us a noontime meal. He tells us to forage in the barn for whatever we can find. We located canned jars in a small cupboard and piles of apples, onions and a few smoked meats. We made a huge batch of apple cider. One of the girls made hot onion cakes in the kitchen and they felt so good in our stomachs. The farmer wasn't too happy about the cider and onion cakes, but he ate more than anyone else did. Said his wife used to make delicious onion cakes and he missed having it this year. He grumbled about his good-for-nothing daughter and pushed her out of the barn before she could share in the meal. He is very rough with her. I noticed old bruises on her arms.

While putting away the apple cider into the cellar well, we found Zurek in a drunken stupor from drinking the *"must."* It took four of us to haul him out of the cellar. Then we didn't know what to do with him once he was above ground. One of the girls said we should leave left him in the cellar because there was no place to put him. We knew the farmer would be back for more cider because he had mentioned he wanted to take some to a neighbor.

We quickly decided to stash Zurek in the hayloft above the senile old man's workbench. However, before we could get him up the ladder, Herr Schuller came into the barn. He grabbed the boy by the collar and hit him hard across his cheek. You could tell the impact hurt the farmer as much as Zurek. His joints couldn't take the jolt. In a flash, he took the belt off his pants and began beating him. Our small group of girls didn't stand around to watch, we headed as far out into the fields as we could get. I heard one of the girls ask out loud…" are we in hell yet?"

Gerti's War

While waiting for our ride, we saw the farmer's daughter trying to comfort Zurek. Already he is black and blue and with one side of his face swollen. She held him as he cried. Then they both cried. I am glad we aren't close enough to talk to him because I don't know what words of comfort I could offer.

We jumped into the back of the wagon when it arrived. As we left the farm, I saw Herr Schuller pull Zurek out of his daughter's arms and begin to kick him on the ground. I closed my eyes and didn't open them again until we got back to camp. I can still hear his screams in my mind as I walked to the showers.

I tried to tell the others what we had seen, but the political news and short program before dinner took a little longer than usual. Frau Ruffin asked if any girls knew how to type with accuracy, and if they did, to come up to the front of the room. Louise and I were some of the ones who answered her request. I hoped to be sent to a local business office instead of back into the fields. Anything would be better than going back to that farm.

Eight girls came to the front of the room. Frau Ruffin took down our names and asked us detailed information on our training.

She asked us if we would like to volunteer for the *Nachrichtenhelferin* (Signals Auxiliary) for the Wehrmacht. All of us said "yes". Then she told us our agriculture service had ended and we were being sent to Stuttgart to learn teletyping for the army. We leave in the morning. I can't believe that I am going into the military. I barely had time to write a note to my parents and pack up my things. Louise and I quickly gave each of the girls the handkerchiefs of hope we had made in a small ceremony on "the stage."

When we finally put the lights out, I heard Jeanette say, "Be careful Gerti and Louise. I heard Stuttgart has been targeted for bombing raids. Be extra careful…" Bombing raids, what do you do in a bombing raid?

Chapter 7 – November 1941

Louise and I squeezed our handkerchiefs as we stepped off the train in Stuttgart. I nervously picked at my awful looking hands while on the train and we tried to clean our thin coats. A matron met us at the train and hurried us into the train station office. Louise pointed out to me that all the windows at the train station, and houses surrounding us, had their windows blackened.

A crude little triumphal arch made up of boughs of pine and wilted flowers hung over the main station entranceway. We were taken by bus to another barracks area for processing. I counted ten girls in our group. We lined up and were measured and handed used uniforms. Thankfully, they were clean and very warm. The green trim on the collars was soft against my neck. Woolen stockings and sensible leather walking shoes completed my new ensemble. They feel wonderful on my feet! They fit!

My training classes are in the afternoons and evenings and we spend our mornings in food preparation and laundry detail. We have limited water usage, but baths are allowed on Saturdays or Sundays. Our coal is in short supply too as we are given nine coals a day to heat our rooms throughout the night.

Our matron suggests we gather supplemental wood early in the mornings or go without heat. It is our choice.

The barracks stonewalls are thick, and its coldness radiates a chill into the air. I always thought living in a stone castle would be warm. I now know how wrong I was.

My wool uniforms are a little scratchy and I have to resist the urge to scratch. Louise and I changed into the uniforms as soon as possible. We have been issued a small package of toothpaste that is mixed with a little peppermint flavoring. Mine has already hardened into cement. I don't care and tried to clean my teeth and my hands as best I could considering.

Lois Buchter

Our instructor says that our six-week training course will be very intensive, with memorization and accuracy demanded always. I have already started studying the forty different coded sentences and abbreviations that must be memorized before graduation. In the larger section, there are over one hundred girls here and the noise of typewriters is unnerving.

Louise and I have settled into the new routine, but many girls here have never been away from home before. We are rooming with eight girls, but so far, everyone keeps to themselves. We have no time for socializing.

They assign our duties by bed assignments on a large chart in the room. The small coal stove in our room barely heats the room. So far, I've been able to see my breath every morning.
The only lighting allowed is a single candle in a bottle on the dresser and it gives the room an eerie glow at night. I lie in bed thinking about Marta and home. If I get lonely, I think about Rolf and I running through the woods to the shrine and that day Papa sang for us.

An 80-plane bomber raid hit Stuttgart over the summer. We are drilled on where to go during the next raid. We sit huddled together in a large underground cellar under the main classroom building. When sirens go off, we stop and run to the shelter. It doesn't matter where you are or what you are doing, even in the shower! The compliance is mandatory for all. The Matron does a roll call in the cellar. Workers added extra concrete pillars for support.

I am having trouble working in the freezing cold classroom and sometimes my fingers won't respond. I thought with all the girls working, we might generate some heat. I moved my chair closer to the girl next to me to see if it will help.

Everyone bundles up as much as possible, but our legs and hands are constantly cold. I am constantly stopping to blow on my hands and warm them up. I wish I had some leather gloves. I wonder if I could type with them on?

The Matron walks by our desks, down row after row. I am constantly listening for her footsteps and the slap of the leather rod she keeps in her hand. Wham! Several times a day she hits someone's typewriter to reprimand them for mistakes or their slow progress. We are tested at the end of every day and our progress is charted at the back of the room. Students with better scores sit at the front of the room. I've already moved up twice. Louise is working hard to catch up with me. I want to stay with sweet Louise.

I had hoped my parents might visit me in Stuttgart, but now Papa's condition has worsened. He is scheduled for another operation to improve his stomach condition. Mutti sent me a warm coat and lots of news from home. Marta has met a nice man injured during the invasion of Paris. He is recuperating at a house near Arnbach and Marta sent me a very complimentary description of her "Paul." She says he is very tall, handsome, and witty.

I smile every time I read her describing him as "full of beans." He must have a very witty sense of humor for her to use that description. I hope he makes her laugh often.

Marta said her father would send travel authorization papers for me if Papa's conditioned worsens or if they can schedule the surgery soon. I am needed at home!

The United States has declared war on Germany. My stomach is in knots. Britain has declared war on Japan. *Kreig*! It has come again. What is happening to the world?

My travel authorization papers have arrived this week, just as I finished my training. I have a five-day emergency travel order! It came just in time!

They were briefing me on our new assignment in Boblingen, just southwest of here, when they handed me the orders. Louise is ready to finish her exams in a few days and will join me in Boblingen before the Christmas holiday.

My heart is filled with joy and apprehension on going home.

I've been so worried about Father's condition, and my feet practically curl over the thought of sleeping in my own bed again and being with Mutti. The time can't go by fast enough for me.

The train conductor just announced that Germany has declared war on the United States. Japan has bombed Hawaii. I noticed none of the passengers celebrated. We are all stunned in our seats. I smoothed and pressed my handkerchief all the way to Pforzheim.

Where are the joyous crowds of happy Germans we hear on the radio or see in the propaganda posters? I have never seen them. What is the truth? I don't know anymore. All I can think about is going home.

I tried to walk in a professional manner from the train station to the house in my uniform, but my emotions won, and I ran the last few blocks to my front door. Oh, how my heart sang!

Papa has lost more weight and he held me in the longest hug ever! I noticed that for the first time in my life I could get my arms around his chest now. Mutti came up behind him and we all had a group hug as we cried.

Papa's surgery will be in Pforzheim and he must go to the hospital tomorrow to check in. Mutti made all his favorite foods for dinner, but he didn't eat much. I told him I would have extra helpings for him and I did. Food has never tasted this good before.

Marta came by and we visited for a few hours before I finally had to go to bed. My eyes wouldn't stay open. A long hot shower and my goose down coverlet has me floating a few inches off my bed the whole night. Right now, I am in heaven.

Marta slept in Rolf's room so that we have the needed time to catch up during my short visit. This morning Marta quietly came in and crawled into the small space between my body and the wall. We both snuggled under the mound of blankets.

She talked non-stop about Paul and the work she is doing at the factory. Her father is trying to get her reassigned out of the factory and into an office job somewhere else, but the political officer at the factory is a Nazi and he has been adamant she remains there. I can imagine the frustration her family is going through.

Marta's father lined up a few office positions, but they don't have enough importance to warrant a change through the political office. Marta hopes in a few months she will be in a more stable position and safer too. There is always a risk she could be sent far away to work in a larger factory. Perhaps even be sent to Poland.

Paul is going to meet us for lunch and we spent an hour fixing our hair and putting on a little lipstick. Marta brought over her new make-up. It is the first time for both of us to wear make-up. Mutti says I must make it look natural or we can get unwarranted attention. I can hear Paul and Papa talking loudly downstairs as Marta and I listened to their conversation from the top of the stairs. They both smiled as Marta and I descended the stairs like royalty.

Paul is very handsome with dark wavy hair and sparkling green eyes. Marta didn't tell me about the deep dimple in his chin.

He told us charming stories about his family in the medieval-styled town of Rothenburg to the northeast. It still looks as it had in the early 1700's. Papa had a picture book of Germany with photos of the town that he shared with us. Paul even pointed out his family's jewelry shop in one of the photos.

Paul has the gift of gab, and able to talk easily with both my parents. Marta is bursting with the happiness she has found with Paul. She told me that he has kissed her once before I arrived.

We giggled over that many times. It has warmed my heart to see her so happy.

Paul and Marta walked with us to the train station and Paul carried Papa's suitcase for him. When we left the train, we walked at a slow pace to the hospital and it took us much longer than we had planned. Papa had to rest and to warm up a little several times.

There was a light dusting of snow on the ground and it makes a good contrast to the blackened windows on every building we pass. Closer to the hospital we saw across buildings and road damage from earlier bombing raids. There are wide craters in the road. A few buildings are just burned out shells of their former grandeur. Luckily, the firestorm from the raids did not reach the hospital district.

This damage concerned me, as I didn't realize so many strikes had hit Pforzheim. When I asked Mutti about it, she said she didn't want to worry me and had not included this news in her letters to me. What else had she withheld during my months away?

We checked Papa into the hospital for his morning surgery.

He will be released after 24 hours and Papa's old boss, Herr Leuschner, told us he would arrange transportation and for us not to worry. I tried not to cry as we said goodbye, but my tears started flowing. I told him we would be there in the morning when he comes out of surgery. Mutti and I slept in the waiting room all night. She told me that I should keep my journal at the house when I went back and I shouldn't carry it with me for fear of someone reading it. I should be more careful.

Papa's surgery went well, and we spent the whole day waiting for him or with him. Marta came by after work. The time home is going by too quickly. Only two days left. Papa is sleeping on the sofa in the living room until he can take the stairs.

I asked Mutti if I could sleep with her, just for tonight and we both laughed over how quickly she said "Yes." Her pillows smell like Papa's after-shave. Mutti told me to take a pillowcase when I left if it would make me feel less lonely. Mutti is taking Papa to a check-up and I will work on an early Christmas meal for us all.

Gerti's War

I loved being home in the house for a while by myself. I put on Mutti's apron and cleaned the house. I made a special welcome-home sign for Papa and put it on his pillow.

If Papa has enough strength, we are going to have some sort of family celebration and exchange presents after dinner. This summer I knitted a scarf for my father and carved a wooden trivet for mother. My carving is very crude and not up to the standards I normally make. It would have to do this year. I told Mutti of the lessons I received from one of the girls at the farm camp, but my lessons weren't finished. I think she will love it.

Paul came by in the afternoon and kept me company as I worked in the kitchen. His leg hasn't finished healing and walking pains him. I made Papa's favorite homemade Black Forest Cherry Cake. Paul kept me laughing all afternoon. I invited Marta and Paul to join us for dinner and he accepted once he smelled the cake. My cheeks are sore from all the laughing. Yes, Marta description of Paul was correct. He is "Full of beans."

Papa couldn't join us for the meal, as he fell asleep as soon as they got home. He looks smaller somehow. Paul and Marta didn't stay long after dinner.

Later, Mutti, Papa, and I exchanged presents sitting around the end of my parents' bed. Mother gave me new shoes and a sweater. Father gave me warm long underwear. It is so practical of him. They were surprised I had managed to make gifts for them both.

After we cleaned up the kitchen and straightened up the living room, Mutti and I laid down on either side of Papa and listened to him snore. I wanted the peace and serenity of this moment to last forever. We giggled over some of the sounds he makes. Poo—breathe, poo–breathe. Ha!

The train leaves at 2 o'clock and I can feel time squeezing the energy out of me. Mutti insisted I take another long hot shower and I didn't argue too much about that. She helped me pack my things. She also gave me a few extra socks and her best leather gloves.

Papa called me into his room and asked me to bring to him a beautifully carved wooden box he kept hidden in his closet.

Funny, but I had never looked through his closet before and was surprised at the number of suits hanging in it. They smelled like mothballs. The box contained medals from the Great War, some coins and a silver men's hairbrush.

He pulled out a small pocketknife hidden in the lining and handed it to me. His father had given it to him when he went off to war and now he wanted me to have it for protection. If asked about it, I should say I am working on my woodworking skills. He made me promise to sew a little pocket into the lining of my suit and keep the knife with me all the time. I kissed him gently on both cheeks and told him I would be careful. It's going to be so hard to leave.

Marta walked with me to the train station. She still has her handkerchief with her. She said repeatedly that she would try to get permission to visit me in Boblingen as soon as possible. We both smiled and hugged each other before I said "Good-bye." I feel we will be together again soon, she is so a part of me.

I took the train through Stuttgart to Boblingen. The agent checked my travel papers at the beginning of my trip and again before I departed. A young lady sitting on a bench in the corner of the authorization office didn't have any paperwork with her.

Her interrogation is causing quite a disturbance in the office.

I am glad to have my papers stamped and get out of there. Travel seems to be more difficult with all the new edicts. Marta's visit might take longer than we anticipate. I hoped not.

Chapter 8 – December 1941

The Communication office building is an immense three-story stone structure near the airport tucked in among the trees at a clearing near the runway. I can see planes on the runway in the distance outside my door. Here, men are everywhere. They must be recruits waiting for orders or for training.

I turned ten shades of red walking past them and felt very awkward. Several men offered to carry my suitcase for me. They look so handsome in their uniforms, but my feet felt two sizes larger as I tried to walk in a lady-like manner past them.

The Communication office is in a building shaped into a horseshoe pattern with a garden finishing off the enclosure. The upper two floors are for lodging, main floor for officer quarters and staff offices, but down two floors underneath the building, this lowest area is storage, training, laundry, and food preparation. A huge processing center covers the entire lower floor where I will join a few hundred girls working the teletype machines. I received my desk assignment and am immediately put to work. A matron handed me a stack of coded weather reports to send out. I had to take several deep breaths to steady my nerves.

Thankfully, Louise found me by the end of the day. She said I stood out with my suitcase sitting beside the chair and gave me a quick run-down of the place. I am disappointed to find out we aren't assigned to the same room, but she is just down the hall from me. I now share my room with eleven other girls. There are three sets of bunk beds on each side of the room. I am shocked to look out the window into the interior courtyard and see the men's sleeping quarters set up exactly like ours on the other side. A few men wave to us from the other side! No curtains!

All my personal items must have my identification number inside including my uniforms. Thank goodness, I no longer have laundry detail and food preparation to do. Dinner is at 8 o'clock each evening and our work assignments start at 9 o'clock. So far, most of the time I send weather reports to squadrons, and sometimes report troop movement and battlefield conditions.

Four divisions divide our big room. A special group off to one side handles the more sensitive reports. My shift is over at 7 o'clock and then I have breakfast and go to bed. My breakfast meal of cold cuts and hard bread tasted great. Louise warned me that there isn't a change for the evening meal. It is red cabbage, white cabbage and potatoes with a little bit of fish sometimes thrown in. That doesn't sound very appetizing.

The bathing ban is still in effect. My military service now allows us to have an additional bath on Wednesdays. There is hot water in this building! The upper levels are not heated during the night while we work and there is minimal heating in our rooms during the day when we sleep. Everyone wears extra layers of clothes and extra socks. The main floor has plenty of heating for the officers.

Louise warned me sleeping would be difficult during the day.

I am trying to get used to the noise and an active mouse problem in the building. Great, I really hate mice. Traps are everywhere.

Fraternization with the men in the area is forbidden unless an officer is present. We can go to town, but there must be at least three of us together plus a soldier to accompany us.

Our matron is responsible for large groups of girls, but the Communication Officer is responsible for the entire complex. He is an officer in full regalia (black high boots, swinging a whip and constantly shadowed by his well-trained German shepherd).

Just seeing him makes my blood turn cold. Other officers in the processing area don't make me feel like ice.

I must stay out of trouble. If I complete my transmissions without mistakes, I should be able to blend into the walls. It is very stressful to work during those long nights. How I wish I

Gerti's War

could say, "Don't stand behind me, so I can work more efficiently!"

I am getting to know some of my new roommates who are from all over Germany. Most of them have been sent here directly from business school training centers. I am the only one who has been to business school and completed my agriculture and women's service. They have all sorts of questions for me about my personal history. I am surprised at the frankness of my reply.

My shyness of the past is now gone. Am I used to the noise of living with others?

Leni has the bed underneath me and is from Cologne. I remember visiting Cologne with my parents so long ago. Some of the girls are too quiet. They won't join us in our late afternoon socials in the park nearby. The socials are a good break from our work. We sing songs and tell stories about our families, but we don't talk about our future. We concentrate on the recent past and things that uplift our spirits. It is an easy way to get to know a lot of people in an afternoon. The soldiers in the area aren't allowed to talk to us, but they listen to our conversations and sometimes sing with us.

For our Christmas holiday service, the Commandant has given permission for us to dine with the men. We can talk to the enlisted men if a higher-ranking officer introduces us first.

The Officers are bombarded with requests from both sides, most of them girls. There must be eight girls for every one man. We decorated a small tree in the lobby and we sang a few songs, but it doesn't feel like Christmas to me.

Most of the men in our area are here for infantry training and tanker training. We can hear the planes from the runway all the time. The Luftwaffe, are using the airport for tactical training of the fighter pilots. They are housed closer to the flight line in a long underground bunker. We don't see many of those men, but sometimes curse the planes when they are too loud.

The flyovers while trying to sleep drives me crazy. At least most of their missions are at night when we are working!

Another Saturday night and a shorter work schedule tonight.

We have an extra hour. Everyone wants to go to town and do some shopping with our ration cards. Mutti sent me one of her ration cards. I'd like to get some wine to celebrate New Year's. Her note said that Papa is doing much better. I want to celebrate his health. I bought cake, champagne and some false coffee. Some of the girls were able to get beer, which has been in short supply.

We were able to get what we needed and gave some cake to our soldier escort.

Today was my first official visit to the picturesque town square of Boblingen. It seems a nice city, but the people are not friendly to us. I heard a passerby say something about "Gray mice" as she passed by us. Ingrid mumbled something back to them that wasn't ladylike. I had to ask her about it and she told me the French soldiers called us "Gray mice--irritable pests always working away during the night...just like mice."

I don't understand why locals don't like us. It's probably because supplies are short everywhere and we get served before the locals. The Communication office has requisitioned supplies meant for the town. What an uncomfortable feeling. I can't give my place in line to anyone. You never know who is watching.

The long cold winter seeps into my bones. My teletype hours are long, and the room is freezing, but it's still better than the training room back in Stuttgart. I've enjoyed meeting more girls and learning about their histories.

Saturday evening socials are the highlight of my week and the dining room comes to life in the evenings. Some girls dance a little when no superiors are looking. Dancing in public has been banned for quite a while. It is a wonderful freeing experience to let ourselves spin and forget about the war. We even had Louise giggling.

I listened to the radio program "*Wunschkonzert*" this evening with the girls. It is our link between homes, families, and soldiers. Personal announcements and messages to families are broadcast throughout the program. One of the girls last week heard a message from her brother in Russia. We now spend Sunday evenings listening to the program in hopes we will hear family names or those of someone we know.

I finally had a Saturday off and celebrated with a beautiful warmer day. Clear skies improved my attitude. Everyone pooled their ration cards and we went on a picnic shopping trip. There were eight of us in our small group including our soldier. We took the cog railway to the top of the main hill in Boblingen.

From there we could see the nearby ancient castle of Sindelfingen. The tight spires looked like rockets ready to fire, but we couldn't sit still very long without getting cold.

Magda practiced yodeling down into the valley below us and we had a wonderful silly afternoon together. I was in a good mood because father wrote that he was doing better.

These teletype machines are a marvel of science. They look similar to my old typewriter I used in business school, but there is a small ribbon coming out the back of the machine. When I finish the transmission, I must glue the message to a long strip of paper. Some of the machines are just for weather reports, but others can do more. The girls handling "top-secret" transmissions have lights on the top of their machines that sound an alarm when they stop typing. An officer stands by ready to review the transmissions going out and those coming in. Those girls received extra benefits and are under much harsher control standards. One girl jumped out of her chair during a transmission because a mouse ran over her foot. The Officer slapped her hard on her cheek for foolishness. It reminds me not to get too comfortable where I am. Things can change in an instant.

No birthday celebration here, it is just another day away from home. No matter how cold we are here, I think of the soldiers in Russia without the proper clothing freezing to death on the front. Reports get worse every day from Russia. My grandfather died in Russia during the Great War by freezing to death.

We had our first air raid here, right in the middle of my shift at 1 o'clock in the morning. We all huddled into the lower bunker in the safe room. The sirens going off are very loud—howling from a low to high pitch. It appears they were mounted right outside our building. We sat clustered into small groups while the matron took roll call.

Most of the girls who knew each other held hands until the all clear siren sounded. It is a very sobering experience to be sitting quietly in the dark while someone tries to kill you. We can hear the planes going overhead, but don't know if they are the Allies or ours.

The buildings shake from the sound of anti-aircraft machinery. They must be somewhere close by. After several hours, we could go back to work, but it is almost impossible to get to sleep at a break. I can see smoke in the distance to the north.

What is burning?

Leni screaming in the early afternoon hours awakened us all. She has been having trouble sleeping too, and when she sat up in bed she saw a mouse sitting on her chest! The covers went flying and we all scrambled for the door. Soon the hallway was filled with girls from every room on our floor to see what was going on. Those crawl monsters must go. A few days ago, I thought I heard one chewing on something, but we can't pinpoint where it is. Now, everyone wants to sleep on a top bunk.

There is no justification for this rationale; it just makes more sense to us that the mice wouldn't want to go to the upper bunks.

We've had constant raids these past few nights and a few during the day. Another wave of planes has arrived for night duty. Our matron has told us that the English are bombing us during the day and the Americans are bombing at night. We cannot leave the Communications complex and walking around the back gardens does nothing for our spirits.

At dusk, we can see a red haze on the horizon to the north towards Stuttgart. We heard part of our flight line here sustained hits. It will only be a matter of time before the planes come back and finish off the airport area. We are right in the line of fire.

The air outside smells burns my nose from burning wood and chemicals. Reports are coming in from all over Germany that the bombing raids are hitting every major industrial city; we know this because it is in some of the transcriptions that we type. Thousands and thousands of people have been killed and many more displaced by the firestorms.

I learned firsthand what explosive bombs, incendiary bombs and air torpedo bombs are. Comments in the bunkers are passed along from officers by the sounds going off. "That was a torpedo" ... "Sounds like..."

I am more apprehensive about my duties now. I have gotten to know so many of the girls here and their towns.

Everyone is concerned about their families. Cologne and Dresden are completely wiped out. Pforzheim has had heavy casualties. I learned 17,000 people died in one twenty-minute bombing raid there. There is no way for me to send a telegram. I can only write and wait to hear from my parents. What about home? Are they still there? How long until I know? I am hoping and praying for their safety.

Marta, Paul; are you okay? Work seems unbearable. We are ragged from our lack of sleep, and yet they still demand absolute accuracy on everything we do. A renewed efficiency has been enforced. The information is coming in faster than we can report it. Several additional officers are stationed in our area to keep up with the details. Two girls collapsed in their seats this week. They pulled the girls out of the room, and grabbed someone off weather detail and had them complete the more intensive reporting. Mattresses have been put on the floor in the corner for officers who remained on duty. We are determined to stay strong, but we are all exhausted and on short tempers.

We've had five days of straight bombing. Stuttgart has been hit hard and we've have some shell damage on our street. Leni and I look out the window across the hall trying to make out the damage when suddenly there is a terrific BANG. We are thrown back into the room and both of us land hard against some of the bed frames. Luckily, we had opened the windows for a better view. I am surprised the windows did not break.

The blast threw both of us off our feet. I have an ugly bruise on my shoulder and Leni has a cut over her eye. At the infirmary, we learned an unexploded bomb went off nearby as they were trying to remove it. It damaged part of the supply building. Two soldiers were killed from the shrapnel blast. They were brought into the first aid station while we were still there. One I recognized.

He was the friendly soldier who accompanied us to the outing on the hilltop in Boblingen. Now he is gone.

The air outside is toxic. I think of it as "The smell of war". The smoke permeates my clothing and my hair. When I go outside, I must hold a wet handkerchief to my mouth. I close my eyes and tell myself I am breathing hope. I tried Mutti's handkerchief, but don't want to bring attention to it.

Gerti's War

These English are relentless. We hear the reports first hand. Germany has massive damage. Louise has been distraught and is on a short medical leave. She isn't alone down there. A handful of girls from the Communication office have joined her for medicated rest. Slowly, information from families is coming in. We console each other as best we can.

It took over a week before I heard from my parents. Arnbach has not been hit. Several friends of mine who worked in Pforzheim are reported missing or killed. The business school where I worked took a direct hit as it was very close to the industrial district. My mother included a newspaper article, listing people dead or missing. At the end of the letter, Mutti put a note that Marta's family is frantic because they have not been able to find her after the last day of bombing. They looked everywhere they could, but transportation has been wiped out.

Walking or bike riding is the only way to get around in the chaos of Pforzheim now. Mutti said she would write more the instant she heard about Marta. Marta can't be gone, she just can't.

Chapter 9 – February 1942

Four days of worry, and still no word from Mutti regarding Marta. I am numb at my desk every evening. Every time I close my eyes, I see Marta full of life and enthusiasm bounding into my room to tell me about her Paul. I must remember to ask Mutti to give me Paul's address. He must be worried too. Marta, can you hear me? I'm praying for you. Giving you all my love and strength…

My transcription duties have now changed. Due to the heavy raids, that scary officer with the German shepherd decided to move us around. They have split up our group. The weather communication groups now work in a school a mile away and another section has moved to Berlin. The elite group will continue in the main building. At least we now have improved the heating in the main Communication office.

My transcription service has changed from constant weather reports to mid-level battlefield conditions and general communications. We will be moving to a barracks house down near the flight line. Great, I was hoping to get away from the flight line. Leni has been included in my group, but Louise will be sent to Berlin. She hasn't come back from her sick leave yet. I have only been able to see her once. Maybe they'll reassign her back into my group. I hope I at least get to say "Good-bye" before she leaves.

Finally received another letter from Mutti, but she shared no news about Marta.

Dearest Gerti,

Marta's mother came by this afternoon. She still hasn't found her little Marta. Gerti, know that she is doing everything she can to try to find her. Her hands were so cut up. One cut was particularly deep so I bandaged her up and gave her a pair of Papa's heavy work gloves from the garage. Marta's father has been notified of her absence and he has requested leave, but they won't approve it. He is somewhere in Russia now.

I am going to go with her tomorrow and help her search. Paul is going to go with us to expand the search area. We know that she left the factory at 3:32 p.m. The raid happened at 3:47 p.m. so we are going to search closer to the train station area.

Pray for her liebchen– pray for all of us that this war will end soon. Received word that Uncle Erwin's two oldest boys have been killed – Otto and Max.

Mutti...... xoxo

Otto and Max were much older than I was and I didn't know them very well. Max gave me treats when I was little. I remember both of them were very involved with the Catholic Church. I think Otto wanted to be a priest. I will pray for them and hope they didn't suffer. Into God's embrace.

The raids are slowing down, and I finally got some sleep yesterday. I'm still having nightmares about the raids and my mind thinks I hear the sirens going off in the distance when they are silent. However, now we hear the planes taking off.

There are twenty-five girls in this new barracks, and we are just starting to get to know each other. I miss the evening socials and I am hoping the mice haven't found this place. The Matron in charge got upset at Leni today and pushed her to the ground. Leni had to scrub the toilets in the men's barracks tonight. She saw some of the pilots and said they were very handsome.

Gerti's War

There was no underground bunker for raids in this area and some soldiers in training are digging ditches a few kilometers from here that we will use in a raid. It will take a while to get there. I wonder what it will be like being outside. The noise must be incredible. They have announced new directions, if you are in town when the sirens go off; you are forbidden to stay on the streets. You must go inside to the nearest cellar available.

All transportation vehicles will stop immediately if they hear the sirens.

I am still having trouble concentrating on my transcription.

Marta, where are you? Can you hear me reaching out to you? One of the lieutenants noticed my hesitations, patted me on the back, and told me to be strong. I hope he stays with our group. His kindness is appreciated. They play a record from the Berlin Philharmonic symphony in the background while we transcribe, and it gives me a small amount of sanity during those long night hours.

I received a letter from Mutti...can't write anymore.

> *My dearest Gerti*
>
> *How I want to be there with you, holding you...just holding you while I tell you this news. I knew you wanted to know just as soon as there was something to tell. They found Marta today. She didn't survive the last bombing raid. Her mother found her amongst some people who had taken refuge in a hotel basement not far from the train station. The hotel had been partially destroyed. The pipes burst and drowned those trapped in the basement. There were forty-two people with her. They found her with a book of poems by Rilke. The handkerchief you gave her was in her pocket.*
>
> *Dearest, please try to be strong and know that the friendship you two shared was a very special bond. You will see her again someday with those who are*

special. You gave her hope-- a very special gift. Please remember the good times. She would want you to be strong and live your life with kindness and beauty.

I found your Rilke book in your room and looked through some of the passages. I thought one of your favorites might help you.

THE SWAN
*This toil and struggle—passing on, ponderous
And as if found, through what remains undone,
Is like the makeshift walking of the swan.
And dying—this letting goes
Of that ground we stand on every day,
Is like his uneasy letting himself down—
Into the water, which receives him gently,
And which, as if happy in its passing,
Withdraws beneath him, wave on wave;
While he, quiet and infinitely assured,
With ever greater majesty and freedom
And serenity is pleased to glide.*

Think of her as gliding into that peaceful serenity, into the hands of God.

All our love,

Mutti and Papa

I spent the last two days in the hospital ward trying to get through my loss. I feel hollow and empty inside. My supervisor has ordered me back at work. Last night in the ward, we had another bombing raid. Soldiers helped get some of the injured into the outdoor ditches. It didn't feel real watching the searchlights looking for the planes. We could hear them, but not see them in the cloudy skies.

We huddled together with the soldiers in the ditches. It was frightening and beautiful at the same time. I felt detached watching the red and green lights of the falling marking rockets.

Gerti's War

One soldier called them "Christmas Tree lights." They seemed to fall in slow motion. Maybe it is my medication, but I felt like I was watching a play and it was happening to someone else.

One of the soldiers stood out among the group. He had a bright smile and gave me his blanket while we were there. I didn't ask him for it, he simply put it around my shoulders and stayed close to me. I didn't even get his name. Will I remember his smile? Was it a dream?

Transcription, transcription, transcription, focus, fills my head with facts and locations. I am beginning to feel like a machine myself. If I open my mouth, will a small roll of paper come tumbling out? I still feel weak and shaky at times.

We had a false raid today. Some of the enlisted men from the flight line hit the alarm because they wanted to watch us run out of the building in our sleeping wear. No one is happy about the false alarm and a lieutenant said he would investigate it and punish those responsible. I hope he starts asking the group of men who were watching and laughing. Bet they won't be laughing when they are in front of the lieutenant.

Working nights and sleeping in the day is very hard. I have mastered the art of wrapping my pillow around my head. I keep Papa's pillowcase close. I am so very tired.

I received a letter from Paul and Louise today. Louise said the whole Communications group, may be moving to Berlin soon. She was "Saving a bed" for me, but there is no announcement from here about moving. Louise sounds lonely and I will try to write her a long note today.

Paul's letter took me a while to get through. I think writing to each other will help us. His leg is better now, and he may get to rejoin his regiment in France. He hopes to get into a communication office and use his French/Italian languages. I need to work on my French and any other languages that I can learn here. I would love to be able to communicate the way Paul does.

What if the Russians win? Will there be anything left of the Germany I recognize? I will never learn Russian!!

It has been almost three weeks since our last "real" raid.

Other parts of Germany have been hit hard. I can't image the 1000-year Reich Hitler talks about. I don't think there will be anything left of Germany if it goes on another year. We are losing so much of our history. My transcription duties tell the real story. Cologne has only the cathedral left standing, and there are so many cities destroyed. Ulm is gone, Pforzheim almost gone, Aachen gone, and Mainz gone. Leni said as we finished our shift "So much glory, so much shame." I think she's right.

Today my thoughts turned to the heavens. Bright blue skies and fans of white clouds paint the canvas over us. We are going to concentrate on the positive and this wonderful day. The early season flowers are out, and Leni brought me a flower to put in our wine bottle vase. We are going to take a short walk and enjoy the fresh clean air before dinner call. We opened the window and I can hear someone singing *Schon Ist Die Jugendzeit (Beautiful is the Youth Time)*. I wonder if Papa has started singing again?

I saw the cute soldier again last night--the one who gave me his blanket. He waved to me from across the yard and asked if I was still cold by gesturing with his hands. I wish I could talk to him. I showed him I am better by turning a few circles and waving back. He wasn't a dream after all.

Our group is going back to the main communication center tomorrow and they aren't telling us why. I will be glad to get further from the planes. We must get our things ready and move after the end of our shift tonight. I wish Louise were still here.

There hasn't been any news from any of the girls from the farm camp in a while.

Things are a bit more stressful with this new setup and now I work in the same room as the elite group, but at the back of the room. The nice lieutenant isn't with our group anymore and they have given us a few more liberties now. We can go around the immediate grounds without supervision and can talk to enlisted personnel in the outer courtyard. On the first day here, I saw the cute soldier waving at me from across the courtyard in his room!! He waves at me every morning since I arrived, but I haven't seen him in the courtyard yet.

The mice are still here!!!! I hate those crawl monsters!!!

Today, I met Sigmund. I looked across the courtyard before work and I could tell that he seemed to be waiting for me.

I was a little nervous, so Leni went with me.

His name is Sigmund Rhinehart and he is an infantry soldier training in the weapon's school run by the Luftwaffe. He's been here one month, and he is from Poland--western Preussen. His Father is also in the army somewhere in Russia. He has two younger brothers, too young to enlist.

He had all sorts of questions about me, but he isn't pushy.

What a gentleman. He kissed both our hands before he left us.

Leni and I agreed – he is very nice and very cute. I know my face felt hot. I bet I was beat red.

I saw Sigmund again this afternoon, but he was listening to an officer and couldn't get away to talk to me. He motioned for me to meet him at the corner at 3 o'clock tomorrow. It's Sunday and I have the afternoon off. Can't wait!

Lois Buchter

What a day! I must write everything down, so I don't forget it. I wish my hair looked better; I'm a mop head. The soap we use is horrible. Leni gave me some French perfume to wear, but I wanted to use some makeup and lipstick. I did my best with my clothes and everything is clean and pressed.

My friends all wanted to meet Sigmund, but only Leni and one of my new roommates, Anita, joined Sigmund and me. A friend of Sigmund's saw us, and he joined our small group. Gottfried is in Sigmund's training class and he talked our ears off. We walked to town and bought cheese, bread and wine with our ration cards and had a small picnic at the park.

It didn't take long for all of us to become fast friends.

We had no time to be shy. How long can we be together? Leni and Gottfried got along well. Anita kept the conversation going.

Gottfried told Anita he has several friends who want to meet her.

She blushed every time he said it and we all laughed each time she turned red.

I learned more about Sigmund. His family has a large farm back in Poland. It sounds wonderful. He painted a beautiful picture of his life back home and all the animals they have. He followed his father into military service and has always felt more German than Polish. His farm had been in Germany prior to the end of the Great War.

Sigmund's first assignment in the army in Wurzburg was to collect the dead and dig graves, but he only had to do that for a few weeks. He spent another week in Merseburg learning weapons and has been here about three weeks. The night we met in the ditch was his first night here.

Gottfried is from a tiny village east of Munich. His family has a small farm in town, milking cows and a few chickens. His father is the mayor. What a heavy smoker he is, and lit cigarettes one after another.

He told us funny stories about his childhood and could make the silliest faces to go with his stories. Gottfried needed little encouragement to be an actor. I asked him if he wanted to be an entertainer and he answered by impersonating W.C. Fields perfectly.

The time passed very quickly at the park. Sigmund asked me to take his arm on the walk back. I could feel a surge of electricity at the point of contact between my hand and his arm and I think he felt it too, but his smile does me in. When he smiles his whole face lights up and I can't help but smile back.

My cheeks and jaw ache from smiling so much.

The sirens went off as we came to the town square and we took refuge in a large butcher shop's basement. There are several people bundled up and sitting in the freezer area when we arrived. Sigmund and I stood just outside the cold area where we watched fresh animal carcasses hanging in the freezer. I didn't want to go in there. Memories of the day of butchery at the farm camp came back to me. I'm not going to complain if Sigmund is with me.

A small family came in behind me and pushed me up against Sigmund. My cheek brushed up against his and Sigmund held me in place. Our eyes locked on each other. The room didn't feel so cold anymore. For the first time in a long time, I felt alive. I don't know how long we stayed there. It seemed like several minutes passed before I tried to pull away, but Sigmund wouldn't let me go. He murmured something in my ear and pulled me next to him against the wall. We stayed there for the next hour until the all-clear signal went off. He held my hand the entire rest of the way back to the center.

I worried we might be in trouble for being gone so long, but Sigmund said he got permission from his *Wachtmeister* to go out with us. His commander said I had nice legs and not to worry.

What would Papa think of a man talking about my legs? Groups of three were allowed passes with a military escort. I am glad both Sigmund and Gottfried are here tonight.

When we got back, Sigmund kissed me on each cheek and kissed both my hands. He bowed to Leni and Anita. Before he went up the stairs, he grabbed my hand again and kissed me on the palm! It felt wonderful. I told Anita I am not going to wash my hand the rest of the day. Does a hand kiss count as a real first kiss?

Sigmund waves at me every morning as I come in from my shift. I hope to have some time with him Saturday afternoon in the courtyard. I held up a sign for him today asking him to meet me and he nodded yes. At least it is something to look forward to. Gottfried has started joining Sigmund in the mornings to wave at Leni too. She thinks he is nice, but he smokes too much.

The Captain in the transcription room complimented me on my transcription speed today. A very rare occurrence indeed! I overheard several officers discussing our group, they are going to take a few of the fastest girls and move us into the elite group. I remember how they treated some of those girls before.

I'm not sure I want to be in that group, but my opinion doesn't count.

I received another letter from Mutti today and Father may need yet another operation. He is still having stomach troubles. Mutti sent me some of her ration coupons and some warm socks she knitted.

It is finally warming up outside and my nights are filled with messages, messages, and thinking of my family, Marta, Paul and now Sigmund. The days go by quickly. Did I dream up the last week? Reality is not a familiar word in my mind.

We had another day-raid today. The planes just went over us, but we didn't have damage in our block. Part of the flight line is gone. I looked for Sigmund and Gottfried in the courtyard, but they aren't there. They must be by the airport close to the training field.

Today six girls from my group start learning the new elite equipment. We will each be given a special patch to wear. Our papers will have special clearance stamps on them and we won't have any problems at checkpoints. At least that's what the commander said during our orientation.

This strange transcription box looks a little like a typewriter and it has all sorts of rotors, sockets and cables on the backside of it. Each evening when we come in, the Lieutenant will set up the cipher rotors of the day. We type the coded messages on the keyboard and they light up on the panel. We must be extremely precise in everything we do. After writing down the messages, we hand it to the Captain. He takes it over to the radio communication room.

The first couple of times I did it my hands were shaking.

Most of these messages come directly from headquarters. We are told that they are top-secret, and talking about the messages to anyone other than the Captain could be cause for removal or something worse. I keep thinking to myself, does this message kill someone?

There are two large stamps on the box; one says "*Klappe Schliessen*" and the other says "Enigma." The Captain in charge and has cold eyes. I bet he could spit nails into the wall. He makes my skin crawl. My nerves are already frazzled.

I can spend three hours with Sigmund today. He brought photographs of his farm and his family. The farm is huge, and so beautiful. There were separate buildings for the animals and even a smokehouse. His family's land has been in his family for five generations. Mutti would love the garden area around the house, especially the big flowerbed in one corner by the house. He burst with pride as he showed off his family photographs. We had a wonderful time sitting together by ourselves in the courtyard.

Sigmund showed me a photograph of himself from a football game. I asked him if he liked to play football. He puffed up a little, and told me he has won many awards and is a champion back home. He is much younger in the photograph, but still had his great smile. Yes, I can see him running around as a young boy playing football. He has a lot of enthusiasm.

Sigmund just received his enlistment photographs and gave one to me. I need to write home and ask for a photograph for him as well. I wish the military picture showed him smiling. He has a stern and very serious look in the photograph.

I told him about Marta today and the reason for being in the hospital. Of course, just mentioning her name brought a flood of tears. There has been too much loss-- Grandmother, Rolf and now Marta. Sigmund held me while I cried. He smelled so good, sort of woodsy with a little hair pomade. It felt right to be in his arms.

I showed him my blue handkerchief and told him the story behind it. Before I knew it, I was telling him about Arnbach, the woods and my friends and family. The words spilled out and my spirits lifted. How I longed to show him my woods. I long to lay on the ground and listen to the canopy singing to me.

I had to report for more training and started work an hour earlier today. When I had to leave, he asked me to call him Sigi, his family pet name. I told him I would call him Sigi-le. In my town, we add that little extra "le" on the end as a term of endearment. He smiled at me, grabbed both my shoulders, and kissed me right on the mouth! My whole body turned into an explosion of tiny currents. Marta, now I know what you were talking about! How I miss you.

I haven't been able to see Sigi for the last several days.

We keep on missing each other. Gottfried told Leni that Sigi's been assigned to another training area for the next couple of days, but he should be back Saturday.

We are having a social for some visiting diplomats and dignitary's tomorrow night. Our group has been requested to attend in full uniform and everyone is excited about it. We still must work for five hours in the afternoon to check the transcriptions but should have enough time to get ready before the party. Now I really want Sigmund to be back in time. It won't be the same if he isn't there.

Gerti's War

What a party! It reminded me of the splendor of old Germany.

All types of military personnel were there. Leni Riefenstahl and her photographer crew took photographs of parts of the party.

She is Hitler's favorite propaganda film producer. I remember having to watch her movie *Triumph of the Will* several times when I was in the Hitler Youth.

Best of all, Sigi came. A small orchestra played and Sigi and I danced most of the evening. I even saw my first famous movie star, Ursula Hohenlohe; she was dressed in a vision of dark sparkling red and wearing lots of make-up. Several of the officers kept surrounding her. I couldn't believe I am in this group!

The variety of food was astonishing. Stacks of lobsters, oysters, and salmon were piled high on the main tables, along with lots of French wine and champagne. Gottfried had all the girls laughing in our small group as he imitated Clark Gable from *Gone with the Wind*. It felt so good to relax and really enjoy ourselves.

Sigmund arrived a little late, right after dinner, but I am still in heaven dancing the night away with Sigmund.

Toward the end of the evening, a group of men sang a few German folk songs. Papa would have enjoyed singing with them. My big surprise came later after we left the party. Leni and Gottfried talked endlessly about the singing group and Gottfried tried to sing some of the songs. He did a terrible job, but then Sigi started to sing. My mouth hung open in the air the whole while. He sings beautifully! His tenor voice would be a good accompaniment to Papa's baritone! It kept everyone in high spirits.

It's going to take hours to fall asleep—I'm so excited. My feet are killing me. I can't get those good night kisses off my mind. I felt like Cinderella going to the ball.

Lois Buchter

The raids over Stuttgart are very heavy today. The Airport was taken over by the Luftwaffe for special training of the ME-109 fighter pilots. I hope Sigi's not sent somewhere else. We had two raids last night during our shift and another one during the day. Leni handed me some daffodils sent from Sigi. They are very cheerful, but not enough to shift my mood. I am tired, jumpy, and not good company. I haven't been able to see Sigi since the party last week. The sky glows red to the north toward Stuttgart. Will this war ever end?

Did I mention how much I hate the food here? If I see white cabbage and onions one more time, I'm going to scream! Leni pointed out to me we should be thankful we have anything at all.

Strict rationing has been imposed throughout Germany. Shortages are everywhere.

Yes, I should be more thankful, but I need to do some hard talking to myself first. I want to do something positive and worthwhile. My energy level has been low, except when I see Sigmund.

Some girls in our section are helping in the medical ward during their time off (a few hours in the late afternoons). Maybe my attitude will change if I do something more productive? I haven't been able to talk to Sigi all week and I am worried about Papa. When will his new surgery happen? Will I be able to go home as I did before?

Leni and I are going to try to go to town for a few hours tomorrow. I think my attitude has been annoying her.

Gottfried accompanied us to Boblingen this afternoon and he helped lift my spirits tremendously. We had some false coffee and cake at a small shop and I enjoyed doing a little light shopping.

One shop sold gas masks! I had never seen masks presented in a shop window before.

Picturesque houses and perfect little gardens are visible in some sections of the city. What a contrast to see one beautiful street parallel to another with loaded heavy damage. I wonder

Gerti's War

if we could start a garden near the compound. Any improvement on our diet of cabbage and onions would be great.

Finally, I have been able to see Sigi for the last two days. We spent the respite talking about the future. Sigi told me how much he enjoys working with his hands. He wants to enlarge the family farm back home and perhaps buy another piece of land and clear it for a small orchard or add a garage to work on farm machinery. He also talked about starting a football camp for boys. We shared our dreams and I could picture it all. A beautiful farm with animals and working with young boys—yes, it all fits.

While he talked, I watched his beautiful hands. Then I started daydreaming about how those hands made me feel. How did he know the right moment to reach out and hold his hands in mine?

He kissed them, and I thanked him for sharing his dreams with me.

When he looks at me with those smiling blue eyes, my knees go weak and butterflies take off in my stomach.

What a tournament we had today! Two squadron leaders had a disagreement over something trivial and they decided to settle the argument by holding a football tournament between the squadrons. I finally got to see Sigi play. He was incredible! He ran so quickly and did all sorts of flip kicks and spinning turns.

The Commandant called him over after the game and congratulated him. He scored three goals! Each time he scored, he looked at me and winked. His teammates took him out drinking afterwards. I was glad to decline the offer to go with them; they were dirty and smelly. All the girls wanted to know about Sigi.

We all had to attend a Social Democratic party meeting this afternoon. It's the first one I've been to since I was a nanny.

They showed us some films and then the officers talked about the "Greatness of Germany" and the unstoppable "German Machine." I felt nauseated by the time the meeting was over. A few of the girls rallied behind the statements and it sickened me to see Sigi with a group of enlisted men in high spirits. We haven't talked about our political beliefs.

I spoke to the ward Matron this afternoon and received permission to start a garden in a sunny spot on the back lot.

She said one of the lieutenants would have a work detail till the soil for us, but we must get our own seeds and maintain the area.

Peppers, tomatoes, schnittlauch (chives), kraut (herbs), lauch (leeks), zwiedel (onion), and kohlrabi (cabbage turnips) will give us a good start. I posted a notice in the mess hall to see who is interested in helping and planting suggestions.

Sigi and I meet down by the garden just about every afternoon. We don't talk much, but he sings to me as we tend the plants. He has so much energy all the time and always has a spring in his step and a good attitude. We talk about football, travel dreams, and childhood stories. His father has been very strict in his standards and doesn't stand for any foolishness. Sigi must have inherited some of that. He kept on saying he had to make the garden look just so. We have access to add gravel paths to separate the rows next week. He wants it perfect.

Since the football tournament, Sigi has been very popular and it's harder to get time alone with him. I cherish our quiet moments in the garden together. If I need a spade or a bucket, he runs and gets it for me, so I don't have to get up. I have never felt so special around someone before. It has been easier to be positive when Sigi is around.

I received a note from Mutti and Papa's surgery went well. I am glad it is over, but I so wanted to be there. He should be home by the time I received her letter. What a relief!! Mutti had help from neighbors and friends getting him to the hospital and back.

She sounded very optimistic about his condition.

I finally gave Sigi a photograph of me today. Luckily, Mutti sent one of my good photographs. I was worried she would send one of those embarrassing childhood pictures.

Gerti's War

Sigi told me his training is almost complete and he will be leaving here soon. We both knew it was coming, but facing this reality is hard. After he told me about his assignment, he kissed me like I've never been kissed before. I still get a little shaky just thinking about it. I had to lean against the cool stone building to get my breathing normal. He makes me feel deliciously warm and comfortable when he holds me, but I can't stop starring at his lips or his hands. Am I turning into bad girl?

Sigi will be leaving tomorrow, and has been assigned to Pommern to be an artillery soldier on the flight line. Gottfried is leaving too, but he will be stationed in Berlin. It won't be the same without them. Leni and I are miserable already. They will write to us. We only have a few hours together tonight before he leaves.

Sigi called me his precious sweet angel and danced with me in the courtyard out on the lawn until it was time to leave. He sang songs in my ear as I tried not to cry. I did better than him and gave him my handkerchief to dry his face. He wasn't ashamed of crying in front of me and told me they were tears of joy from knowing me. I had so many words to say and did not want the moment to end. His station is only about two hours northwest of here by train. I promised this isn't good-bye forever, just good-bye for today. I have his address in Pommern and his home address. My arms already feel empty and heavy.

I received a long letter from Paul today and he's been assigned to Paris. He is now working in a branch of the Communication office. They put out a monthly publication for the *Wehrmacht* and he is the new official photographer for the publication. I think he has some real potential because the photographs he enclosed of the gargoyles on Notre Dame are good.

A Nazi communication officer comes into our transcription area every night. I can hear the dog's paws clicking on the floor in the hallway before they enter the room. My whole-body tenses up just hearing the clicking coming down the hall. I can tell from the transcriptions that things are more tense; Japan has been losing in the Pacific and our troops are moving closer to Stalingrad.

Today is Midsummer's Eve. I wonder if they are celebrating in Arnbach? Papa, are you feeling better?

I joined a small group of typists and went to a Catholic Church service this evening in the neighborhood before my duty started. I felt peace and serenity with the crowd inside. I said prayers for Grandmother, Rolf, Marta, Sigi and Papa and all my family and friends.

I gave my offering to a refugee family sitting at the back of the church instead of the church. When I did, the wife grabbed my hand, and thanked me. She had tears running down her cheeks.

My worries are tiny compared to the worries of so many around me.

I wrote a long letter to Louise and my mother today. Mutti has been asking about my availability to come home, and hopes they will be able to come visit soon. Everything depends on Papa's healing time. He can get around the house now for a few minutes at a time but is still having a lot of trouble with his stitches.

I've sent two letters to Sigi but haven't had a reply yet.

Today I re-read my journal entries from the last few months and I've noticed that I am responsible for my attitude. Marta always tried to get me to be more outgoing. I must control my reactions, even if I can't control the situation I am in. From now on, only a strong and positive Gertrud Leicht will be present!

Gerti's War

I spent a lot of my time this week working in the garden. I tried to help at the hospital clinic, but the antiseptic smell made me sick to my stomach. Maybe I should try a children's school? Where is my place in all this madness? I am going with a group that will be cherry picking this afternoon. Maybe it will lift my spirits. I must remember to be strong and positive. Now I wake up in the afternoon saying, "strong and positive," but by the end of my shift I don't feel very strong.

Finally!! I've gotten a letter from Sigi!!! I've read it about twenty times. I wrote it into my journal, so I don't forget a word.

> *My dear sweet angel,*
>
> *I miss seeing your smile, but I see it when I close my eyes. Your photograph has a position of prominence in the front of my journal. Remember our dance my Gerti-le, and keep my songs singing softly in your ears.*
>
> *Pommern is a good size airbase. My squad leader is a grandfatherly-type of man and the men in my group look up to him. It seems to be a good bunch of guys here. Last week they caught a civilian trying to cross the forbidden zone and two of the men in my squad were able to go on short flights in the 262s.*
>
> *This is a new holding area for the planes. It hasn't been hit too much by raids. There are bunkers and shelters all over. We are close to the Rhine River. On clear nights, I can see the moonlight reflecting off the river and the planes. Everything sparkles. Yes, Gerti-le, I am being careful.*
>
> *My squad is called the night hunters because we patrol the flight line. We are charged with protecting the beautiful Messerschmitt 262s. They are such incredible machines. I can only dream that maybe someday I'll be able to take a ride in one. Rows and rows of their cigar-shaped bodies are lined up ready to go. We haven't seen many of them take off because*

there is such a shortage of fuel. Seeing them for the first time at night took my breath away. I am proud to be out here guarding these magnificent machines. What a sight it must be to see all these planes in the air.

I hope that you are still tending "our" garden.

Let me know how the lettuce is coming along. Thank you for your letter and I wait anxiously for the next one.

I am always, your Sigi-le...

There has been much confusion around here lately. Trucks and armored divisions rattle as they pass our building. New faces show up for our evening socials in the garden. I have requested several times to visit home, without success. I am still hopeful Mutti and Papa will be able to visit me soon. They have sent another group of transcribers to Berlin this week. Louise writes we will join her soon. I wonder if that could really happen. I miss Louise and her stories.

Leni has been seeing someone new, Otto. He is attached to a Para trooping unit with the *Luftwaffe*. He has the broadest shoulders I've ever seen. Leni said dancing with him is like dancing with a bear. Some soldiers took several of the girls in my squad to the cinema in town last weekend. I miss having Sigi's hand in mine. We laughed all the way back to the center. Today the war seemed very far away.

I received a package from Mutti today. She sent more material, so I could make a handkerchief for Sigi. I decided to try to find some red thread and embroider a little red heart intertwined with the "H". It will be a special touch for my special soldier.

We've only had a few raids this month, one with damage. My transcription messages continue to be more negative than positive. I worry about all those families losing fathers and brothers, especially those in Russia.

Gerti's War

Great news, my leave request is granted! Five whole days at home! I can leave tomorrow morning after my shift ends. My parents will be so surprised. Leni and I have been requesting a leave every week for the last two months. She is very disappointed her request hasn't come in and says it's probably because I've been working in the top-secret division and she hasn't. I don't care for the reason, I am just glad it came through.

My trip home was both wonderful and sad. I noticed a change in Arnbach as I walked up the hill towards home. The people who used to spend their afternoons outside working in the garden or visiting with friends are absent, but several people greeted me as I walked by. I could feel a change in our town. Frau Hoffsteadler, who is always so cheerful and welcoming, turned when she saw me and went into her home. I think she was crying.

The town seemed empty and quiet without Marta and my other friends around. The lively spirit of youth has floated away. The children I saw are staying close to their mothers. The little ones I used to watch and play with a year ago no longer recognized me. How odd to be a stranger in my hometown.

I went to church service with Mutti and again had a feeling of being on the outside looking in, even inside the church. I saw emptiness on many faces. Several family friends hugged me as I left the church. Afterwards, a small group of us were crying in the vestibule, as stories of loss flowed. I hoped I would be refreshed and de-stressed after this visit, but I am very emotional and heavy-hearted. My stronger-positive attitude feels further out of reach with each day of my visit.

I tried to go to the cemetery to visit Marta's grave, but could only make it to the small park adjacent. I sat on the grass where we used to practice our Olympic breaststrokes and hugged my knees. I couldn't go any further. The velvet grass felt wonderful against my skin.

I could see Rolf's grave and my grandmother's from there, but there were too many new graves to spot Marta's. Maybe on my next visit I will plant some yellow flowers on her grave. Death and reality have hit me hard like a mallet in the chest. I visited with Marta's mother, but I don't remember walking home afterwards. It's all a blur.

Papa's wound hasn't healed as fast this time. He looks ten years older. Has it only been six months since our last visit?

Mutti stays busy canning everything in the garden during my visit. The pantry is completely full and overflowing into other parts of the cellar. I did bring back a few jars of her applesauce and sauerkraut (for emergencies) when I can't stand the menu. I took some family photographs from Mutti's favorite collection, and have posted them on my headboard. I left my journal at home and am starting a new one.

I finished embroidering Sigi's handkerchief today and posted it to him with a long letter. At dinner, our matron notified the whole communication group we will be moving to Berlin at the end of the month. Now I am anxious about going and a little excited.

Berlin is THE city and I have never been there before. Stories are going around about the theater, opera, restaurants, people, and politics of the big city. It will be a big change from the small town of Boblingen. Leni received her leave authorization and will be gone in the morning. I am happy for this small kindness. Her enthusiasm over her leave has helped my spirits.

I will be glad to leave these mice! Because of all the packing and moving activity in our building, the crawl monsters have multiplied overnight. Is there a place they can't get into?

I discovered evidence they had been in my suitcase! They caused quite a disturbance in the shower area yesterday. Three mice decided to make a run for it. I probably would have slipped and landed on one of them!! A few of the girls can kill the vermin, but I haven't been able to do it yet.

Gerti's War

Some of the officers attached to our unit have already left the center. We will be leaving here by military transport on the 28th. Only five days away!

I received this short note from Sigi today. It's easier to be strong and positive when I get a letter.

> Dearest Gerti-le:
>
> Thank you so much for the lovely handkerchief.
>
> The workmanship is of the very best quality. I will make sure that I show it to my mother when I get home.
>
> This treasure will stay in my pocket, to give me hope and to think of you.
>
> A few friends and I went to Strasbourg, France, on our afternoon off. It's my first trip to France and it's the farthest west I've been. The city was beautiful, and the huge gothic cathedral spire could be seen from miles away. It was a long walk from the train station to the church and I thought how nice it would be if you were walking with me holding my hand.
>
> Have you ever been there before? It's so close to your hometown that I thought maybe you've been there with your family.
>
> I wish I could enjoy our garden together. Think of me often and know I'm thinking of you.
>
> Your Sigi-le

I wrote home and to Paul and Sigi giving them my new address on *Margaretenstrasse*. This address is different from the mailing address I use for Louise, so we won't be in the same area. I will try to see her as soon as I get settled. The entire communication group will be taking a special transport train together to Berlin. No civilians will be allowed onboard. Our matron has told us we must stay inside the train cars and keep to ourselves always. I am looking forward to seeing more of Germany on the way to Berlin, but it will be further from home. *Auf Wiedersehen* all you awful mice!

We made it to Berlin. The military transportation train is a large one with two luxury cars, six general seating cars and ten boxcars full of supplies. The seats were incredibly thin, as was the threadbare carpet spotted with cigar burns.

It took most of the day to pull into Berlin. We only stopped twice. The first stop was in Nurnberg for lunch a necessary break. The green and hilly countryside changed to flat lands just north of the city. The beautiful fields of poppies covered everything and yellow fields of crops another. If I squinted my eyes, the flowers looked like big colorful blankets spread across a field of green. The scene reminded me of the postcards Mutti had taped inside the kitchen cabinets at home. With a full stomach and the tranquil scene out the window, I fell asleep.

Somewhere around Leipzig, the car jerked to a stop and I slowly opened my eyes. The abrupt stop didn't wake me; it was the awful smell coming from outside that covered everything inside the cab. The putrid odor made my eyes water and my throat dry.

Dull gray clouds of dust outside the window were a stark contrast to the beautiful fields of flowers I had seen before I fell asleep. At first, I thought I was having a bad dream, but after a few coughing fits, I realized it was real. I tried to close the windows to keep out the smell and noticed everyone around me had handkerchiefs in hand. We couldn't see much outside the windows, as the trains blocked our view on each side.

The oppressive smell combined with a very hot day and the closed windows made us all shift nervously in the car. Finally, on an adjacent track, a train moved off and showed us the reason for the smell. Long lines of thin filthy men unloaded cargo onto wooden wagons. I couldn't make out exactly what they were unloading; a huge swarm of flies flew overhead.

Gerti's War

I didn't know where to look – the men working beside us, the cargo shipment, the guards, barbed wire enclosing the camp, or the men working in the fields on the horizon. Guards with weapons in hand and a few with guard dogs watched the men and shouted orders. More men worked on the hillside around the camp. They were of all ages and wore gray and black-striped clothes that were torn and stained. They looked like walking skeletons. Their skin had a strange greenish hue I had never seen before. I was shocked to see some young boys in amongst the work crew, they couldn't have been older than 14.

At first, I couldn't comprehend the scene outside. What had those people done? What were boys doing there? I rubbed my eyes a few times and coughed. The images remained. Throughout the train, no one said a word. A few of us looked out the window, but several of the girls just stared down into their laps.

As we pulled out of the station, we passed another long column of workers and the horror continued to the last prisoner who pushed a wheel cart. There were men lying in that cart. It's something I never thought I'd see. There was such complete hopelessness on a massive scale in every direction I looked.

Tears ran down my cheeks. The Commandant slowly limped through the car and his eye caught mine. He had a leg injury and walked with a flashy silver tipped cane. As he made his way through the cabin, he saw my tears and stopped beside me. With the tip of his cane, he caught my chin and asked me if I had a problem looking at the Jewish scum. I told him the smell was causing my eyes to water and he accepted that response and slowly walked to the luxury cabin where the officers were seated.

As soon as he left, my whole body began to shake. I had to sit on my hands so the girls around me wouldn't see how upset I was. My heart beat hard and my temples were bursting. I closed my eyes and didn't open them until we reached Berlin hours later. I was still shaking as we walked off the train. All those people…families…children. I have no more words.

Chapter 10 – September 1942

Berlin doesn't have quite the charm I expected. People move constantly on the streets and with a population of 4 million people in the city, I feel as if I've entered an ant mound. I feel a quiet hurry up behind the people around me. The city itself is nice, but it's too modern and formal for me. I prefer the older architecture and stone walkways that give Germany its character and history.

I have heard the buildings around the cultural district are very nice and I hope to visit there soon. I can't wait to go to the opera or Philharmonic and maybe do some shopping. I think I am more suited to a smaller town and I miss seeing familiar faces in a crowd. Maybe I'll change my mind after I've been here longer. The air smells dirty, like a furnace that needs cleaning.

The shopping must be great, if only I had some money to spend and coupons to use! Surprisingly, I've seen little bombing damage in the area around our complex compared to the devastation of Pforzheim. It's just a cluster of little neighborhoods all pushed up against each other. Busy, busy, busy.

My new home is a three-story marble estate with intricate hand-tooled ironwork that looks like lace. One of those eagle sculptures holding a laurel-wreathed swastika in its claws hangs over the entry in the vestibule. I shudder every time I walk under it.

The sleeping quarters are on the upper floors and flow into an adjacent building. Willow trees ring a quaint pond on the grounds behind the main center, which has a few black swans. These swans are not friendly. Yesterday I saw them chase two girls who got too close to the water. From a distance, it seemed comical and Leni and I laughed out loud. Leni is on the same floor as I am. My five new roommates have been very polite.

Helga is the friendliest and very chatty. Thankfully, we can shower two days a week here! No sign of mice yet, thank goodness!

This complex is huge and must hold close to six hundred girls working in all areas of field communications. I am still trying to find my way around the building and the small neighborhoods between the center and the train station. There are a few nice little restaurants close by and even a cinema. Last week Leni and I took the new S-Bahn train to *Potsdamer Platz.*

It's filled with pedestrians, shops, and many restaurants. We went into a few stores and couldn't get over the selections. It seemed each business was nicer than the one before.

Buses occasionally fill the streets, but there aren't many cars. All personal motor vehicles were confiscated due to the lack of petrol. The flow of people continues in the streets and on bicycles. How refreshing to see a variety of foods to select from again. Can I hope things will ever get back to normal?

Yesterday I caught up with Louise. She hugged me for an hour. We spent the afternoon together at a small coffee shop that had "real" coffee. At least it tasted real to me as the mellow flavor coated my throat. I quietly told Louise about my train ride into Berlin. She heard rumors of camps like the one I saw but didn't believe they existed. I found it hard to get the words out of my mouth. My beautiful handkerchief has almost been destroyed due to the crushing I've been giving it lately. Last night I dreamt I saw Papa's face among those prisoners.

I finally found something constructive to do in my free time, helping the Red Cross distribute food to small neighborhoods when they have emergencies. They call them the **NSV**. Mostly I'll be helping feed people who come by free soup, coffee, and cigarettes. Helga, my new roommate, has helped in these types of programs before and invited me to join her.

She said it gives her some comfort to help. Seeing the faces of hungry children can be hard, especially when food supplies run short. Thankfully, there aren't many children left in town—as many have moved to safe places in the country.

Gerti's War

I haven't seen one raid here since I've arrived. There are six different shelters in the complex area that I've found so far and each are reinforced with massive concrete partitions. Why don't they tell us where all the shelters are? A map would be very helpful.

I have filed my change of address with the BDM and must keep my file clean and to date. I don't want any Nazi's knocking on the door for me or my parents!

I had the afternoon off today and wrote my family and Sigi.

I miss them so much. I joined a large group of girls from our floor to go sightseeing in town this afternoon. We saw the *Brandenburg Gate* on the east side of the city. The columns supporting the archway are massive and impressive. The sky, crystal-clear blue today, hurt my eyes to look up at the gate. We all took turns taking photographs in front of it.

Afterwards we went to the *Zoologischer Garten* and it seemed as if we walked for hours looking at the animals. Helga often talks about her love of animals and she giggled the entire time there. She wants to take several of the silly monkey's home with her. It felt good to have such a long walk. My legs needed it, but my muscles will be screaming tomorrow. I have been sitting in the communication office too much and it has made my bottom soft.

We've had raids the last two nights. One hit very close, and dust and bits of earth shook loose inside the shelter on top of us. I was glad that I took my blanket. The walls already have the feel of winter to them and radiate a deep cold. The quiet in the shelter makes you watch those caring for others and huddling close to keep warm.

The officers in our group are more compassionate than the men in Boblingen; at least it seems so when the Commandant isn't around. Everyone focuses on their tasks, but there is kindness in their eyes when we come in. Maybe it's because the summer offensive in Russia isn't going well and food harvests have increased. I don't know. I am glad the Nazi with the German shepherd is not in my area anymore. Good riddance!

I helped with my first NSV station these past two days. From last week's raid, one bomb landed only three blocks from our center. Today it was cold, windy, and people were appreciative for the warm soup. We ran out faster than expected but people continued to show up. I haven't noticed many children since the war started. Strange, I never registered them on my consciousness before now. How do you convey the meaning of war to a child? How do you comfort them when there is nothing to eat? Their eyes reflect a deep loss and sadness and I don't know what to say to them. I try to keep hard bonbons in my pockets for the little ones. I want to hold them and comfort them, but I'm only a stranger. Any extra pocket money I get goes for sweets for the children.

Our NSV station is close to a cemetery and last night and we watched an evening All Saints Day parade. Small clusters of people walk through the graveyard carrying candles dressed in Roman togas. The huge mausoleums in the graveyard shadowed across the lawn and a light fog covered the ground.

We could hear them singing, but we couldn't understand the songs. Helga said her brother would have loved it. He is an amateur moviemaker and enjoys eerie black and white horror movies. I expected to see monsters walking among them so close to All Hallows Eve. Helga and I both wished for protective handsome men to escort us home. We giggled and held hands all the way home.

Before I went to bed, I pulled Papa's pillowcase from my suitcase and put it on my pillow as a preventive measure from nightmares. When I close my eyes and hug that pillow, ahhh, I can still smell home. Papa, Sigi, Mutti...

Gerti's War

I received a small red card with a hole in the middle of it with my ration card this month and I am supposed to hang it on my radio to remind me not to listen to foreign radio station. I smile as I think of Mutti's reaction to such an edict. To be caught listening to a foreign station is now a crime punishable by death.

I went to an outdoor concert of the Philharmonic this evening with a few of the girls. The building is one of the most beautiful that I have ever seen. The music floated over us in waves taking us on a cruise in warm, calm waters. I tried to keep my eyes closed and escape Berlin for a few hours, but the laughter and applause brought me right back.

I watched one couple who seemed so in love much of the night. My hand reached for Sigi's in the dark. I wish I had something better to wear out for special occasions. My shoes are so worn looking. Leni wore some silk stockings she received her from a boyfriend in France. I saw several young ladies wearing silver-fox fur coats. Leni said they were serving girls who had received gifts from soldiers on the front in France.

I don't have the opportunity to meet young men in this environment, unless I seek them out and that will not happen. I am lonely without Sigi and his friends. With so many women here, you would think maybe the men would find us. I think there is a tank training school a few blocks from the barracks, but it is rare to see any enlisted men in our neighborhood. Maybe if I yodel they will come running? ... Yoo-hoo!

I need to be more guarded in my entries and who is around when I write. A Captain in our unit found a diary on the floor in the communications center. The girl who owned the diary accidentally let it drop out of her bag. We were berated for nearly an hour about the importance of our work for the Fatherland and how even the most innocent entry, if found in the wrong hands, could be disastrous. I must hide my book from now on and watch who is around when writing.

I miss my comrades from the work camp and the easy banter we exchanged. I feel as if I am stuck tossing and turning—as if I'm caught in a dream, or is it a nightmare? The restlessness of my new routine keeps me awake many evenings. Sometimes I think I hear planes going overhead and the warning sirens going off in the distance, but it is only my imagination. Thank goodness, we are transcribing during the day now.

The loudspeakers in the dining hall come on weekly with a loud *"Achtung, Achtung, wir bringen Ihnen eine Sondermeldung* ("Attention, Attention, we bring you a special announcement").

The Fuhrer is about to address the nation – we sit at attention and wait for the final announcement to begin. The *Sondermeldung* precedes a moment of silence before the radio announcer says, "From the Fuhrer's Headquarters, the Supreme Command makes known…".

These announcements are like listening to an opera where you can't understand the words. They are all the same anyway. I try not to listen to the actual words. It's as if a madman is leading an orchestra in a controlled fury of squeaks and well-timed silences finishing with a crescendo of kettledrums. Opera has never been this bad.

Leni talked me into going shopping with her this week. We went to the *Kurfurstendamm* and *Tauentzienstrasse* shopping district today looking for Christmas gifts. The beautiful boulevards left us speechless. West Berlin must be for the very wealthy. We walked through the beautiful Aldon Hotel and Hotel Bristol – for movie stars and people who only want the best.

Someday I would like to stay there. Maybe when I'm a little old lady! I read the menu's posted outside and wished for enough funds to eat such a fine meal.

Gerti's War

Every business and restaurant is decorated in festive boughs of garland with a light sprinkling of snow, like powdered sugar. People wear their Sunday best. Even the street noise is softer. Mutti would have enjoyed our outing very much.

We saw such beautiful embroidered skirts and vests, but they were out of my price range. I purchased some wooden carved Christmas ornaments for my parents. It is all I can afford. Leni and I did have some wonderful rich hot chocolate before we came back. The aroma of good food we enjoyed throughout the day is a big letdown when we sat down for dinner and had white cabbage and onions. Ugh!

I know from my transcriptions that things are not going well in Russia. So much of my day has focused on Russia and the campaigns in the deep winter cold. I can't imagine being in a hole somewhere in Russia with Christmas right around the corner.

Nevertheless, my hands fly sending the orders and receiving the updates.

Several large maps fill a corner of the main room now. A cute corporal keeps it updated with troop movements. He never looks my way. The battalion changes are identified by different colors (red – Russians, white – Allies, black – Germans).

Army High Command has a station inside the communication field office monitoring the maps. I can just barely make out the changes on the maps from my work desk in the back of the room.

The enormity of this campaign makes my head swim. Hitler is a greedy child who doesn't share and only communicates with temper tantrums. He would get along well with Petra! I can't get this image out of my head.

Our Christmas passed, and I feel empty and depressed. How I missed my family on Christmas Eve and the times we would spend opening presents in our circle of unity and love. My arms feel very empty. I spent my Christmas working, boxing supplies in a field office. I did receive a small package from my parents, but no word from Sigi. We've had two raids these last few weeks. How surreal to be huddled on the floor, sitting in a cold, damp, dark room singing "*Stille Nacht*" as the room shakes. Will I ever be able to sing that song again without a cold bomb shelter coming to mind? It used to be my favorite Christmas song.

A small group of girls from my floor went to a Greta Garbo film last night. The cinema building was enormous! The theater decorations gave the feel as though you were sitting outside.

We watched newsreels on the progress of the war filled the propaganda agenda. I ignored the campaign updates because I live it every day in the center. Nevertheless, we had a good time watching Garbo being so elegant and dignified. Each one of us tried to imitate her. We practiced walking and smiling just as she does. I did a terrible imitation of Garbo, and everyone laughed at me.

Only Giselle could do it perfectly. Now we call her "Garbo." On the way home, we walked by the Sarotti Chocolate factory and let the sweet vapors of chocolate surround us. What a great smell! Louise squirmed as she pleaded for "just one bite". We stopped in a café and had tea and rolls and I used up the last of my ration coupons. We passed a cabaret house and a partially bombed out theater that are continuing performances in the shells of the building. "The show must go on!"

Today is the ten-year anniversary of the Third Reich regime. We listened to broadcasts about supporting our armies especially those on the Russian front. The announcer said, "Save our culture and religion from the hordes in the East." I don't think the leaders care about religion.

Gerti's War

Happy Birthday to me! I feel much older than 19. Helga has agreed to teach me French. I know some basic phrases, but the chance to become truly proficient in French is on my "life list."

We have already started working our lessons when we help in the NSV, it will keep our minds active and focused on something positive. Mutti pressed some of my favorite flowers into the card they sent. More smells of home, peace, and hope.

I received a short note from Sigi last week, wishing me good things and a smile in my heart. He didn't write a very long letter, but it is good to know he is safe. Paul sent birthday greetings and another wonderful photograph of him in front of the Arc de Triomphe. I wrote long letters back to both. How I wish you both were here and could meet.

Tonight, some of the girls are going to take me to a cabaret. It will be my first time in a nightclub. All the girls on my floor are talking about it and I think quite a few girls will go with us. Josephine Baker is no longer doing her nude shows, but it should be very educational! They won't tell me which club we are going to. Spontaneous cabaret shows are performed on the floor for my benefit, especially on the way back from the showers.

There has been a definite change in the Communication office.

The campaign in Russia has ended in surrender and it fills me with horror and despair. Goebbels came on the radio and asked us for three days of national mourning. He won't say how many men were lost, but it must be a lot. It's always the people to blame, never the government.

I had to put in lots of extra time this week. The updates are coming in faster than we can handle them. Every day there's been another announcement from the Fuhrer. His political machine is in full swing. Three raids this week on the west side of the city. I can smell it in the air.

I was so glad to get out for my birthday as it may be the last time for a while. We had a grand time at the cabaret. The costumes were naughty—and the dancing and singing were great.

"Lilli Marlene" was the favorite song of the evening. I even smoked a few cigarettes but coughed too much as the room was filled with smoke and music.

Some enlisted men came and joined us for a drink, but they had to return to their unit. We didn't get back until curfew. I thought one of the men VERY cute. His name was Gottfried. He kissed me on the cheek for my birthday kiss, but his hair was greasy, and I noticed I had pomade on my hands after they left. Yuck.

Some of the girls went to the Golden Horseshoe Bar and watched women ride a horse to music and show their legs above the knees. The men in the audience shouted encouragements out to them. Several of us went inside for a few moments, but we didn't have the courage to stay.

It seemed strange to be out on the streets at night absorbed in the darkness of the blackout, like staying up late without permission.

Helga and another girl from our floor were walking a little ahead of us and saw a large rat sitting right in the middle of the walkway. They both ran down the street screaming. Their voices echoed down the alley. I laughed so hard I had to hold on to my ribs. Someone said, "Helga, we thought you loved animals, it's only a rat!" The image of her running and screaming continues to make me giggle just thinking about it. By the time we arrived back at the barracks, she was laughing over the ordeal. Today someone put a rag doll on her bed made up to look like a rat. Poor Helga...

Today I walked to the *Tiergarten* this afternoon and spent the day sitting in the sun, walking, and reading a book. Helga joined me on this rare warm March day. I picked up a small book of love poems and enjoyed the freedom of reading what I wanted.

It was glorious! Would Sigi ever write love poems like that to me? Helga read a book called "The Vampire," which her brother had sent. We exchanged verses back and forth. They were so different from each other.

Gerti's War

I love the sound of walking on gravel at the *Tiergarten* as we wandered through the old oak groves surrounding the lagoon.

Monuments and fountains are scattered in the woods around us. I don't know how many times we walked around the garden. It refreshed my soul as I cleansed the destruction from my mind. If I close my eyes, I can still feel the cool air inside my lungs and the sun on my cheeks.

On the way back, we noticed the large guns in the Theater Center area of the gardens. Huge anti-aircraft cannons are mounted at the top of the tower. Thankfully, they are quiet today during our walk. The sounds coming from them must be enormous.

Today is a Memorial Day for those killed in all the wars.

We lit candles for Marta and my cousins and for the thousands we've lost. Everyone at the center has lost someone close to them. Papa, I am so glad you are safe at home now. Sigile, please get through this safely.

Wave after wave of planes fill the sky above us. Even in cloudy weather, the planes fly low. Over one thousand planes flew over Berlin this morning. From our shelter, it is hard to distinguish the droning of the engines from the bombs exploding.

The anti-aircraft guns never stop firing and my ears are still ringing.

The air smells heavily of gas and smoke and it's hard to catch your breath. It is strange to see raids in the day-—true destruction in front of you. People cluster in small groups and we aren't sure when to leave. I heard an officer say groups of planes must assess the damages after each raid. There is massive damage even in our area. One corner of our building has collapsed, but no one here is hurt—just some minor scrapes.

There are anti-aircraft flak pieces all over the ground.

They just notified us that a bomb has been found in the pond. They hurried the evacuation of the whole area until the bomb squad removes it. Some of us are heading to barracks further south of the city. Louise may go with that group. I hope not--her nerves are just about shot. They gave us bracelets yesterday with our blood type and identification numbers on them.

Our Top-Secret clearance gives us top priority if we become wounded. What about the rest of the girls here?

I pulled a muscle in my lower back yesterday working at the NSV and now walk like a little old lady. I can't get over the damage from the last raid massive. People seem to be coming from everywhere for soup. The lines are so long that you can't see the end. We melted snow for our murky, weak coffee. It tastes like an ashtray. I heard some of the beautiful villas on the southwest side have been completely wiped out. If you listen carefully, you can hear people asking about news from different areas of town. We've started posting notices at the main NSV station to keep people better informed. I don't know how many people were left homeless or killed this week. Berlin seems very gray.

I picked up a German propaganda flyer this week that talked about a mass grave found in the western part of Russia. It said, "4,400 Polish officers captured by the Soviets during the campaign of 1939." All the officers had been shot in the back of their heads. I wonder if Sigi's father could be in this group? I can't remember when Sigi last talked with him or received word.

I sent him the flyer with a note attached. It's been two months and no word from Sigi. Papa, are you safe at home in your bed?

Working with the NSV is now the focus of my week. The kind people I volunteer with are extraordinarily friendly. We are *"compagnons de malheur"* (companions of misfortune). My French lessons are coming along. I am surprised at how many people speak French. Helga and I try to communicate only in French, at least to each other. I am determined to get good at this!

We did something naughty today. On the way back to the barracks, as it was getting dark, we found a pile of *"Der Sturer"* (The Storm Trooper) tabloids sitting off to the side at a newsstand. Helga and I picked up the whole bundle without being seen; smuggled it a block away, and threw it on a pile of burning debris. I can't believe we got away with it! I can't stand that rubbish, always lecturing a vicious anti-Semitic campaign. Now, it is rubbish! Papa you would be proud of me today!

I met Louise at an intimate café off the *Weinstuben* and feel so at ease talking to her. She loved my little sabotage tale.

What a relief to share it with her. I noticed Louise has picked up a nervous habit of chewing on the corners of her fingernails.

They were in tatters. I asked her several times how she was doing. I think her mind is sick. She kept patting my hand—and seemed jumpy. I finally got her to tell me she hasn't been sleeping and is only getting a few hours rest at night. The last daylight raid dropped a bomb close to her bunker and two people died at the entrance, one she knew well. I don't know how much longer she can hold out.

It's May Day this week, but there's no celebration here. It seems a lifetime ago that I was one of those happy children dancing around the Maypole. We had another horrendous raid last night. One of the officers said there were at least fifteen hundred planes in the swarm that covered the city. Thousands of bombs were dropped.

The English are doing a good job of stopping the transportation centers. Last night I was physically paralyzed with fright. It has never affected me so much before. My throat tightened, and I kept swallowing repeatedly. My ears grew two sizes as I listened for the next explosion. Phosphorus bombs can take out the whole district in an evening. The fear of fire makes us all shudder as we watch flames burning high in the sky. Those tiny phosphorus packets look like thick, wet business cards as they fall to the earth. When dry, they ignite and cause a small fire to burn for a few minutes. You don't hear them, but the fear of fire consumes everyone.

All our communication lines are down now, and we are confined to our dorms. Will it ever end? Will I ever get home?

Germany is no more.

Our army in Africa has surrendered--Unbelievable.

Helga has been so worried about her family from Hamburg, on the coast. Her mother sent one of the leaflets the English dropped saying women and children should evacuate the area. They are trying to get to relatives in a small-town east of Munich. I promised Helga I would go with her to train station. She was able to get transportation documents. They tell us the trains have started working again. It's complete madness and chaos anywhere near the switching yard.

Several of the roads in the area are blocked with rubble and we can still smell gas. No one is permitted to smoke outdoors in our area until they find the gas leak. With nerves on edge and these smokers around, I keep thinking we will go up in a huge ball of flame from a smoker sneaking a quick puff close by. Gertrud Leicht, killed by a smoker, R-I-P.

It was absolute madness at the train station, an indescribable situation. People were hanging on the sides and sitting on the top of the train, they are extremely overloaded. Some people had their faces smashed up against the windows. One woman cried uncontrollably in the arms of several passengers. Her daughter was pushed from the train just before it arrived. She walked right past me trying to walk back down the tracks. I saw several people burned or covered with soot with their clothing partially burned off as well. They carried no suitcases or belongings. People tossed all parcels out the window to make room for more bodies on the train. I got stuck in the crowd with people pushing and shoving. Helga and I stayed until the

Gerti's War

soldiers moved people back. We watched the Police remove two bodies of passengers who died on the way.

Raids have started in Hamburg. *Der Montag.* The newspaper says 25,000-50,000 people were killed. Another headline reads "Thousands of children homeless and wandering the streets looking for their parents."

This is one propaganda message that may be real. I saw those people on the train. Newspapers always slant the news—the British are purposefully targeting residential areas to bring the German people to their knees and, Germans are only attacking military objectives. The usual propaganda rubbishes! However, why would they completely decimate an entire town? What military installations are in Hamburg? These people are only shells of humanity.

We couldn't find Helga's mother amongst the mass of bodies.

It's so important for Helga to find her. They haven't seen each other in two years. There was too much noise -- shouting, pushing, and tear-streaked faces of those shuffling along the walkways. Where would these people go? I told several groups where the nearest Red Cross station was. I knew they wouldn't be able to do much for so many. We both felt drained by the time we got back—and older. Helga didn't want to leave the station.

Helga and I have started singing as we work at NSV; it helps keep her mind off things. Germans love a good song and sometimes we can get people in line join in. It warms my heart to see they still wear the small pins on their shirts, which says they have given to the Wartime Winter Relief Fund.

We saw several high army officers' speeds down the *Tiergartenstrasse* to the War Ministry office in the *Bendlerstrasse* today. There were eight carloads of them. Everyone stopped and watched them go by.

I was close to the yellow-brown Chancellery office today and I have never been there before. I decided to see what it looked like. Numerous guards keep you away from the side of the street where the house is. I heard that the enormous bronze doors on the front were removed and melted down for the arms industry, and replaced with big brown wooden doors. I saw them removing the doors in a movie reel the last time we went to the cinema.

The stone courtyard held three large buildings four stories tall. Stationed guards are everywhere. Each window has Swastika flags hanging from bottom of the windows.

A small crowd of people mingles outside the Chancellery. They are waiting to hear a word on the war or peace. One woman said she had been there every day since the war started. I wanted to yell, "Wake Up! You are Destroying Germany!" But I kept my mouth closed and went to pick up my monthly ration card instead. Weakling!

A massive fifteen-hundred-plane raid hit hard last night.

The officers in the bunker said it is the largest grouping of planes they have seen so far. Searchlights and anti-aircraft gunfire lit up the sky well before the sirens went off. Now, when I hear the rumble of planes, my throat tightens, my heart beats fast and my ears focus on the sounds above us.

We spent five hours in the shelter and afterwards I couldn't sleep. One of our barracks had a direct hit. The bomb stripped the roof off and compressed the top floors. The rest of it is only a heap of rubble.

Everyone keeps asking for information, "What was hit?" "What have you heard?" The NSV is setting up a station in our backyard. We are alive! As never before, I feel I am alive and must do what I can to help others. Mutti are you okay? Paul, Sigi ... is anyone left out there?

Chapter 11 – July 1943

I received a short note from Paul. He will be leaving Paris and sent to Berlin! How wonderful to see him again. I hope he hasn't lost his sense of humor. Hope… Be positive … ugh! All mothers and children received orders to leave Berlin immediately. Fear grips me in the stomach sometimes, but I try not to show it.

The streets are almost passable again, but in some areas, it's just a narrow strip of dirt surrounded by piles of rubble.

Women and old men scavenge and dig through the mounds looking for valuables and some work for food coupons. The NSV has set up large metal drums at stations asking people to donate any spare copper, bronze, brass, tin, lead or nickel for the war effort. I donated my small metal tin used for carrying loose valuables in my suitcase.

Louise, Leni, and I strolled around the *Tiergarten* this afternoon. It was a wonderfully hot day. Leni received a marriage proposal from Otto—that big burly man. He is still in the Luftwaffe training paratroopers at a base in the North. If she accepts, they would get married by proxy and it would take two months to complete the paperwork. Otto would be bound to the marriage contract immediately, but women get two months before its official. She's considering his offer. They have been writing to each other for a year. I had no idea they were this serious. Does this mean she and Otto have a future?

It's getting harder to tell the districts apart anymore. When I first arrived, West Berliners were very apparent in their fashionable clothes and neat appearance, while the East Berliners were factory workers in common clothing, and not well kept.

Southwest Berliners are impressive--the true nouveaux rich in secluded villas with servants. Mixed in are many of the transplanted workers from other countries. Now everyone walks about with wet towels over their faces or scarves covering their nose and mouth. Our clothes are dirty. Whites are more gray than white. Berliners are just Berliners—there is no class distinction. If I didn't have my duties at the NSV—I would probably just stay in the small area around the complex rather than venture away. Italy has surrendered to the Allies.

A day of clean air finally arrived, even if it is windy.

Many people are out on the streets today. It is a small reprieve, one week without a raid. Most of the fires have been put out.

Helga and I work the soup kitchen at a children's school today. We walked quite a way to get there. We wished for bicycles, but they are expensive. I have heard that people steal them at any opportunity.

Our long walk took us by a structure being rebuilt. The sign at the front said, "New Headquarters for the British Embassy." A large propaganda poster on the building said, "England will be giving in soon." It is sad to see them building this monument.

The school building, we worked in was nothing but a shell. All we could do was shake our heads. It all seems so pointless.

The war seems to be turning against Germany. First, the surrender in Stalingrad, then Africa, and now the Americans invade Italy. Could the war be over by Christmas? People are talking about a new secret weapon Hitler must have that will win the war. I want it to end now.

Paul sent me a note today and we will meet at the beautiful Aldon Hotel for tea tomorrow. He told me to bring some cute friends along with me. I asked Helga and Leni to join us. Louise doesn't want to go out anywhere and prefers to stay near the barracks.

Gerti's War

Our meeting with Paul raised our spirits. He brought two friends with him and we had a great visit, Paul kept us laughing and is still quick with his jokes. He makes me think of home. I had to hold my cheeks on the walk back because we did too much smiling. It had been a long time.

Paul and Leni really hit it off. I don't think Leni is going to accept Otto's engagement offer. She didn't say anything more about it. I noticed that sparks were flying between Paul and Leni. We could all feel it. Is love in the air?

Paul's orders now have him attached to a group of documentary offices. He must take photographs of Berlin and categorize the photographs on file. He said there were so many photos to go through it would take him years to finish the project. Organization is important.

He took several pictures during the day today and said he'd send them to us. I asked him to take a few extra of me –for Mutti and Sigi.

At the hotel, we had some Ersatz pastries. They tasted bitter. It was awful. Paul asked for some hard liqueur to put in his tea, but all the bottles arranged in the hotel bar contain only colored water. The elderly waiter told us "that today, just today, they had run out of the ingredients."

Paul and his friend Heinz surprised me last night and waited for me down in the courtyard. Paul wanted to take me out to a play at the Prussian State Theater and wanted to know if Leni could join us. I think he really came just to see Leni. Word spread fast and soon three girls joined us. Leni and Paul walked arm in arm on the way back.

We saw Faust-- Gustav Grundgen played Mephisto. He is very famous throughout Germany—I have heard of him many times. We could hear music coming from some of the darkened clubs we walked by. Dark, formless bodies easily hid in the shadows. Twice I almost ran into light poles in the middle of the pavement. It is easy getting caught up in the night; we all want to forget for a while. I enjoyed the light in Paul and Leni's eyes. Sigi, I am missing your hand in mine.

On the way home, a guard stopped us, asking for our *Kennkarte* documents (identity cards) and *Wehrpas* (military passes). It seemed too clumsy in the dark fumbling with your paperwork and trying not to lose anything. We were all cleared. My heart thundered in fear. What would they do if our paperwork weren't correct?

I can see small fires burning everywhere in the little neighborhoods around us. We had another phosphorous bombing last night with less heavy bombing. The cards have ignited the coal supplies delivered to get people through the winter and now they will have no heat. Once those coal piles ignite, it is impossible to put out. Fires are inextinguishable, even in the rain. Thank goodness, our coal is inside. We must pray for a mild winter and an end to the war.

I received another letter from Sigi and he said that his father is still in Russia. The letter was dated back in May. He hasn't heard from him since. Could he be a prisoner of war?

Sigi loves getting my letters and apologized for not writing more. Every day he takes out the handkerchief I made him, spreads it out and says, "Hello Hope, keep my Gerti safe today." It is hard for me to picture it, but it sounds nice. He sounds bitter about the direction the war is going. It is the first time he's mentioned anything political.

A new proclamation was posted and sent out over the radio. All young people must stay in Berlin. Leave requests will now be stamped *verboten* and returned. I would desperately love to go home for Christmas and now Mutti will be very disappointed. Will I ever get to make my own decisions?

Gerti's War

Another heavy raid this week filled my days. The main topic of conversation everywhere you go consists of "Which district, which building, how many people injured?" Questions and answers change all the time. I saw two huge groups of transfer workers being led down the street. Some come from Russia and others from France. I can tell by their clothing where they are from.

Helga and I discussed the group as they went by. One of the officers said the Fatherland is gathering people to keep the factories working. There must have been over two hundred in both groups. They looked longingly at our soup. I said a prayer for them.

A paper in the dorm said millions of people are being brought into Germany to work in industry and agriculture service. The nightmare continues, for how many millions today?

Horror, today I saw madness. Helga and I walked to our NSV station assignment and we saw a man shot and killed by an SS officer. The Officer and work detail crews were moving furniture from a home and they found a frail old man inside. We heard them say something about hiding and in a blink of an eye; he was shot through the head. He lied on the cold stone courtyard bleeding to death. It was horrible.

Helga held me back against the corner of the building, so we would not be seen. I don't know what else to say other than to document that it happened at .22 *Linkstrasse* at 4 p.m. The Officer who fired the weapon was tall, thin, blonde hair, and had large scar on chin. He looked about 35 years old. The old man was at least 75. The Officer didn't seem slightest bit concerned over the incident. They threw his body on top of the furniture when they left.

Christmas is right around the corner, but I still see the murder in my head. I dreamt it was my grandfather lying there. He was someone's grandfather or father. I know I shouldn't, but I am going to try to find out the family's name. Helga says forget it. How can I find out? Can Paul help? He has access to information. I would have to tell him what happened. First, I must see what I can find out on my own before I involve Paul or anyone else. Where do I start?

We've had five days of heavy bombing and I think I've only slept six hours in five days. The Americans are bombing in the day and English are bombing at night. We can't leave the area to help the NSV. The droning of planes going over is all we talk about if we speak at all. I try to concentrate on the words of a prayer, but my mind refuses to respond. It is bitterly cold today and my chest stays tightened from the stress of the raids. Am I getting sick? Will we have another night of fear and terror? How many nights before it's over? Please God, make it stop, make it all stop.

They brought mattresses down into the bunker for us to use, but they are too filthy, and I can't lie down on them. I do most of my sleeping sitting up with my head on someone's shoulder.

My schedule these past two weeks consists of, report at 8 o'clock, work for a few hours until sirens go off, then running down into the shelter until the 'all clear' sounds and transcribing until evening. Sometimes we are working at midnight if we are behind in transcriptions.

Our meals continue with less variety and we are getting smaller portions from the kitchen. The water tastes chunky and is a light brown. Ugh! Everything stops at midnight for cipher changes. Am I a machine? No more smiles – work, work, work.

The English raids have started in the middle of night, ending three hours later. I haven't been able to fall back asleep after 4 o'clock as my adrenaline is pumping too much. I am too exhausted for words.

Gerti's War

Finally! A day free of bombing! Some communication lines are down and groups not working must help clear the compound. Two structures in our area have severe damage. Six buildings have been demolished this past year. I haven't heard how many people were killed in the past two weeks. That wonderful Italian restaurant around the block is gone, along with the entire family. The whole complex of shops went up in a phosphorus firestorm. I have survived the devastation of Berlin. Surely now things will stop.

Outside you must wear a wet towel wrapped around your face just to breathe. The sweet smell of death burns the back of my throat. It is terrible and bitterly cold. Be thankful, Gerti.

I'm one of the lucky ones. I still have somewhere to sleep, a warm bed and something to eat. Will those things disappear tomorrow?

I worked at the NSV station outside our building for only an hour today. The silence on the streets gives me goose bumps.

Street after street consists of burned out houses and businesses. People line up and shuffle in silence to get something hot as if they are emerging from tombs in the ground, rather than homes.

My coughing won't stop and for the past two days, Helga and I have been at infirmary. We have horrible coughs from standing outside and just when I was grateful for sleeping lying down again, now I must sleep upright to breathe. We both shared the same cot at the infirmary. Now I know Helga very well. I had her feet in my armpit the whole time. There were so many here for treatment. We both felt like sardines in a can. A wall and dresser give us each a brace to lean against.

Helga heard from her mother and she made it safely to relatives. She seems better now that she has word from home.

The rumor around the complex is that over 10,000 were killed in last raids. Some people here are horribly burned. Paul came to see me today. He is in the area to see Leni, but I am glad to see him. Even though we looked awful, he cheered us both. He told us to be prepared once we are allowed out of the area. Nothing looks the same. Heavy, heavy damage everywhere.

One of the girls stood outside in the dark and yelled at the top of her lungs, "Stop it!" I agree with her. The matron slapped her across the face. I felt like joining in the yelling.

No one is talking about anything other than the Russian front these days. I've been back at work for four days now; my cough is still there, but it is finally getting better. My fever is gone.

Today I overheard two officers talking about the situation in Russia. The Russians are fighting like criminals, putting up a white flag, and then when Germans approach, shooting them at close range. They are even shooting the Red Cross workers trying to remove the wounded. I shudder when I hear "Russian."

One of the girls in our unit asked to resign and return to her family. Her parents have been badly burned and she wants to go home to take care of them. One Officer overheard her request, stepped in, and ordered her taken to the front to help with the wounded, "Where she can do more good for Germany." Terrible!

Just terrible. She asked the right officer but had the misfortune of the Nazi coming up behind her and overhearing her request.

She left in tears. Leni is quite upset over it. The girl is one of her roommates.

Finally, I've received a day off. I can't remember the last time I wasn't plastered into my chair typing. I walked outside briefly and saw the devastation around us. How much more miserable can it get? Groups of grey women picking through rubble piles, looking for valuables and things to burn to keep warm swarmed over the piles. "Watch your step. Don't lose your way." Mutti, your words are echoing in my mind. I am being as careful as I can.

I found the same neighborhood where we witnessed the shooting. Nearby we saw a banner hanging from a window –

Gerti's War

"Our walls may have crumbled, but not our spirit!" Just more propaganda trash to decorate our crumbling walls.

I took a deep breath and replayed my strategy to find out about the murder. I had some donation pins from the NSV and a tin cup for cash donations, so I started knocking on doors asking for donations to the War Relief Fund. My hands shook with each new door I tried. Some secret agent I am!

It took six stops before I found someone who was willing to talk about people in the neighborhood. Luckily, a worried mother started talking about her boys that she missed, and I found out who the murdered man is. His name was Peter Muller, a retired writer. He had strong political views and the Gestapo asked about him on two occasions before. The Frau thought him harmless. His son is also a writer for a newspaper in Madrid. His name is Peter, Jr. Before I left, she gave me two brass candlesticks for donation. I am glad to get out of there.

Now I have the information I need. What do I do with it? I will never do that again.

There is no more city transportation. The City center is a battered town square with carcasses of burnt-out buses and shells of trams tossed to the side. Walking is the only method of transportation left to most, including me. I saw a makeshift Emergency shelter made from a demolished building. It is icy cold these days. Where do you put all the people?

"Have you heard of any new shelters?" "Is the electricity being fixed?" "Do you know of anyone with room to spare?" The questions come one after another. It's endless.

Yesterday someone was caught standing in line with their pockets bulging with coal. Soon shoving and pushing started in line and people tried to steal a piece of coal. My countrymen are cold and hungry. Manners are dropping into the gutter, just like Germany.

Paul visited us yesterday. He looked so tired and gave me photographs taken months ago, or was it years ago? I will send one to Sigi and one to my parents. After the first couple of heavy raids, I would write home quickly letting them know I was safe. Now, I write every two weeks and hope the mail continues to work. I saw Leni and Paul holding hands and walking around the grounds after he visited with me. I am glad they had more time together.

My transcription news gets worse every day. The Russians are moving closer to us, and they are now in Poland. Sigi, I am saying prayers for your mother and brothers. We now have guards posted at the communication building entrances and I must keep my paperwork with me always. I sewed a pocket into my uniform to keep it safe. The guards are looking younger and younger to me.

It is freezing in here and my fingers are having trouble working. The telegraph lines are down again, and I notice we do not have the sweet music of church bells ringing in town. They have all been melted for production of war materials.

Paul came by again and took Leni and me the Aldon Hotel for tea. There is no more coffee in Germany. He said we'd better enjoy the beautiful hotel before it is gone. There are only two items on the menu, and one of them was crossed off with pencil saying they had just run out. We Had *spaetzle* and *Lachs Galantine,* it tasted like soggy salmon rolled in sawdust. I thought the prices were too expensive, but we're all starving for some real food. Paul is such good company and he helped me to relax for a few moments. I am tired of being scared.

Yesterday's raid hit the Hotel Bristol during a military dinner. Several generals and high-ranking officers were buried alive in the rubble. Italian work crews are still pumping air into the basement when we passed the hotel on the way back. We kept out of the way. Their bodies were lined up on the sidewalk. It caused our celebration come to a quick halt and brought reality back.

Gerti's War

I don't want to get out too much and I stay close to the center. It helps to drop in on Louise and check on her. She loaned me some books. I try to escape into a book when I can. It helps. I tried to get her to go for a drink or something hot, but she refuses. There is no more chocolate to entice her.

We had two more small raids this week and are just about out of coal in our building. The workrooms will be kept heated, but our sleeping quarters have no heat now. I wear three pairs of socks and one pair on my hands to keep warm at night.

Families must come by to get two pails of their allotted water a day. There is no light, no gas, and no coal. Rationing keeps us on the verge of starvation. The few children here are thin and lifeless. There is no more singing in the NSV lines, we've no energy. I have no more bonbons in my pocket either. They're all gone. Each face seems so pale, unhealthy, and white, with red rings around tired eyes. I've noticed many of us are starting to lose teeth.

I work when the lines are up, run to the shelter and then stand and dish out soup or *Ersatzkaffee* if we can get it. Most supply trucks are having trouble getting to us or receiving food in the first place. We run to the shelter and see if the telegraph lines are working. I sleep when I can. What a life!

Mutti, I'm still here. The Americans are bombing during the day; and their friends hitting us at night. It never stops. I run to the shelter. STOP IT! STOP IT! Please God make it stop!

The *Wehrmacht* has withdrawn from Rome and now it's called an open city. Will their heritage be saved? OUR architectural history is gone. Is the Roman history obliterated as well?

I wonder what is left outside to bomb? The partial frames of buildings now fall indiscriminately on those digging in the rubble. The Rothchild family I worked with in the food line was crushed a block away. They were regulars at the NSV. I considered them friends. Now they are gone. No coffins are available. Wood is too expensive, and is used for kindling.

We said a small blessing for the family. I heard they were all buried together in a wardrobe chest. It is so sad. Go with God. I will remember you.

Leaflets were dropped in our section by the Americans.

"Give up." Yes, I give up. Hitler will never give up. Run to the shelter. *J'ai peur* (I am afraid).

I write in my journal by candlelight, no light, no water.

Each room is given one bucket of water a day for six people. They announced 'no more hot showers' at the meeting yesterday. I haven't had warm showers for months. Did they forget that when they announced it here? Thank you for reminding us.

It's been quiet the last few days. Maybe the warmer weather is helping things. Spring is beginning to show. I am glad the flowers and budding trees don't work on a war schedule.

The neighborhoods around here are congested with craters and building debris. The streets are lined with carpets of glass and concrete chunks. Glass shards sparkle in the daytime light, tricking the eye. Windows shattered by raids in the past are no longer fixed, just left open and jagged. There are many open roofs here and there, as you walk around. Sometimes you can see right into living quarters with people walking around. Am I becoming a voyeur? I can't help but watch for a minute or two as people handle private matters in their homes. Is someone watching Mutti at home?

The transmission lines are up again, and it's been frantic at times. The radio in the communication office used to play music as it helped quiet our nerves. Now it stands silent until a news flash is announced. We all prefer the music.

Brick dust is everywhere, even in my teeth. I can't get clean. I taste it in my mouth and try not to smile, not that there is much to smile over. I've been trying to save my leftover washing water to wash my hair once a week. I look disgusting and wear my handkerchief every day! I hope for peace and a cleansing shower to wash all this choking air away. I never want to be this filthy again.

I didn't use my ration card during the Easter holiday and hoped to get chocolates for Louise for her birthday next week. It should cheer her up. The window display at the chocolate shop has beautiful boxes tied with pink and blue ribbons. The sign in the window says, "Not for sale." Leni and I will go tomorrow.

My scarf does a good job of covering my ugly hair. I cut it short and now it sticks out, skinny, dirty, and now ugly hair. Yoo-hoo...boys! I'd even scare away the Russians if they looked closely at me. If I see a mirror, I stick my tongue out at the reflection. It isn't me anymore. What would Sigi say about my appearance?

Today is Hitler's birthday and they've ordered flags to fly all over Berlin. What a waste of energy. Meanwhile the army is losing on every front.

Soldier work crews are covering areas of town with wire netting covered in mottled strips of green gauze. They've even decorated the lampposts to look like trees, but the winds cut into the netting and it makes a mess of everything.

The trip to the sweet store was interesting and I even managed to get a little box of chocolates for Louise. She loved it. The storeowner is very nice. He apologized for selling us old chocolate. All his shelves are bare. He hasn't had sugar or cocoa deliveries in two years.

When he saw my NSV patch, he asked me about our supply loads. I didn't know much myself, so I couldn't tell him anything. He gave me some hard bonbons for the children and told me not to tell anyone. It was a simple kindness in this madness. Be thankful for what you have.

Another May Day goes by, but we had no celebrations, no Maypole, just flowers blooming amid the rubble. I wished to walk by the beautiful rhododendron bushes in the city park and breathe in deep pink and orange. Nature finds a way to remind us rebirth is possible, even in the worst situations.

The *Bombenfluchtlinge* (bomb refugees) have been put to work clearing rubble so military vehicles can pass. Even the smallest children work all day for a single meal. I don't know where they all stay. I am thankful that it's warming up. We had no raids this week.

Because open windows don't shatter as easy as closed ones, we've been instructed to keep our windows open if we have any more raids.

American planes are visible very high in the sky. Sometimes the sirens don't go off so we all run to the shelter if someone calls out, "Alarm! Alarm!"

An American plane crashed in the *Tiergarten* last week. They never found the pilot. Paul took photographs of the plane. They were in the paper.

I daydream as I work in the NSV. I float over meadows of brilliant flowers. What a contrast to the dirty people in line.

Women have been wearing men's trousers throughout the winter to keep them warm. Everything is covered in a fine layer of gritty soot, ashes, and brick debris. We are all shades of gray. My uniform is shabby these days. There are thunderstorms in the distance, maybe it will clean the streets, and the people, and we will have color again.

Gerti's War

I took a very cold shower in the runoff rainwater as it fell from our roof. Several girls joined me and we showered in our clothes. They also needed cleaning. Some of the girls were humming songs. Soon playing in the downpour took over the whole group. We filled everything we could find with water. It rained all evening and relaxed our guard since planes don't fly in this weather.

Good news from home, papa is finally feeling better and can go for short walks in the neighborhood. Papa, can you feel me reaching out for you? For the moment anyway, they are safe.

As I write this, I can hear trumpets heralding a victory song on the radio. They have had successful raids into London with the new V1 jet propelled rockets. It's been so long since we've heard a victory song. There are no more victories. Everyone loses in this war.

Many people were killed taking shelter in a subway tunnel during a raid. The city looks better after the cleansing storms last week. Ash from the new raids leaves a light film on everything. Now we have 'political talks' to help our spirits during the noonday meal. It's the same old story and makes me feel more hopeless than energized. I don't have the discipline for this. Why is this war still going on? There is nothing left.

If you choose war, it will destroy you. Ruins and dust as far as I can see fill my mind.

We had blue skies today. I remember Mutti saying blue was the color of hope. I try to look up and not around me and listen for peace. Listen.

We had a talk today given by a soldier from the front. He has a leg brace, head wound, and his arm in a sling. What a waste.

He told us how important our work is for Germany and about the heroic life of soldiers on the front. The American and British forces are now in France. How much longer? I give up. I am tired of waiting. I just want to help the people outside and go home.

There is a new play opening in Berlin and the proceeds go to help the Red Cross. Who still has the energy to go theaters and cinemas? Are there any buildings left standing? Paul took Leni out last week, but I didn't have the energy to go with them. She twisted her ankle walking near a crater site and Paul carried her back. I think Leni liked Paul rescuing her. She glowed with happiness about him carrying her in his arms. I noticed she didn't talk much about her ankle. I spent the evening playing cards with Louise. Her hands shake all the time now.

The Russian offensive has been relentless. The Allied troops are making slow progress in the west. How many more will die for this campaign of madness? This war is crushing us to death.

Yesterday, a storeowner in our area was murdered in his shop while trying to protect it from vandals. The people cleaned the shelves within minutes. Hunger in this form is a sign of the desperate conditions out there. It's rampant and getting worse.

A raid this week hit the zoo. What chaos! There were exotic animals running free. Several squads were sent to shoot the big cats and apes. One alligator almost made it to the Spree River. What a sight that would have been to see an alligator in the river! Some monkeys are still wandering in parts of the *Tiergarten*. Paul took photographs for the paper and told us about it.

The Red Cross received some of the animal meat for soup. I wonder what they served us today. So many of the animals were starving or suffering—all of them were shot. Paul came by to tell Leni about the event. Helga was very distraught over the loss of the zoo. I'm more worried about people than animals right now. So many are starving, including me. We get one meal a day now. I heard them say in the kitchen that no new supplies are coming in.

Gerti's War

The Allies are coming. Will they get here before the Russians? I hear so many horrible stories whispered about the brutality of Ivan—their massive murder sprees and rapping's.

Please God, let the Americans get here first.

Letters from families in the east describe their assault of towns where girls are being raped by entire squadrons in front of parents, families, and children. Over twenty girls at a small school in the southwest committed suicide rather than being captured by the Russians. For Louise, it is too much to think about.

There are no more mild sedatives available and she may have to be heavily medicated. She stays down in the infirmary all the time now.

I want to go home. I've been told that survival with the Russians depends on how you react to their request of "Frau, Komm!" (Come Here) Letters from parents tell us to submit to the Russians and when they have their pants down; run away as fast as you can. I desperately want to go home.

Someone tried to kill Hitler yesterday. Goebbels said, "Only God Almighty could save Hitler's life." They announced it over the radio *"Totaler Kreig"* and closed all superfluous shops.

There's nothing in them anyway. There is a new decree for all men ages 16-60, to pick up weapons and fight to the end. Not only will there be no more Germany, there will be no more men either. Will Father be called on to fight? He is still much too weak. Oh Papa, I need one of your bear hugs right now! Please stay safe. The *Volkssturm* doesn't need you.

I can't stand transcribing more and more bad news--troop updates, shifting strategies, shouting, pressure to keep going, and shouting. That nice Corporal Max was knocked out of his chair when he handed another bad update to the Commandant yesterday.

Tempers are short everywhere. I shuffle into work and try not to look at the update maps. Is it worse to sit in the bomb shelter or sitting at my desk? I don't know anymore. I keep my handkerchief spread out on my lap; it helps me to focus on hope – not war.

Roland Freisler, whom many secretly called the "Beast of Berlin," was hung by meat hooks for his involvement in the plot to kill Hitler. The photographs were in the paper. More than twenty generals were also killed. They have picked up thousands for questioning regarding the Hitler conspiracy. No one is above suspicion. The Gestapo pulled one of the officers from our office out of the building last week and we haven't seen him since.

More raids this week. Windowless apartment buildings are everywhere. Their torn blackened curtains flap in the breeze.

Most shelters have messages written on the sides giving families messages about where they have gone. Grey hunched forms search the rubble and people seem blinded by the loss of humanity.

These are the people I help and we are completely out of food at the NSV. All we could offer was bad *Ersatzkaffee*. It was so very weak. We tried to stretch out the small amount we had.

I must remember these events carefully. While at the NSV station with Helga today, a single American aircraft flew very low over us. I could see the pilot's face! We had no warning or sirens. He began shooting at those in the line. We scattered as quickly as we could looking anywhere for shelter. Helga and I took refuge in a nearby cemetery and hid behind tombstones. My heart beats so fast.

The tombstone I cowered behind was hit with bullets! I could hardly breathe. I was shocked to see the miserable SS officer who had killed Herr Mueller in the group taking shelter near us. His officer name badge said "Glueck." I got as far away from him as I could. The plane took three passes before it left. Two people were killed and six injured. Stretchers carried the injured around craters in the road and debris to get to us. My hands are still shaking. They were shooting at me!

The headlines are full of the actions of *Volksgericht*-- a court to deal with those responsible for the assassination attempt. Two judges and three SS officers killed thousands involved with the sabotage. It's more Germans killing Germans.

It never ends. My mental movie sees Hitler having one of his tantrums again, "Kill them all!" Last week they called another one of the officers from our center for questioning by an SS group and marched off. Could he be included with those responsible? Who is next?

I received word from home. Papa will not have to join the *Volkssturm*. His Doctor gave him the necessary paperwork discharging him from duty. He has started working with the local Red Cross for a few hours a day from home. Marta's father is out there with the *Volkssturm*. This worries me.

No more single airplane fly-bys, I keep having nightmares about it. I feel better now that a small group of us went up to the roof and screamed as hard as we could until we couldn't scream anymore. The officers watched us and shook their heads. We didn't get in trouble.

We had Helga's birthday yesterday. I picked dark blue Enzians and white star daisies for her. I also harvested some primrose blossoms and have them drying on newspaper for tea. It is a perfect evening tea to settle our nerves. They fill our room with the sweet fragrances of flowers instead of the burnt smell of ash. I hope it lasts a while. When the sun fills the room, it makes you forget the dark clouds of war surrounding us. Helga gave me a haircut and I feel a little better about my appearance. Now we all look the same.

General DeGaulle is back in Paris. The Russians have gone through Lithuania and Latvia. The Americans are coming from the west. Can anyone stop this madness!

More propaganda directives have come from high command, no more cinemas unless they have 'approved' newsreels or are German-made movies. We have no more refuge into the fantasy world of American movies. No Garbo, Gary Cooper, Claudette Colbert – we will miss you.

Paul brought a work associate Eduard to visit and a basket of FOOD. I think we sat there looking at it for five minutes before we touched anything. I can still smell the hard Landjager sausage, sweet cheese, wine and crackers. It was food of the Gods!

Leni and I joined them near a small cluster of trees by the pond in back. I had to force myself to eat slowly. My stomach grumbled with every bite. We all laughed! I later got sick to my stomach from eating real rich fat again. I am used to the weak filtered restaurant grease leftovers they use to flavor our foods.

I gave Paul and Leni some time alone and Eduard and I walked around the park. He was wounded early in the war, and has lost most of his hearing. We practically yelled back and forth. He asked me how many women were stationed with us, but it is half the amount from when I first arrived. I think he is lonely for companionship. I haven't heard from Sigi for seven months. My thoughts are full of him, not Eduard. Sigi – where are you?

This war has lasted five years. I stare at the calendar wanting it to tell me how much longer until we all go home.

Winter is knocking at the door and again we have no coal. The NSV is taking donations of clothing, blankets, and shoes. Everyone has a quota to fill, no exceptions. My assignment had me going door-to-door for the offerings. There are few landmarks or street signs left.

I had a push wagon to load supplies in, but did manage to get clothing and shoes, but not many blankets. I donated some socks and a jacket and skirt that no longer fit. My clothes hang on me.

They hang on everyone. We are losing weight. I use three safety pins hold my skirt up.

Louise is a mess. The Russians are approaching her hometown. She shakes all the time. I talked to her matron yesterday and she suggested we take Louise out for a walk. She sits and mumbles with a blank stare. I don't know what to do. Mutti, I wish you were here to help. You would know how to help her. I just hold on to Louise as she cries on my shoulder. Goebbels cries over the radio, "Hold out! Total victory is at hand!"

The Allies have taken Aachen near Belgium —Charlemagne's city. It's one of my favorite towns, so old and picturesque. Is it still standing? I don't know. More history has been lost forever. There is loss and retreat on so many fronts. The only victories have been the damaging bombing raids of the V-1 rockets in Britain. Retreat goes on in Romania. I feel like a whale caught in a net. I know the end is coming, but it's a slow dark death.

The raids continue sporadically, but there are not many buildings left standing in Berlin. Louise is a little better. She was able to get a phone call through to her family. Her Mother didn't tell her much, but hearing her voice helped her. I tried to reach home myself for the hundredth time, but the lines must still be down. Mutti, are you still there? I've had no letter in three weeks. Our post responses are few and far between. There is so much worry and misery around us.

I've still had no word from home. I sent two letters this week and I know that the Allies are only an hour away from Arnbach. The town is so small maybe they will pass it by, my last letter said they had very little bombing damage. When I close my eyes, I see so many faces of the people grew up with.
Where are they now? Be strong, be smart – have hope.

Lois Buchter

The sighs and screams of the falling bombs rock the inside of our shelter, but I am terminally exhausted and hungry. We've unending periods of wait-and-see. I dream of raids, it's with me all the time. I dream of food—Mutti's chocolate cake when I can sleep through the lighter raids.

It's cold, very cold and I've had little word from home with only two short letters this month that were written months ago.

I am surprised mail is getting through at all.

They have stopped posting work schedules. We report first thing in the morning and stay until we are dismissed. Sometimes we are going until midnight. We now have required check-ins after raids and each team of six girls must go to different areas during raids. Helga and I are still in same squad of six.

I feel like a prisoner and must have permission to leave the compound. All the trains are for military transportation only-- No civilians. There are no military passes for us. Giselle, "Garbo,"

cries all the time. Her family is from Fussen in the south. The Russians have already advanced through her town. She's had no word from her family in months.

It's a cold November day, and we've no water, no heat. It hasn't rained since the middle of July. My skin is cracking from the constant rubbing to warm up. I cut the fingertips off my gloves and now can wear them while working. Our last winter was mild compared to our average temperatures so far this winter.
The only movement outside is the gray masses of people scavenging for food. There is no food. No shipments. No farms. I live in a world filled with *"nein."*

The Allies have taken Pforzheim and Arnbach as well. It is strange to see white markers on the map over my hometown. We all search the papers for news on what is happening. I wish we had a small radio and could listen to the BBC, even if it is a death sentence. The not knowing is driving many of us mad.

Paul is trying to find out more information for me. He brought us some newspapers yesterday. I think he has access to a radio but won't tell me anything specific. We should all pray to the Allies liberate us. The news reports about the Russian atrocities follow the markers on the map and now I see faces of the girls here, when I look at the map. Whose family is the Red Army swallowing today? Many heads stop working to see the updates, especially in the east.

Leni showed me a Spanish newspaper article Paul gave her last week. They included photographs of the horror of death camps in Poland--piles and piles of naked thin bodies everywhere. *Oh, mein Gott*! This horror is worse than what I saw coming into Berlin two years ago. No German papers are reporting this massive barbarity. It made me physically sick, but I didn't have enough food in my system to vomit. I am careful not to let Command see this. How many more pockets of inhumanity are out there? Several girls are going to the chapel to pray this evening. What do you say to God over this? A lifetime of prayers would not be enough.

Ahhh, letters from home. Finally, I have word they are alive. Papa had to fill out lots of paperwork with the Allies verifying his status in the Red Cross and his was wounds. The kept him for twelve hours for questioning. Papa says the Allies have been very civil. They have set curfews that are enforced.

Food supplies are extremely low for everyone. Most ration items aren't available in Arnbach.

A refugee family of five is now living upstairs in my and Rolf's rooms. Everyone must help with boarders. Mutti was able to trade a few jars of her preserves for some flour and wheat. Be thankful—be thankful. Thank you, Lord Jesus. They are safe. Keep Sigi safe.

I sent my old journals home by post. If captured, I don't want anyone going through my private thoughts. The less I have the better. Mutti will be comforted reading them.

Nothing in Germany is beautiful anymore. A dark cloud of gray has settled over the city. We are all freezing and starving.

Will I be home for Christmas? Will I ever see home again? I put a note in the front of my journal asking that it be sent to my parents if I don't survive. I hope to see tomorrow.

It's as if your breath freezes and stays up in the air in this bitter, bitter cold. What do people exist on? The French Army have liberated their own. I can picture it very clearly in my mind. We know through our communications that the German Army has taken refuge in the mountains in Italy. Russia moves on through Bulgaria and parts of Prussia. The radio command still talks about Hitler and his wonderful V-2 rockets. What is happening? I almost started laughing over the latest update. It's so ridiculous, so sad. He thinks he will win the war. Am I going crazy?

Merry Christmas to me, I survived another horrendous raid that went on for six hours last night. I stuffed my blanket in my ears and tried to sleep through it. Someone cut a small tree from the nearby woods and we had a Christmas tree with little bits of yarn tied on it. I don't know who cut down the tree and put it up. People are burning everything to stay warm. After we sang we cut it up and burned it in our little stove. No one feels like celebrating. Silent prayers for those who have survived, are exposed, lost, homeless, rescued, helpless, hungry... my list could go on forever.

I got permission to work at the NSV today. It was so very, very cold and I stood in deep snow. Somehow, we had thin soup and gray people were everywhere. One little boy had so many layers of clothing on that he looked fat. When I asked him about it, he said he was wearing everything he owned. I squeezed my last bonbon into his thin hand. What a wonderful smile he gave me before he ran off. It was my Christmas present.

Paul came by and wished us a, "Happy New Year," but no one felt like celebrating. There were no families skating on the pond and the streets are deserted. Leni and Paul are getting serious.

I still no word from Sigi and it's now almost nine months. I write to his home address hoping to hear some word about him.

More bitter cold runs through me, the temperatures are way below freezing. The flu is traveling through our group and many of the girls are sick, I am weak but haven't started coughing yet. We are all quarantined to our center until the all clear is given. Starting tomorrow we will be working straight through to help cover the shortage of personnel. I can't believe they are still giving us political talks to keep our spirits elevated. Ugh!

I finally got through on the telephone lines. Papa, it was wonderful to hear your voice, but it makes me long for you even more. I can picture the look on your face talking to me and it made me smile deep on the inside. I had so much to say and all I did was ask about you and Mutti. Now I can't remember much of what you said. The time went by so quickly. I feel calmer, more at ease now that we've spoken. My hope is still alive.

Raids are increasing again. Dresden is gone! That beautiful city of baroque architecture, cultural center of art and music is now a pile of rubble. The radio says over 200,000 civilians were killed, including 20,000 allied prisoners of war. The Allies are at the shores of the Rhine and the slow death of Germany continues. Russia pushes through East Prussia. How can our soldiers continue to fight? There has been so much loss.

Helga has been visiting with Corporal Max. The simple kindness shown to him over last few months has finally loosened his tongue. Now he looks in our direction occasionally and smiles. He's been here almost as long as we have. Now have a friend at the front of the room.

I saw Louise this week and thought she had birthday greetings for me, but then she handed me her letter from one of her sisters. Russians repeatedly raped her sister Margot and that later she hung herself orphaning her two small children. The news from her town is very bad. I read the letter from her mother as Louise couldn't talk about it. She thinks she may be able to go home. How could she think this? Going home to the Russians—unthinkable! A few girls received passes to leave the area. The critical staff will have to stay until the end. I am included on the 'critical list.'

Hungary has signed an Armistice. Budapest has fallen to the Russians. 20,000 died in the last bit of fighting there.

The Russians are deporting thousands to Russian factories. Could this happen to Louise? Paul brings us newspaper reports and communications that aren't well known. We already know there is a big difference from what is printed in the paper and what is going on.

Max tells us the Russians, English, and Americans are meeting and discussing how to partition Germany after the war.

Every day I come in expecting to hear the end, surrender at last. The German positions on the map get smaller and smaller. Will I ever know what happened to Sigi? It's been a year with no word.

I had my birthday and didn't celebrate at all. I told no one. Why bother?

I worked at another NSV station today near the Red Cross hospital. I heard some American pilots were there. I could see them through the window in the hallway. They looked harmless. I didn't see the face of the pilot who shot at us in the park. One pilot waved at me. Unconsciously, I waved back.

Louise will be leaving on the 20th. I will go see her tomorrow, for possibly the last time? She was my connection to all the girls from the work camp. I haven't had much communication from them. Little Jeanette from Heidelberg was killed in a raid last summer. What will happen to Louise in Garmisch-Partenkirchen? There's been no message from Margret or Annemarie in over six months. Cornelia hasn't written to anyone since we left the camp.

It was a tearful farewell to Louise as I walked her to the *Hauptbahnhof*. I gave her all my extra pocket money. She looked so frail squeezed into the cabin. This image is clearly burned into my mind. Three times, they checked her papers before allowing her aboard the very overcrowded train. How long would it take her to get home? No one knows—there are so many lines down. Go with God, Louise. Be safe. *Auf widersehn*.

The Allies have crossed the Rhine and there is fighting around Cologne and Bonn. Close but not close enough. The Russians are moving faster toward us. Soon the two armies will link up and it will end. Please let us be on the American side. I've decided to use Papa's pillowcase as surrender flag if needed. It's been endless waiting for peace.

My hair is falling out in big chunks and I try not to comb it but once a day. Stress, lack of a varied diet, poor hygiene conditions, maybe it's all three things to blame? My scarf keeps everything plastered to my head. Leni is better at hair styling and is trying to help. My scarf is the only solution.

Goebbels continues to shriek, "Berliners, the German Army is approaching. Rescue is coming! Hold Out!" We know from the communications that no army is coming to our rescue. They want people to stay in the city to help defend it.

It's so cold. My fingers are too stiff, and I can't type very well. We are almost out of coal for the whole building. I stay wrapped in a blanket at my work desk. The communication lines are down often. Our one meal a day consists of a watery soup with a slice of black bread. I am light-headed, and it is hard to climb the stairs in our building. Grabbing the railing, I focus on the wooden steps, taking them one at a time. I remember home and all the walks through the woods and the feel of sun on my face – it is a good memory when I feel faint. I must get stronger.

Helga shared some white cheese Max gave her. I took tiny bites to make it last. I will never gulp down food again if I have it. I try to remember the incredible meals Mutti would make. We all have taken so much for granted.

The *Gauleiter* announced over the radio, "Upper Austria must stand to the last man." Hearing it makes me look at the maps and I know the true hopelessness of our soldiers. Why are they sacrificing so many? Do the soldiers know how bad the situation is? Rumors are flying. Hitler must have a secret weapon that is more powerful than the V2 rockets.

The air raid sirens lasted all day. The explosions rock the earth under my feet. From the rooftop on our building, you can see for miles. Nothing but shells of buildings remain. Only a handful of three-story buildings remain on the horizon. All the landmarks are gone. How many people still survive in the city? Where are they living? What are they eating? More refugees arrive daily fleeing to the west away from the Russians.

Max is feeding the coal stove in the main workroom with paperwork, confidential reports, and parts of an old wooden desk. Yes, the end is near.

Paul told us to keep one small bag packed and be ready to leave anytime. He is trying to get travel passes for us. When I asked him how, he said, "Don't ask." I told him about the troop maps in the top-secret room. He isn't surprised. He gave me an old bar of chocolate for the two of us to share, but said I needed it. What a present! He kissed me on the cheek and said, "Happy Birthday." I ate one small piece and saved the rest.

More girls on the floor are going home or leaving. Some have passes, others don't. Trains don't run much anymore, there is no coal. Will I have to walk home, by myself?

I have started looking for small maps of Germany, anything with directions on it.

My essential things fill a small bag, no suitcase for me. It would be too heavy. I feel the warmth of spring outside and hope to see small buds beginning to appear on the trees.

Goebbels speaks to us every day. Is he Minister of Morale as well as Minister of Propaganda? He tells us to be strong.

"Germany can rebuild all that has been destroyed. The Allies are broken with the loss of Roosevelt." How can he say these things?

One of the girls in our group started laughing during his speech. She was hysterical by the time they removed her from the dining room. It is hard not to start laughing myself. We are all on the brink. Just a little push and we all go over.

I look for Paul every day. Leni says they will marry when the war is over. I will go with them if I can. Helga is going to stay close to Max. No one knows what will happen.

Hitler's birthday was yesterday. Goebbels said, "The Fuhrer is within each of us and each of us is within him." If I'd had food in my stomach, it would have come back up.

The Russians are bombing areas of the city just north of us. The Allies are close. Everything will end in Berlin. Will we survive? What will the new President of America do with us? Will I be sent to work in a factory in Russia? I still have no word from Louise. The post service is no more.

More horror to my eyes as I walked friends to the station. I saw two young boys in makeshift military outfits and one older officer hanging from lampposts near the old train station. They had signs pinned to their chests, which said, "Traitor" and "Coward." The boys looked to be only about twelve years old.

Our Army has been cut in two with no possible escape. Hitler is finally knocking on the gates of Hell. Paul came to give us the news in person. Hitler is dead! Goebbels is dead and now we hear Hitler was married? Is this propaganda, a cover-up story? Can it be true? Who is running what is left of Germany?

I feel nothing, absolutely nothing. The shelling continues. Why doesn't the war end now? No one seems to know what to do. I've been given permission to leave, but Paul's paperwork has not cleared. I won't leave without him. Leni and I stay close together. Helga and Max are leaving tonight in the dark. His family home is to the north, in the American-English sector. Everyone is trying to get north or west. We will head in that direction too. Tomorrow? Watch for Paul. Watch for Paul.

Someone ran into our room to tell us the Russians are only three-kilometers away. We grabbed our bags and ran downstairs.

It was just getting dark when we found Paul. Now is our time. He tells us we have transportation on a truck leaving to the north, but we must hurry. We keep to the shadows along the way. I overhear a German officer talking about a group of girls he is going to give to, "Service Russians". My blood turned to ice. I know this officer. We used to call him, "The Watch Dog."

Carefully we made our way. I could see Russian troops on our street! They have captured some German soldiers. We heard them say, "*Germanski kaputt!*" My body and mind freeze when I hear "Russian" spoken. Paul pulls me along and whispers into my ear, "Stay focused and very quiet." We took off our shoes, so we made no sound. I don't care if my feet get cut, just keep moving! My heart is pounding so loudly!

Gerti's War

We got to the truck just at it pulled out. Paul threw us into the back before he climbed in behind us. We passed a film crew with cameras and bright lights. Everyone strained to see what was going on through the slates on the truck. They were interviewing people on the street. We saw movie actress Ursula Hohenlohe talking to them. Her makeup and clothes were beautiful, but from behind, I saw a large burnt hole in the back of her mink coat.

We were on the last free street in that section of Berlin. The people in the truck were quietly talking about the Russians, taking no prisoners. Most of the streets were deserted. We had a narrow one-way passage through the ruins and dust. It is hard not to cough and my lungs burst trying to keep quiet. After a few minutes, the truck finally stopped at the American side. I closed my eyes and said a prayer of thanks before climbing out. We made it!

Chapter 12 – May 1945

The American forces make us sign forms stating what we did during the war and list our hometown information. Leni whispered into my ear to change the name of my hometown, so it would be hard to track personal information. Even now, we fear being sent to Russia. The Military police have taken control of our small group. They divided us into men's and women's. Leni was in tears saying good-bye to Paul, and my cheeks are wet as well.

Auf Wiedersehen. Be safe Paul. I hope we will meet again.

I am now classified as a Prisoner of War, but I am thankful the war is over for me. They told me I will be sent to Lubeck in the north at the end of the week by military transport for processing. There are ten girls in my group. We know we are the lucky ones. My thoughts remain focused on those left behind to be used by the Russians. The Americans have given us real food and hot coffee. I am jittery from the caffeine overdose or from my escape. I don't know, but it keeps me awake.

Tears of joy, the war is finally over! I can see Mutti and Papa sitting in the kitchen celebrating and being worried about me. I say silent prayers and then in the next moment I feel like screaming it to the heavens! I hope to be processed and cleared as quickly as possible. I don't know how long it will take.

People outside of our complex have been celebrating by firing guns into the air. Two soldiers kissed me before an officer told them to leave us alone. Yes, Peace is quite noisy. I smile on the inside as I watch others celebrate. I hear songs all over the camp. By God's mercy let the souls of those lost rest in peace.

Before sleeping tonight, all the girls in our room held hands and said a prayer of hope for the future of Germany and all those affected by this war. Leni and I stay close to each other. We've no other choice, as our room is 8'x 8' for all ten of us.

From our camp fences, we can see trenches and barricades made to hold the Russians back. People come by the Americans asking for food or for permission to dig through the rubbish containers.

A soldier now patrols to keep the crowds calm. Imagine, guarding rubbish?!! I couldn't resist trying to see what they picked up. I am slightly tempted to join them if I could. Will that empty hole that is my stomach ever be filled again?

We've been loaded into the back of a transport truck. The soldiers are on one side and girls on the other. It's a very slow and bumpy ride. Some girls have tried talking to the soldiers, but we've been told not to socialize with Americans. *Verboten*.

On the way, we've seen many, many families walking along the road with belongings. One woman carries a huge iron caldron in front of her followed by three small children. What could be so important about a large pot? There is nothing to eat! Nothing to drink! The river has bodies floating in it. It is disgusting! The smell overwhelms us!

At one stop, we saw bodies being collected near an underground rail station, which had been flooded. Over a hundred bodies were stacked up, mostly women and elderly people. Many had used the underground places for bunkers. Hitler ordered them flooded, killing his own people. I don't understand it. So many are gone at the very end. We can't get water anywhere. It's all contaminated. You try not to look at the water when we pass, but the debris and floating bodies makes you glance.

Some of the soldiers have offered to share their water with us, but many did not. It is humiliating to pee with men guarding us. Several of the men laughed at us. Tomorrow we arrive in Lubeck.

Gerti's War

We slept on the ground last night in the open. No more worries about raids. The stars looked beautiful under an ocean of deep blue. Sigi, do you see the same sky tonight?

The air still smells of death and destruction, but the heavens have repaired themselves in all their glory. The refugee families are everywhere trying to make their way, to where? It's an endless stream of wretched looking people moving very slowly. It's a desperate situation for all. What must my family be going through? What will we find when we get home?

Occasionally I see pieces of furniture or suitcases lying beside the road. I guess people got tired of carrying them. All the faces look so tired and hungry. In one small town we passed through, townspeople were burying piles of dead people. For most, the last few days of the war had brutal bombing runs. At one junction, I saw German officers under guard being forced to bury civilians. I wonder if they were Nazis or just POW officers.

The *Wehrmacht* did a good job of destroying all the bridges and roads. Hitler ordered everything blown up and almost every bridge or overpass of importance gone. It is taking a long time to reach Lubeck. Every time we stop, I think we have arrived, but it is another delay. One of the soldiers sitting across from us makes my flesh crawl. Again, I try to keep my eyes closed or look up at the sky, but there seems to be nowhere to look. Will Germany ever come back to life after this beating?

I am riding through the devastated countryside that was once Germany. It is hot and steamy today. The view out the back of the truck shows mangled forests, scattered war materials, deserted vehicles, wrecked tanks, soldier graves, and dead horses. The stench of death in the air. A toxic cloud hangs over all of Germany. Where do we go from here?

Lubeck and the smell of the ocean, the air is cleans here. Many houses have white flags hanging so they won't be bombed or destroyed. We were given second hand clothes today. I wanted to burn my uniform, but they were collected. I couldn't get my small knife out of the secret pocket before it was collected.

Piles of uniforms of all types were displayed in corners of the camp. My shoes are so torn up they wouldn't take them. The clothes almost make me feel normal again. Some of the Allied soldiers were asking for medals, armbands, hats for souvenirs.

We've been housed in a nice Swabian woman's home, all ten of us. I've not had a shower in ages, but maybe it will rain, and we can clean ourselves that way. Heaven tonight was thick cold barley soup with carrots for dinner. No one complained. Tonight an elderly British captain guards us. Tomorrow they plan to give us socks from the soldiers to mend to keep us busy. The Captain is friendly and smiles easily. Everyone is slowing coming back to life the war is over!

I've spent the last week sitting in the sun on a bench leaning against the house mending socks all day. I am getting good at this. My tiny stitches will never come out.

We still cannot post a letter or call home. There is no mail service at all and no infrastructure to get it to us. I wrote a small note and envelope to my parents. I keep it in my pocket just in case opportunity presents itself. Everybody is in a light mood these days. We've had fish soup for dinner again. It's hard to communicate with the English captain, but he speaks a little French. Only one of us speaks a little English. The Captain tells us it's good for us to keep busy. Today he showed us pictures of his family. Everyone wants to go home.

We've been transported to Hamburg in a large truck, but there is nothing left of the town. We had a full-days walk to Ulm where we stayed at another household. A soldier with a rifle stays at our door while we repair socks and uniforms. Once a day we eat soup at the Red Cross. Sometimes it is very good soup, sometimes they have nothing at all. The Red Cross helper there is very nice. They have no beds available, so we sleep on the floor. They gave us food coupons, but there is no food available to buy. There are twelve girls in our group now. We are hungry, but happy and we are beginning to hope that we will see our families again.

The Red Cross gave us coupons to get second-hand outfits in town. They issued us papers saying we are working with the English troops and they must serve us before others. The townspeople don't like us. Our guard takes us to town to buy little things if we can find them. Today we were able to get a few handfuls of herring fish to share for dinner.

A friendly Swabian woman let us use her kitchen to cook one meal a day, but ugh! We found rat droppings in the cabinets.
Mice are bad enough, but RATS! No more sleeping soundly for me! Have we been eating this all week?!! We might be processed this week. At least the weather is good here.

They finally presented us to some English ladies today. They released Leni and she will get some transportation to the south with 'free soldiers'. My paperwork is different from Leni's because of my 'top secret' clearance. They say I'm bad and my case takes further review. I'm not bad; I didn't have a choice. We barely had time to say, "Goodbye." I gave her the letter for my parents hopefully; she will have more luck than I will. For now, they are sending me to Marburg and then to a German POW camp. My stomach is in knots and the shaking in my hands has started again. I just want to go home.

Today I saw an American General riding in a jeep. The camps are full and there are refugees everywhere. He stopped our group and told us we couldn't cross the river. The bridge isn't safe. We had to go quite a way to cross at a low water crossing. Along the way, I saw two girls from our camp in Berlin. It is good to know they made it out of Berlin.

I

The English gave us potatoes and salt again. We slept in straw last night in the remains of a barn. There is no roof and only a few walls remained. We noticed the straw filthy with dried blood when we woke in the morning. We are so tired from walking that we didn't care. The mice are everywhere! I hope it isn't our blood on the straw. Quickly, everyone checked our bodies before we left, but we had no bite marks.

We have arrived in Marburg. It's a big place surrounded by wheat fields as far as you can see. When I see the fields I don't think of food, I think of MICE! Here there are many different POWs. I can talk to men through the fence. They are ragged and haggard looking. They tell us to be proud German girls and not to forget where we came from. Sometimes it's hard to look at them. I wonder if that awful Nazi officer is somewhere in the back of the crowd? How many are in the military because of forced military service? How many are radical Nazi's? I look for faces that I know but see none.

The man in charge wants me to undergo medical tests. I won't do it. I saw the look on his face and he made me feel dirty. I gave my address as Stuttgart, in the American zone.

I don't want them to be send me on a rebuilding campaign into France, but Arnbach is now in the French zone. They won't release me until they verify my 'top secret' clearance.

I miss my friends and worry about them all. Olli has joined us. She is from Berlin. She confided in me that two Russian soldiers raped her not far from our compound, but she managed to escape before they came back for seconds. I try to soothe her, but what can I do? She is so ashamed. I heard some of the POW men talking about the massive raping going on throughout the German empire. The Russians are so angry about their losses

Gerti's War

back home and seeing the splendor of what Germany used to be, they are taking it out on any women they see. They are raping women not once, but six times, ten times, twenty times. Families are encouraging wives to commit suicide and hiding daughters wherever they can.

We invaded their country, killed their fathers in the Great War, and carried away their belongings and dignity. People in Russia were told how poor German people were. They thought our suffering and hunger must be greater than theirs must. I heard that when they came to Germany and saw our wealth it was too much. Maybe Stalin told the men to re-seed Germany with Russian children? I don't know.

Some Russian enlisted men came over to the fence yesterday and taunted us. Their victory was evident. Ivan will never understand. No one has won in this war. Olli covered her ears and cried. She is worried that she may be pregnant already? I feel nauseous as well. It must be the heat. An American captain told the Russians to wait in their jeep and to be quiet.

Today they finally verified my paperwork, but I still won't take the medical exam. They want to physically examine me by three slimy American soldiers. That means I must stand naked before them. For what?! When I asked for a woman to do the physical they laughed at me. Olli will do the exam today. Her dignity is gone. She doesn't care anymore. She will take another letter to my family with her. I am hoping to give it to someone going south.

Every day I deny the medical exam. Maybe they will bring my case to the attention of someone with morals.

We get war updates on the battle still going on in the Pacific. America, England, and China are pushing hard on Japan. Loud speakers tell us news every day.

I spend my days ripping the seams out of old uniforms and making piles of cloth to re-made into regular clothes. The wool is hot and scratchy to work with in this heat. Wool dries my fingers so much that they are bleeding and cracked.

I try not to watch the POW men walking around. They look deserted and lost. Some have lost arms, legs and other parts. They are walking ruins. I watch for the inhumane Nazi Glueck in the faces across the fence. I will never forget that face. How many Nazi's are watching me now?

More POW's have arrived this week. I hear the men talking about Russians taking German POW's back to Russia. Many feel they intend to shoot them as soon as they are in Russian custody. Could Sigi somehow be in Russia?

We had more women coming into our cabin this week. Several of them had been raped. They spit on the ground whenever someone mentions the Russians. Workers with the Red Cross came by to see us today. I got to talk to someone in charge and told them of my work with the NSV. Would anyone give me the physical, so I can leave? Five of us are resisting the physical. One woman took our names. Maybe soon.

Leni, did you make it home? Paul, are you safe? Louise? Sigi? Work crews of POW men now go into town to rebuild the roads and build a makeshift hospital. Disease is spreading, dysentery, and typhoid.

On the wheat hills nearby, summer flowers are scattered amongst the fields of gold. Cornflowers, blazing red poppies have an urgent need to live. I wonder if the cherry tree in my yard is full and heavy with fruit? Home, I just want to go home.

Many townspeople congregate around the officers' mess hall on the other side of the fence. They are catching what they can to take away. I have seen several soldiers feel sorry and give them canned goods or leftovers. People are no longer disgusted when it comes to rubbish. Flies, dust, and heat fill my days.

My *fragebogen* questionnaire is complete. They finally verified everything and more Red Cross people came in camp today. I waved at the woman who took my name before. I am hopeful.

Gerti's War

The men who sit across from my mending area talk about Hitler betraying their trust and loyalty. They curse Ivan and his physical victory on women. There is a constant whining about the injustice of their fate and inexhaustible self-pity. It's the same men with the same complaints day after day, they complain long into the evening after their days of road clearing. One man draws in the dirt a map for me showing how to get home. He was a map specialist in the *Wehrmacht*. He has been kind to me. I took a piece of paper from my journal, and made a good map and keep it inside my sock.

This morning the Red Cross came through and offered to do physicals for some of the women. I think those Americans in the medical office were tired of my refusals. A woman gave me a brief physical. Afterwards, they called me in with my paperwork sitting on their desk. Now I have FREEDOM!! I will dress as a man to travel.

    I bound my chest and put my hair up in a cap. If they don't get too close, I can pass as a man. I am tall enough. Yes, I will walk home if it's the only way.

    I walked along the train tracks; or what used to be train tracks. Mangled tracks with gaping holes and loose wiring tangle my feet if I don't watch carefully. Hidden holes are a real hazard. I have no water or food. I do have some coupons and money, but it's not worth anything. The sky seems even closer than before. I can almost touch it. I'm free and on my way home! The quiet of this night is odd. Be strong. Be safe.

This morning beautiful rain began to fall. I walked in the rain enjoying the feel of water on my skin again. My last shower was a rainstorm in Berlin, but I can't remember my last hot shower, maybe it was at home. "*Dreaming of a hot shower*", "*dreaming of Mutti's Black Forest Cake*". I sing silly songs to keep me company and my mind off food. I found an apple tree with a few wormy apples. It gave me stomach cramps.

I passed a family cemetery today with six fresh graves. A sign said "Family Leicht". Could they be relatives? I walk through the forests and stay on country roads. Thank goodness, I have an internal sense of direction. I think it safer to stay off the main roads if one can even call them roads. I don't want to be part of the thousands clogging the main thoroughfare.

Strange to see so few people when I've been around so many. I wished for Papa's little two-inch knife and have a sharpened stick in my waistband for protection and God's grace.

I was caught by an American Third Army patrol today, but they found my paperwork okay. One of the soldiers gave me a small tin of peanut butter. I've never had this food before. It is very good. I was scared at first when their jeep came over the hill. They were nice and told me to watch where I sleep. The bottoms of my feet are so very sore. I can feel every pebble when I walk, but I must be thankful for little things. I could be walking even farther from the north from Lubeck. Sometimes I take little steps and say out loud, "Each one brings me closer to home." Last night I tried to sleep in the ruins of an old barn but could hear things moving in the night. I slept deeply and then woke up with a start.

I made it to Wetzlar today, my first real town. I traded the last of my peanut butter for an oilskin bag. It's so hot and I am dying of thirst. I met another girl walking the back roads this afternoon. Maria is from Wiesbaden. She's been on the road for almost two weeks. We are going to try to go through the Lahn Valley. We will have to get across several rivers on our own, but it will be a shorter path. It is such a beautiful countryside here, very wooded. The air smells clean and fresh in this forest. I find myself taking deep breaths. It smells like the woods at home. We got a ride on a wagon from a farmer all the way to Diez. What a treat!

I picked berries in a thicket for breakfast and we found a few wild mushrooms to have later. We crossed the Aar River this afternoon. The cool water felt wonderful on my feet and I swear I saw steam coming off them. We saw the intact Schaumburg Castle to the west of us. Some jewels of architecture and history have survived. It's still there sitting in the sunshine, almost as if sunbeams were lighting it up for us. Maria grew up close to here and knows the area very well. It's been a tough rocky walk here and we must rest often. My energy reserves are gone, and my mind wanders to large plates of food.

Maria is an angel! We found a natural hot spring this afternoon. I wanted to soak my feet forever. I rinsed my hair repeatedly. I feel refreshed but wobbly. My feet say, "Thank you."
There are several hot springs in this area. Maria promised to find another one close to her house to get me out of the water. One more long day of walking and we should be close to town. Maria hasn't heard from her mother since the Allies invaded. Her Father was killed in 1943. She has two younger sisters still at home. We found some ugly apples for dinner and ate wild carrots. Thank goodness for my gardening skills. I can identify plants.

We made our way across the Tanus near the Rhine. We hiked up very steep slopes. There is evidence of heavy bombing in this area. Maria cried over some of the devastation. Small pockets of architecture still survive, but not much else. The streets are passable.

We got a lift to the south side of town with some American GI's. We were so happy for the ride, we sang for them. Maria's apartment building is gone, but we found her mother with friends nearby. I cried with Maria and her mother. We had hot soup for dinner and will sleep on a real mattress tonight.

Lois Buchter

I am giving myself one day of rest before going on. The many elaborate hotels that made up the spa neighborhood of Wiesbaden are gone, but it's still a beautiful city despite the damage.

Marie's little sister Margot, is healing from a foot injury. We are all confined to the small room that serves as living room, bedroom, and kitchen. They don't need two extra bodies in here. I will leave as soon as possible.

There are at least ten families living in an old bank building next door to us. The bank closed when the victors cleaned it out. Marie's mother has been trying to set up a makeshift school in the back of the room. She is teaching reading, writing, and arithmetic on slate boards.

Marie and I walked to the vineyard on the hill, to forage something for dinner. Food is almost non-existent here. They have a small meager garden with potatoes, onions and tomatoes, but watering the garden has become a problem. The city water supply is contaminated, and the drought is making it worse. We carried back two pails of water each.

As we were coming back from the vineyard and hot springs we heard some people talking about a freight line still working. Now I sit writing this while riding in the back of a freight car taking me to Heidelberg, I hope. There are three other people in the car, two older men and one young man, Wilhelm, about my age.

I shared my small bag of plums Marie and I picked with them. I am so happy to be riding instead of walking. We share polite conversation, but Wilhelm doesn't join in.

Through the wooden slats of the car, I can see the devastation of Germany. Small snapshots of the old Germany come to mind. I am overwhelmed at the new wasteland of Mainz and Worms. I can smell the pockets of humanity before we see them.

Gerti's War

More people enter our car when we reached Worms. Their clothing emanated a foul odor. Cattle once used our car and they complained about the smell, but it's coming from them!

What a terrible night. The train stopped outside Heidelberg just about dark, and I ate my last plum for dinner. I found a soft spot under a tree near the tracks to sleep. In the middle of the night I awoke with a man on top of me. His hand covered my mouth. I used my sharp stick to cut the back of his hand and cheek. When he released my mouth, I screamed and screamed for help. Two elderly men from the car came to my rescue and pulled Wilhelm off me. They roughed him up and tossed him away from me. He swore some obscenities at us and disappeared into the night.

Herr Vogel and Brandt said they would stay by me. It was comforting to know they were close, but I can't sleep anymore.

I saw a sign for Pforzheim today! I am getting close. We are walking back on the main roads and many *Ostfluchtlinge (Eastern Refugee)* families are on the move with us. There are many nationalities of Lithuanians, Latvians, and Estonians walking with the caravan of people, wagons, and goods. The walk is full of hungry and tired children. I gave the last of my marks to a woman with three small children. My money is worthless. Maybe she can use it somehow.

My stomach has been upset for three days and waste pours out of me. Was it bad water or too many plums? I am very tired today.

There are more signs for Pforzheim, and I will be there by the end of the day. I am one step closer to home! Herr Vogel left our walking group to go home. He smiled and wished us good health. What a nice man. *Servus*! Herr Brandt says he's heard there is a displaced persons (DP) camp in Pforzheim. Can we get food there? I sucked on a blade of grass most of the day to keep my mouth moist.

Lois Buchter

We arrived in Pforzheim late last night just before 9 p.m. curfew and given very weak soup at the DP camp. At least it was hot. Pforzheim is not recognizable. As far as you can see, it's nothing but flattened sections of the city. Makeshift city road signs are posted on the sides of crumbled buildings. I traded my oilskin bag for a ride on a wagon to Birkenfeld. I am fidgety. Faster. Faster. Home.

Tears fill my eyes, but I am so dehydrated that they don't fall down my cheeks. The Enz Valley, my valley. Edel Pines waved a greeting to me on the wind. It smells of home. Irmgard passed me on her bicycle. Someone from home! She was traveling into Pforzheim. She told me everything is good at home. My legs can't go fast enough. A man with horse and wagon gives me a lift to the road to Arnbach. I ran down the hill all the way to my street. HOME. I collapse into the arms of my parents. I am never leaving again!

Chapter 13 – September 1945

I've slept for two days straight and the sofa in the living room has never felt so good. My old bedroom is now the main living room for the Schwartz family. So much has happened since I've been gone. I don't know where to start or when to stop.

Both my parents are noticeably thinner. Papa keeps looking at me with a broad smile on his face, but his checks are sunken with weight loss. Words of what I went through in Berlin come out in waves. I tell him about the narrow escape from the Russians and how much Paul helped me. He keeps saying, "He's such a nice young man," every time the tale is retold.

Neighbors and parents of friends stop by. There has been a constant stream of people here. Marta's mother has been here every day since I came home. A few letters from my friends are here waiting for me, but not one word from Sigi. No one knows when the regular post service will start up again. Letters are random and sporadic.

Food is in drastic short supply. The horde of canned food in the cellar is almost gone. The garden is almost finished for the season, but Mutti says with all the additional mouths, she hasn't been able to can much. She has been supplementing their ration cards with garden items. There are now five more mouths to feed with the Schwartz's, and now me. How will we manage?

Papa has told another family of three they can stay in our garage if they will help keep guard over our garden. It's essential we get as much as possible from it this year. Mutti has a potato patch hidden in a clearing off some land near the woods, by our old cherry orchard. It's far away from the main road. We will probably wind up feeding the 'garage' family as well. Then on top of everything else, we've had no rain in this part of Germany. Everything is withering away.

As I sit here writing, these words come to mind; "Enjoy the war, peace *could be worse.*" There is nothing left in food, homes, or in human spirit, just an abundance of love from my parents.

Lois Buchter

We can't buy fresh bread anymore from the *bakeri* down the street. They are unable to get wheat and flour. The only commodity today is some stale bread. It quenches hunger pains longer.

The three Schwartz children have become my shadow. Georg is nine, Yakob is seven, and little Katarina is four. They follow me every morning and we stand in line together hoping to get bread or potatoes. Mutti gives Katarina tomato soup in the afternoons for extra calories. She is malnourished, but she will only take the extra food if I eat it too. Her smile lights up the room, but she also seems as tired as I am. We take a nap together every afternoon on the sofa. Our electricity comes and goes. Papa makes a small fire in the backyard and heated some water for me, so I could take a hot bath. I owe him a thousand kisses. Ahhhhh.

Mutti brought me some old newspaper articles about the death camps. The pictures are horrific. I told them about the train ride when we stopped at a work camp. She hadn't known about them, but when I pressed Papa about it, he said he knew about them when he was in the field hospital with his injuries. He had seen a camp when they picked up some soldiers.

He tried to deliver some Red Cross packages to the prisoners, but the Commandant gave the packages to the guards instead and laughed him out of the office. I am glad to see the reports that the war in Japan is finally finished. Is it over?

There are more refugees on the streets around our tiny village. Our house sits on the main road and every day someone comes to the house asking for a meal, water, or any food. Mutti is friends with a farming family nearby. They gave her a large bag of ground wheat as payment for midwife services. It is our prized possession, but already I've noticed a difference in the supply.

It won't last long. Today Papa helped a refugee family bury a child who died on the road.

Today I received a letter from Leni and Paul! They were able to get to Rothenburg and are now married. This good news warms me up all over. They are living with Paul's parents. The shop and town were spared from the bombing raids. Another little German jewel has survived.

Papa told me the day before I arrived home he saw a fawn in the meadow and knew it was a sign I would be coming home. Sounds like something Oma would say. She had a real gift in predicting special future events. They received the letter I wrote at the POW camp. Leni's efforts gave them some comfort knowing I wasn't in Berlin.

Prices at the market are doubling every day. We can't afford eggs anymore at 5 marks apiece, and now they are asking 1,000 marks for a pound of butter! Mutti is now going to the market and doing our shopping. She is better at negotiating and stretching our money. All the banks are closed, and everyone's accounts are frozen.

Papa will testify at Herr Koska's denazification hearing.

Marta's father can't return to any sort of work until they clear him. They are classifying him as a third-level offender, which would not qualify him to vote or hold any sort of good paying job. This means low level approval on ration cards as well. Yes, he was an officer, but everyone had to join in some sort of capacity. The French tribunal has not been sympathetic to anyone in our area. We are all Nazi's in their eyes.

I filled out another *Fragebogen* questionnaire and had to give detailed descriptions of what I did during the war. I counted 131 questions. Everything will be checked and verified once again, just like at the POW camp.

Papa isn't allowed to testify at the tribunal. They aren't allowing any defenses or arguments. He did get them to accept a letter he wrote on behalf of the Red Cross, and maybe it helped get Herr Koska's status reduced by one level. This only slightly raises the level of his food-rationing card, which is essential for their survival. We are surviving on less than 1000 calories a day and most daily rations are gone before we can pick them up. Papa gets in line at 5:30 a.m., but many supplies aren't coming in at all.

Mutti has asked me to start going with her on deliveries. I think she wants more of my company and doesn't really need my help. For the past year, so many babies born die shortly after birth or are stillborn. There isn't enough nutrition to keep the mothers or babies healthy. She has seen a lot of death. It is so hard to hold a dead baby, I know, I did that today.

Mutti and I stopped by the hidden potato patch and started harvesting the larger spuds. The few onion plants are pitiful, small, shriveled balls. The drought has taken its toll. This is the worst looking crop I had ever seen come from Mutti, the amazing gardener. I will come back tomorrow with Papa to finish clearing.

Our produce has been harvested. When Papa and I went out in the woods, we found a refugee family digging up our potatoes. I think they had just arrived, because we didn't find the loss too extensive. They ran off when we got close. Papa left a few of the smaller potatoes for them. We also stopped by the Kleins' home and gave them potatoes. She is a widow, elderly and has two DP (Displaced Persons) families living with her. Her husband had been a friend of Papa's.

Frau Schmidt (Lotte) and her mother Oma already feel like members of the family. It's nice having another Oma around.

Lotte and I will start making the weekly trip to the farm to trade or purchase whatever we can. Mutti saved a set of twins born two years ago to the farmer's wife. She gave them daily care for the first several months of their lives. They give us a small tin of milk for Lotte's children every time we go, and sometimes some eggs and meat. They hired a local man to sit outside, day or night, and guard the smokehouse at the farm because Horst lost his leg in the war and can only hobble around with a lot of pain. I check his still oozing leg wound each trip and clean it for him.

Sometimes I have a small jar of Papa's homemade wine and Horst gives me salami, some type of hard meat or fat trimmings. They are precious foods and my mouth waters for them, but I know that it will only cause me to be sick if I eat it. My stomach isn't used to the heavy fats.

More good news, a letter came from Helga and Max! They are getting married and have set their nuptials for the end of the month. They are in the American zone outside Berlin and never made it further north. Max's father is in an American POW camp and they aren't releasing him. He is very distraught about it. Helga has a job working as a secretary for the Americans. Her English is very good. Wish I could be there for the ceremony, but I don't want to leave home yet. Pforzheim still seems too far away.

This week we collected mushrooms and Beachwood seeds in the woods. The children were a big help in getting everything we could harvest. We can press a small amount of oil out of the seeds. Papa even had the children gather acorns and chicory to grind to use as a coffee additive. It improves the taste but is very bitter.

The newspapers cover articles in every paper covering the Nuremburg war tribunal cases. Newspapers are too expensive to buy with our limited funds, but they post them outside the beer hall down the street. There is always a small crowd of townspeople milling about the area in front of the building. It's the place to keep up with town events and news. Papa goes by every afternoon after his nap. He still tires very easily. The missing persons list gets updated often. People trickle home or leave forwarding contact information there. My name is on the list, but it has a line through it and the word *"heim"* (home) printed very small besides it. It still makes me tear up when I see it.

Mutti and I have gone through all our old, boxed clothes and what we still had of Rolf's for the Schmidt children. They are overjoyed with the sweaters, worn shoes, books, and toys. They only brought one change of clothes with them when they left Munich. The Russians killed Lotte's husband in front of their house, then raped Lotte and Oma. Thankfully, the children were in hiding and didn't witness the event. They won't talk about it to me, but they have told Mutti. Lotte was pregnant with a Russian baby when they arrived. She miscarried later.

We have a new garage refugee family. We have moved many household items into the garage, but Joseph, Margot and Dorothea now sleep on the floor of the living room. Winter is starting early, and it is too cold for them out there. Joseph, a professor of literature before the war, spent the last year of the war in a POW camp. He is still very thin. Margot is in her 50's and she won't say much about her past. Dorothea is fourteen. She fits into my old clothes and I am glad for her to have them. More mouths to feed.

Herr Buchter told me they are resuming postal service throughout Germany. I asked him for a job, but he didn't have anything to offer me. No international parcels yet, but mail is getting through. We received word from distant cousins in the United States asking about our situation. They sent real U.S. dollars to help us. For us it's a fortune! Papa says we will use half the dollars for coal and the other half for food. Joseph and Papa have been cutting down wood in my beautiful forest every morning. We heat only the living room. We have moved more furniture to the garage to make "people space" in the house. Thank goodness for the thick carpets in the living room.

Some of the schools are starting to reopen. Joseph takes the boys to school across the street. After inquiring numerous times, he is now teaching the English courses. We are lucky to find him a job.

I don't remember winter starting this early before. It is very cold and blustery outside. In the evenings by candlelight, we alter clothing and coats to make do. We cut up my linen dirndl outfit to make underwear. I never got to wear that beautiful dress. I saved Oma's apron from the scissors by hiding it with my journals. Mutti has two dresses to her name. There are too many women and not enough material to go around. All the beautiful materials and goods in my wedding chest were given to our clothing campaign.

Papa found out about a position at the Center for Displaced Persons office in Neuenburg. There is no salary, but a higher coupon rating on my ration card. Every little bit will help us.

I'm going to talk to them in the morning. Rumors say they will be cutting ration card eligibility unless you have a job.

I now have a job at the DP office and have started work immediately. It seems strange not to need a work permit or authorization. All my life people have been telling me what to do, teachers, parents, tradition, or the government. Tradition, habit, local mandates, religion, and political direction and stifling German bureaucracy have regulated my life. Now I can see how easily the Nazi's took control of Germany; they took control of the paperwork and the children. It has always been our way to follow rules, orders, and regulations.

My new job at the office requires the same focus on organization. Lists are everywhere. Cards are typed up with family names, history, city information and missing relatives.

Everything is to be cross-referenced. I type from the moment I come in the door in the morning until I leave for the day. It's not bad. I'm used to typing and the room is heated. Today I helped re-unite a lost family with relatives in Paris. That feels good.

Unbelievable! I received a letter from Sigi. It is dated July 1944, a year ago! He was captured by American forces at the air base. After he was processed into the POW camp, a German farmwoman handed him farmer's clothing through the fence. She helped Sigi and two others walk right out the front gate of the camp! He walked home to Poland from the Rhine River to the Weichsel River. It took three months walking at night to make the journey without money, food, or water. He hid in the woods by their farm for two weeks until he thought it was safe before approaching the farm. He was worried about being labeled an escaped prisoner and thought people were looking for him.

The Russians took everything, including their farm and now a different family is working Sigi's farm. His brothers now work at a neighbor's farm. When the Russians came through they told Sigi's mother and brothers to leave or be shot. They couldn't take anything with them, not even a change of clothes. His mother, brothers, and Sigi are living in a one-room apartment in town. They are working menial jobs and starving. He is very bitter about losing the farm and their seven generations of hard work lost. He had sharp words about failing Germany and the promises Hitler failed to live up to. I agree with the needless ruin and stupidity for everyone. He sounds so devastated and lonely, but he's alive. Now I know.

DP's must have the lowest rank in the hierarchy of mankind. No one wants them. These people are so traumatized. Before I take down their information, I must hear their stories. It helps them to have someone listen to them. I think half the world must be displaced. No one is where they should be or where they want to be. No home, no future, and they are unwanted. Most have hardened hearts. Their dark eyes stare at me with a fathomless depth. These people have lost hope and are surviving at the edge of humanity.

We have started a collection and distribution center for clothing for refugees in our office. It's not much, but at least we're trying to do something.

Das Goldene Blatt ("The Golden Paper") gives a weekly listing of people looking for others with photographs and addresses. I send them an administrative packet every week. The photographs are emaciated shadows of the people they were. There are so many children listed. It breaks my heart.

Russia is demanding billions in reparations from Germany to pay for the damage the German Army did in Russia. They want to be paid in industrial plants, people, products, and land. We have nothing. German POWs are being sent to Russia by the thousands. Will we ever see those people again? Everyone knows it is a death sentence.

Field detachments of Allied Military Government (AMG) personnel are helping run local affairs and keep what little order we have. This is more of a problem in Pforzheim than around here. Laborers are clearing roads, repairing bridges, restoring electricity, gas, and water, and building shelter housing for the millions on the streets. There isn't much I can do for the DP's, but to take their information and tell them where the nearest aid station is located.

Mutti is very concerned about the women DP's. Public health officials have decided a woman who aborts a fetus or kills her unborn child is to be punished with imprisonment up to five years.

If Mutti assists in this matter, she will also be imprisoned for at least six months. If you force a woman to have relations or cause a death while doing so, it is punishable by imprisonment of ten years. Mutti says she hasn't met one pregnant DP who wasn't carrying a Russian child. I've seen hundreds of them since I've been home. Where is our human dignity? What about these unborn children? *Mein Gott.*

Papa's decision to buy more coal on the black market is a good one. People are starting to freeze to death in their homes.

We have little electricity in many parts of town. There is no water, and no coal. The temperatures this morning were fifteen degrees below zero and ice crystals seemed to freeze in mid-air.

At night I keep on my coat when I get home and sleep with little Katarina next to me. We both barely fit on the sofa. She is so small.

Lotte, Margot, and Dorothea now make the weekly trip to the farmer. Margot is a skilled seamstress and makes underwear to sell. Lotte negotiates the supplies needed, and Mutti's old foot pedal sewing machine is working again. It brings in a little extra. Papa qualifies as unfit for work and gets 35 marks a month. It takes 21 marks to buy a food card.

We had such a strange Christmas. I made an early learner reading book for Katarina and we gave the boys some of Rolf's books. Mutti repaired a very tattered pair of gloves found in the garage and we gave them to Dorothea. Our rations have been cut and we now only get about 800 calories a day and most days it's even less. At night when it's quiet and we are trying to sleep, you can always hear stomachs grumbling in the dark. It's not coming from anyone in particular; it's coming from all of us.

Papa bartered the last of his spice wine for two chickens.

They tasted wonderful. We pulled them out of the oven just as the electricity went out. Chicken by candlelight. Mutti surprised us with apple preserves baked in a dark crust. Merry Christmas.

Gerti's War

Papa stopped by to see Frau Klein this morning and found her frozen in her bed. The DP's in her home didn't want to notify the authorities for fear they would be put out on the streets again. They said she died just after Christmas.

An elderly DP man stands on our street corner with a sign "I must eat. I will do anything. Please help me." Mutti brings him warm weak tea every morning. It is such a sight to see on our street.

We received another letter from the cousins in New York. They say a care package is on its way and included $10.00 in United States money in the letter! Cousin Magdalena, you are an angel! She said she would work on getting us sponsorship if we wanted to come to the United States. We've been discussing it, but we don't want to leave. Mutti isn't quite sure.

The trains in our area are beginning to run again. People crowd the stations for food runs or bartering trips. Papa took the train to a farm on the other side of Pforzheim, into the American sector. This was an old friend of Oma's—some distant relative. He traded $5.00 for a can of lard, bottle of *Kirsch*, bacon, eggs, and a bag of flour. He had trouble carrying everything and sadly broke one of the eggs on the way home.

All Nazi Party memberships are being checked against past work histories. No NSDAP members can hold jobs of responsibility and there are few jobs for residents. I can't find work for the DP's. Somebody must have an answer to this problem? Prices for goods are skyrocketing and we survive by bartering. People are selling heirlooms for a pound of butter and selling them eagerly.

Uncle Ritchie came by today. I expected Aunt Charlotte to be with them. They are distant cousins, but we've always called them *Tante* and *Onkel*. They live on the other side of Pforzheim and we don't see them often. She always makes Mutti laugh. I haven't heard Mutti laugh in a long time. I found out Aunt

Charlotte was killed last fall while working in her garden. A single American pilot swooped down out of the sky and shot her. Uncle Ritchie had to bury her right away. It was horrible, she was in pieces. Mutti can't talk about the tragedy. They didn't have any children and spoiled me with attention when I was little. He brought several items he wanted Mutti to have. A china set, silver tea service, and a beautifully woven golden tablecloth.

He and Papa disappeared in the cellar for quite a while and when he left, he wouldn't take anything with him. I found Papa crying later in the day and he said Uncle Ritchie was giving up on life. He couldn't go on anymore. He wanted Papa to give him our old revolver to end his life. Papa couldn't do it.

Relief organizations are trying to send food to us. We received our first shipment of canned food from the UNRRA (United Nations Relief and Rehabilitation Administration). The *Burgermeister* posted a notice on the public board. We will be receiving cows, seeds, and more canned goods next week. Most of this aid will be to help us re-establish our agriculture base. Everyone is talking about the news and who will get the livestock. Already the arguing has started and it's not even here yet.

We had a small family birthday celebration. Papa bartered our typewriter for a pair of shoes for me. What a wonderful gift. I don't know how he found the right size! I still wear my old shoes to work and then put the new shoes on at home. I don't want them to get dirty. A precious gift. I won't take it for granted.

Allied forces are cutting down timber near the Rhine and shipping the wood to England. People are outraged about it.

Photographs were in the paper and Germans are crying out about the harvesting of trees hundreds of years old. An entire black walnut grove has been slaughtered. This wood is very expensive and takes generations to mature. Is it part of the spoils of war?

Dorothea is going to be working at the farm where we get our supplemental supplies. She will be living there and earning 60 marks a month. Joseph and Margot have encouraged her to take the position for the improvement in her diet.

I received a letter from Louise. She doesn't say much other than she made it home. She had to walk almost three weeks through the mountains. She is taking care of her sister's children, but the family restaurant is closed. There are no supplies. She doesn't mention the Russians. Louise, I am thinking of you.

Tonight, I listened to a radio program called "Daily Announcements of Lost People." A whole hour dedicated to locating missing friends and families. I heard Cornelia's name mentioned, no one has heard from her since she left the farm camp. I miss my bunkmates. How different our lives are now compared to when we met so many years ago.

What is it in a human being that can change a family man into a monster against humanity? The Nuremburg atrocities disgust even the hardest of our friends and family. War makes a monster out of everyone.

Are we part of this collective shame? The world watches us and shakes their heads over these trials. We lost our power by staying silent as the political wheel turned, giving us false stability and order. The "if only" questions and thoughts tumble in my mind. Class hierarchy must be dissolved.

It bothers me to see the *Burgermeister* treat Papa with a lack of respect. He has been mayor for so long, he despises anyone beneath him who opposes his wishes, or tells him what to do. That was the beginning of our problems with the National Socialist Party. The best form of government for Germany is to start at the bottom of the government ladder and elect the ablest man interested in good government, rather than party government.

Papa and I talked long into the night yesterday about the trials and the future of my homeland. It must be a different Germany, one without a thirst for revenge. Humanitarian democracy, respect for others and a re-education of the youth must lead the way to freedom. Papa has been talking to the boys at the school one day a week about their studies, values, and being someone, they can look up to. Joseph asked for the help and Papa is much happier on the days he works with the children. So much needs to be done and people are still very caught up in surviving each day, rather than thinking about tomorrow.

Papa is thinking of running for some type of political office. He has some information about the Allied chemical bombing raids. The Allies deny this type of warfare, but Papa has documented statements from DP's talking about the shriveled and burnt bodies of their families. Thank goodness, it doesn't seem to have been a widespread occurrence. He still tires easily, and his stomach continues to give him trouble. The doctors want to do another surgery. I am worried about his health. He keeps telling me, "It's nothing".

We've received word that Uncle Ritchie died. He left his house and all its contents to the Red Cross. Papa is very upset over this news.

President Truman has approved a European recovery aid program giving financial aid and supplies without any strings attached. There will be no new debts piled on top of the 80-year Great War debt. God must have touched the hearts of the people behind the Marshall Plan. The newspapers are praising the efforts of the president. We have the details of the relief program printed in many languages in our office for the DPs. It is a glimmer of hope on a little piece of paper.

Gerti's War

My future with Sigi died today. I received another letter from him written at Christmas. He is alive, but says he has no future, and worse, no future to offer me. Wants me to get on with my life and remember him with loving thoughts. He briefly talked about working in a printing factory for a meal a day; and how bad things are at home. His father died a few weeks after arriving home, after spending the last three years in a foxhole in Russia. Thank goodness he wasn't a POW, but living in a hole isn't much better.

He sounds so desolate and angry at the way things have turned out - desperately trying to survive and help his family. Our dreams may have been shattered, but I will always hope the best for you Sigi. You take a piece of me with you. I will miss you.

Chapter 14 – April 1948

Mutti has noticed a change in my attitude. I talked to her about my letter from Sigi and how much he meant to me. I feel better after our long cry. She made me think about my vision for the future – marriage, lots of children and a happy home. Yes, it's still possible. I can only control the actions I do and how I feel.

Everyone in town is talking about a shipment we received from an import-export company in Holland (two dozen goslings, a dozen small piglets, three calves, sacks of grain and a variety of seeds) all came to the attention of the *Burgermeister*. This came from an anonymous person who grew up in our town. A note said the calves should be raised by a group of older children and the milk products used for the school lunch program. What a wonderful gesture. Who could it be?

Only the racketeers have the purchasing power to buy and sell anymore. The black market is becoming stronger as more people barter to avoid paying huge taxes. I can't earn more than 1,000 marks a month in a job or the marks above that go directly to taxes. The fabric for Margot's underwear sewing business cost 6,000 marks for a bolt of fabric. Dorothea manages to barter an exchange of fabric and thread for a painting in our Livingroom, some preserves, six pairs of long underwear, and a pair of men's galoshes. With some tight maneuvering on cutting the fabric, we should be able to make 2,000 marks selling the underwear. Mutti is going to donate her wedding dress to the sewing fund. I think the curtains are next.

My work at the DP office is now a paying job--300 marks a month. I am glad I have a job when many still aren't working. Also my French is getting better now that I regularly communicate with a woman in the Paris DP office.

In the Ruhr district to the north, in the English zone, people have demonstrated against the rapidly deteriorating food situation. Strikes in factories alternate with marches against hunger and lack of coal. Our coal supplies come from this district. We still have a long way to go before Germany is on the road to becoming self-sufficient again. We are tired, hungry, and have forgotten how to use our minds. 15,000,000 DP's would strain anyone to the breaking point.

Papa went on another train run, but this time took a small cart, so he would be more careful with the eggs. He said that the train station was overcrowded with people with empty bags looking for food. They asked repeatedly if he knew where they could get potatoes. Lotte is going to go with him on the next trip. People are calling the train's names depending on the food to be found in the area (Potato Train, Calorie Express, and Nicotine Line).

Uncle Erwin came by our house this evening ranting and raving about the DP's. He never came to see me when I returned.

He always looks for someone to blame his troubles on. It used to be the Gypsies and then the Jews, but this time I had to leave the room before I embarrassed my parents. I am no longer a little girl cowering in the corner when he is around. Someday he will have to account for his cruel words and actions.

We received a care package yesterday from Cousin Magdalena. The large box was wrapped in a sewn feed sack (we will use it for more underwear). We crowded around the box as Mutti opened it.

Coffee! She sent two pounds of coffee, a variety of planting seeds, an American magazine, socks, slippers, canned Spam, cigarettes, and chocolate.

I think Uncle Erwin came by because he heard about our package. Cousin Magdalena didn't send him anything. Papa gave him a package of cigarettes. He is too generous.

Gerti's War

Someone stole one of the calves the city received last month. A reward has been posted. Before the war, we never had to worry about anyone in Arnbach stealing a thing and now many are pointing fingers at the DP's.

We still haven't received the (UNRRA) agricultural aid distribution they told us about last month. Many cities around us are getting deliveries of cattle and seeds. Hopefully, we will be able to replace the lost calf.

One of my friends from school will marry a widower who is older than Papa! Her parents were killed in Pforzheim. She told me she is lonely. He is too. Will this be my fate? A few soldiers are starting to return home. Most POW camps have been holding them through the winter for processing. We can't feed them, but many still are unaccounted for.

We had a small May Day celebration at the church. There were no ribbons and food, but we had some flower decorations and sang songs. It was the nicest day we've had in a long while. Little Katarina loved the garland I made for her hair. For her, it's her first May Day. She still insists on sleeping on the couch with me. The boys are outgrowing their clothes again.

The tribunal cases sicken me. We have forfeited our reputation in the world following an insane obsessed man. Still, the trials continue in an unending stream of barbarity.

Papa was able to barter some good supplies for a few of the care package items. We've already started germinating the seeds and will sell the ones we don't use. What a variety! Magdalena's husband survived the Great War eating only turnips for a year and her note said they wanted us to have diversity. Still don't know what we will buy with the coffee. It's our most valuable possession.

I took a long walk in the woods with the children today and showed them all my special places. We gave an offering at the shrine in memory of Oma, Rolf, and Marta. I tried not to let

Katarina see me cry as I listened to the boys playing tag along the path. We spent the entire day outside in the sunshine and hiking. It brought back many memories. I thought I heard Rolf's laughter several times.

The children made colorful drawings to send to America. We are so thankful. The ground has warmed up enough to begin our summer planting. Papa and Joseph are preparing all the beds by the house and our hidden plot near the woods. We've been discussing using the coffee to buy or barter a small plot for more planting. I like planning for the future. It keeps my mind off the present.

I took one of each of our little plants to Marta's parents. We visit every Sunday afternoon. It is still hard to see the loss in their eyes. They both are so weak and thin.

We had a small Feast of St. John festival in town this week. Again, we had no food, but we enjoyed the companionship, religion, and sports for the children. Katarina and Yakob had a very good time. Georg is quiet and didn't participate in the games with the other children his age. He prefers to draw and read. The celebration has changed in format from what I remembered as a child. Will it ever be the same?

Papa asked me to go with him to Pforzheim yesterday. I was able to get the time off from work and we took the train part of the way. Nothing is recognizable in the city. There are miles of rubble in every direction, with street signs posted on wooden boards in handwritten script. We took some of our seedlings to a refugee camp on the south side. The American soldier at the gate did not speak German, and my little bit of English from school didn't get us too far. We had to wait until someone could translate for us. A refugee woman from Poland helped us donate the seedlings. She was grateful for the plants. We talked with her briefly about the conditions and the population of the camp. She said the Red Cross visits and they are now about half full. They are starting to give incentives to encourage people to go home, a small stipend and a loaf of bread for a family. That won't get them very far. We took the rest of our potential produce to a makeshift Veterans club in Neuenburg. People are planting small plots anywhere they can. Papa sang with a small group of men before we left. It's the first time I've heard him sing in years and it was music to my ears and my heart.

I finally wrote a letter to Herr Peter Muller, Jr., in Madrid. Papa and I stopped at a newspaper vendor while in Pforzheim and I looked through all the Spanish newspapers I could find. *El Mundo* listed Peter Muller as a reporter. I wrote him a short letter asking if his father lived in Berlin and that I had information regarding his death. Papa and I discussed it several times on the way home. He offered no answers but hugged me and kept his arm around me the whole way home.

Today I feel the weariness of a DP. So many people continue to go through our office. The dull eyes of the children follow me around the room while I work. They are so thin and pale that I can see blue veins on the sides of their faces. Two children came in today with distant relatives looking for their parents. After so many months of working with the DPs, my mind and body still ache for a method to ease their suffering. I don't want to become apathetic to their situation. Each case is different from the one before. I used my French and gave them a small lead through the Paris office.

The local food distribution is starting to get better. Bartering on the black market enhances our diet, but prices continue to seesaw back and forth. The wet summer has helped our garden grow and we have fresh vegetables again. Margot's sewing business is beginning to make a regular profit. Lotte and Oma now sew for her full-time.

A few POWs are returning to Arnbach. The lucky ones were captured by the English forces outside of Germany who treated them the best. Max and Helga sent another letter. He was very upset about the conditions at his fathers' POW camp, Camp *Rheinwiesen Lager,* in the American sector lead by General Eisenhower. He heard from another refugee that his father starved to death inside the camp.

The British effort to step in and help, failed. Gunther, a friend of Rolf's, returned home last week. He had been held in a camp run by General Clark. He visited with Papa yesterday afternoon. Max sent a newspaper clipping regarding the camp his father was in, thousands starved.

When I came home from work yesterday, I had a visitor waiting for me at the house, Herr Muller. He received my letter and wanted to know what information I had about his father. The newspaper sent him to Germany to do some reporting and photographing of the Tribunal cases. He stopped by on his way.

We sat in the living room and I told him everything I could about his father's death. He took notes and asked me to write up a letter with the information. My parents signed the letter to witness its content and he took it with him. I don't know if Herr Glueck will answer for this crime in our world, but he will answer to God.

Today I watched a football game in Neuenburg. Many people were there and caught up in the frenzy of a good game. Each small community is trying to pull together enough people to make a team. Not many young men were able to play, but one caught my eye several times. I am sure he smiled right at me. My heart hasn't beaten like that since Sigi held me in his arms.

Papa has decided to purchase a small plot of land with our coffee and use the remaining funds to supplement our coal supply. We will receive a small allotment of coal this year and hope it won't be as cold as last season. The newspapers are saying over a

Gerti's War

million people died in Germany from the cold and starvation, over six million throughout Europe. Sixteen people died last winter in our small town Arnbach, including Frau Koenig. Food supplies are getting better and with some delivered coal supplies in most cellars, we can pray that we've survived the worst and things will be better.

Katarina said her prayers last night asking for, "A better world with no war where people can just love one another." Such wisdom coming from a five-year-old!

I've gone to every football game now and my feet are freezing. My shoes aren't thick enough to keep out the cold. We invited Hugo Zimmermann for supper tomorrow. Papa enjoys going to the games with me, Hugo introduced himself to us two weeks ago. He plays goalie and papa says he is a good man.

Hugo is 26 years old, my height, nice looking, with brown hair and blue eyes, but his shoulders are massive, like a bear. Papa says he has a strong back and that's good. I am slowly getting to know him. He grew up in Calw, and now his family lives a few towns away. When I look at him, my stomach does flip-flops. I wish I had a new dress to wear for his visit.

Before the war started, Hugo worked on an orchard farm until they drafted him into the infantry. After being captured in Belgium by the English, he spent the last two years of the war in Scotland cleaning up bombing debris sites. He is also a talented engraver and made jewelry from spoons while at the POW camp. He gave Mutti and me spoons he fashioned into rings as a gift.

Our dinner wasn't anything special, but Mutti did make one of her good cherry cakes with white flour! Hugo makes me nervous. I am glad for Papa's conversations. Hugo is strong, gentle-mannered, and can hold his own point of view with Papa. Not many young men could do that!

Hugo and I had a few minutes to ourselves after dinner as we walked around the block. He invited me to go with him to the library in Pforzheim before the game next week. We will have to leave early to get there and be back before 3 o'clock. The library was bombed during the war, but some of the books have been salvaged. The church is running the distribution side of the library until the city decides what to do. One of Hugo's cousins is working there.

I had a wonderful time with Hugo in Pforzheim. The dread I felt going into the city before with Papa vanished with Hugo beside me. He told me more about his family and his two brothers, Helmut and Rudger. Helmut is newly married and inheriting the family farm. Rudger is studying forestry and walks with a cane because shrapnel shattered his leg.

Hugo wants to use his talents in engraving as a career. He's been working two jobs for the past months—welding scrap metals during the day and sorting rubble waste piles after work.

His hands are very strong. I could feel the strength in them when he held my hand on the walk back into town. They are very rough and reminded me of my own rough hands from working at the camps.

Joseph and Margot told us today, they will be moving to the farm after the school year finishes. Margot may leave earlier if their accommodations are finished by then. Dorothea announced she is engaged to the farmer's brother. He is twenty years older and adores her. They are building a small house on the property. They intend to add additional space so her parents can live with them.

Margot will continue the sewing business in a section of the barn when she moves. Oma and Lotte will still be doing sewing work for her but will stay here to do it.

Gerti's War

Joseph and Margot feel like family. It will be hard to see them go. He will keep the job at the school even though he will have a long commute each way. The boys really look up to Joseph.

What will things be like when Lotte's family leaves someday? Katarina has taken a part of my heart. I want to have five little girls just like her. Since the weather turned cold again, she has snuggled up against me again on the sofa at night. She makes little comforting noises when she sleeps. Papa heats the lower floor and we aren't as cramped now with our sleeping accommodations anymore. What a luxury!

Hugo and I went to a dance last weekend. Afterwards we stopped at a small café and had drinks. Hugo told me about losing his best friend during the war. While parachuting into Belgium, they spotted haystacks in a farmer's field. Hugo's friend, Dieter called out laughing he was going to have a soft landing and went for the haystack. Hugo found him dead impaled on a pitchfork. An English unit captured Hugo weeks later. It was an emotional conversation for him and I told him I would tell him my experiences another time.

He had some good things to say about his two years in the POW camp. As a part of a military band, they would march weekly through the little Scottish town. It was very wet and cold, but he made many friends in the camp. He fashioned a spoon into a piece of jewelry for one of the officers' wives and soon had a small business going in the camp. What a change from the conditions Max said his father went through!

Slowly Hugo and I are getting to know each other. He is kind, thoughtful, and determined to have a better future for himself and Germany. His brothers sound more like Uncle Erwin in their attitudes about the future and blaming others for the problems we are going through. I haven't met them yet and I am not looking forward to it.

Lotte heard about a shipment of fabric from one of her contacts, and before I knew it, we were on a train and heading for Wurzburg. Our business trip was successful with four bolts of fabric, but it got late, and we couldn't find accommodations in town, so I called Leni and we took the train to Rothenburg. How wonderful it was to see them both. Lotte slept, while Paul, Leni, and I stayed up all night talking. Leni is three months pregnant and looks healthy and happy. They both do. I told them about Hugo and the work I was doing with the DPs.

Paul enjoyed showing off parts of his historical town. An American general had been to the town prior to the war, and due to his intervention, he spared the city from the raids. Parts of the town go back to the tenth century. A medieval wall still surrounds the city. The family store is in a building built in the 1200s. The family jewelry store looks like something from a fairy tale, and Pinocchio should be sitting in the window display instead of jewelry and watches.

When I admired a watch in a case, Paul pulled it out, put it on my wrist, and said it is now mine to remember them by. Leni cried off and on several times. She blamed it on her pregnancy.

The trains are still not running well, and it took almost the entire day to get back home. I am never taking that watch off! Leni called out to me as I left that they would come to my wedding. I miss them so much.

I went shopping today and had actual money in my hand and there were items on the store shelves available for purchase! I gathered up some Christmas items for the children. Soft warm boots for Katarina, sport shoes for Yakob, and colored pencils and paper for Georg who has taken over Rolf's architecture books and drawings and spends most of his free time studying. Rolf would be pleased to see him interested in his things. I spent three months of salary on the items, but still have a little money in my box at home. I can't wait to see their faces during the holidays! For Mutti I purchased white flour, sugar and wine, and for Papa tobacco for his pipe. He hasn't smoked in years. Hugo enjoyed carrying my packages for me. What am I going to get for him?

Hugo and I have spent more time together, especially on weekends. I told him about my time in Berlin and losing Marta and Rolf. The loss still feels fresh when I say the words out loud.

He has invited my family to join his for dinner during the holidays. Papa and Hugo get along very well. I will have to warn Papa about the political views of Hugo's brothers before we go over there.

Hugo kissed me this evening! My feet haven't touched the floor yet. Mutti saw the flushed look on my face when I came in the door and we giggled about it, as I got ready for bed. They approve of Hugo. Thankfully, Hugo is a patient man. Every time we are together, we get a little bit closer. I asked Mutti if she had any suggestions for a present for Hugo and she said she would talk to Papa about it.

I have changed considerably from the young girl who started writing in my journals so many years ago. I spent the last few days re-reading the entries. How different I feel now that the war is over. When Rolf died, I needed the journals to find a reason, a direction for my life and to put my thoughts into some sort of order. It has given me internal encouragement to go on and keep hope alive for a future for my family and myself. I am safe and slowly we are building a future. I have had loss, but I have also met such wonderful friends. With my work at the DP office, I feel I am making a small difference in the world.

"Life is to be experienced, good and bad" as Oma would say. I am ready for my future and whatever God wants me to do. I put it in all in his hands.

Chapter 15 – PART TWO – JULY 1992

Danuta bends over and pulls open the door of the cabinet, knocking over a box filled with loose papers, photographs, and journals. "Gerti." She called out, "Where exactly are the candlesticks?" She gathers up the spilled items and takes one more look inside the cabinet. Moving the last box out of the way, finding the silver candlesticks shoved in a corner and calls out, "Never mind, I found them."

Gerti enters the room and helps take some of the scattered items from her hands. She holds them against her chest and places the papers on the dining room table nearby. Gerti set long tapers into the silver holders, put the papers on top of the cabinet, and returns to the kitchen. Danuta follows her. Their steps are light as they walk on the thick woolen runners down the hallway.

German Folk music plays on the radio in the background.

Gerti stands by the stove, cooking the last batch of Spaetzle and stirs the rich gravy for the pork roast. "This kitchen smells wonderful." Exclaims Danuta. "I didn't mean for you to go to all this trouble."

"No trouble at all. It's nice to have someone to cook for and it's about ready. You can go ahead and start putting the meal on the table and I'll bring the spaetzle in as soon as it boils."

Steam fogs her glasses as she leans over the pot.

Behind her, a built-in table is set for two with her good bone china. An embroidered tablecloth and a small bouquet of red and pink poppies from the garden fill the center of the table.

Gerti and Danuta sit together at the table and fill their plates.

Gerti lifts her wineglass and offers a toast.

"To good friends and happy futures." Says Gerti as the glasses clink together. "I hope you will enjoy your new job."

Danuta smiles with the toast and takes a small slip of the wine. "Gerti, how will I ever be able to repay you for all your kindness?" She moves the food around on her plate and an awkward silence fills the air briefly. "No one has ever done so much for my daughter and I. Finding the position at the home care facility will improve my financial situation immensely." She pauses, "You don't know how difficult it is to be paid in good money." Danuta reaches out to Gerti. "It still doesn't happen in Poland. My doctorial medical degree pays about the same as a nurse."

Gerti looks at Danuta with warmth. "Nah, it is nothing. I made inquiries on your behalf, that's all. It's your education and background that made them accept you."

Danuta continues to move the vegetables around, not yet taking a bite. "I know it's only a fill-in position, but I will be able to make more money in these three months than I would in a year back home. Eva will miss me, but she loves her grandparents, and time will go by quickly. Please, let me pay you something for letting me stay with you. Can't I even help with the food bill?"

"Okay, you may give me 20 marks a week for groceries, but that is it. Now, eat, it's getting cold, and you haven't taken a bite yet." They both smile and began to eat.

"I'm sorry I knocked over that box of papers. My knees have been giving me trouble and sometimes I lose my balance. Can I help you put that mess together when we're finished eating?"

Danuta says as she points to the box.

"Oh, it's just some things I kept from the war. I haven't looked at that box in years. I think it's full of some of my early writing efforts and some old photographs. Maybe I'll show you how cute I was in my younger years, not this old woman sitting beside you." Gerti says with mischief dancing in her eyes.

"You don't look a day over 55, and I bet you can beat me up the hill if we are to race! I am supposed to exercise my joints more." Gerti leans in close and moves a lock of silver hair out of the way.

"Well, I'm 67 and I might just beat you up there. I walk it almost every day and my legs are still good." She pulls her leg from under the tablecloth and shows a shapely, muscular calf.

"Not bad for an old lady." Gerti exclaims with pride.

Gerti's War

After cleaning up from dinner, they ease into the padded chairs in the dining room and begin to flip through the photographs on top of the pile. Danuta sits close and pulls a nearby lamp to the table. Gerti slowly looks at each image. It takes her a few moments before she speaks. There are photos of her parents, of a young Gerti standing on the front porch step with long dark blonde braids and a big smile, another walking in a work camp, and another in a group photograph with aged friends.

"I still meet with my friends from the camp once a year."

Gerti says. "We get together in Stuttgart and talk about old times and family happenings. Our group gets a little smaller and a little older every year. Here, look at this photo." She passes the color photograph to Danuta. "Almost twenty girls and a few of their husbands came to visit me four years ago, after Hugo died.

They knew I needed the company." Old friends are hard to replace.

"Do you have any photographs of Hugo?" Danuta says. "I see some photographs of children over there in the windowsill, but where is your handsome husband?"

"My favorite of him I keep on my nightstand, so I can tell him good night and good morning. We never had children. Those children are from good friends. I like seeing their smiling faces during my meals. They keep me company." I wanted children very much, but in those days, we kept on trying, hoping next month would bring good news. Children are a gift from God. You are very lucky to have Eva." Gerti said.

Danuta pats Gerti's hand. "I'm sorry you never had children.

Yes, you would be a great mother." Danuta puts her arm around Gerti and gives her a hug. "What are these drawings?" She pulls out a handful of aged colorful children's sketches. "Yours from your youth?"

"Oh, no. We had a displaced family living with us for years and their children made some of these. I can't believe it. Those children are now grandparents. Bits of my poetry are in here too."

Gerti hands Danuta a hand-written poem. She blushes lightly and exclaims, "Oh my, I'm such a clever writer." They both chuckle over the last silly line of her prose.

"Gerti, I love it." Danuta says. She reads through the poem again and smiles at the ending. "I never did well with poetry. My nose was always in a medical book. How did you manage to keep your sense of humor?" She asks, "Wasn't it awful during the war?"

"Yes, it was bad for everyone. Just as the war started, my brother died. Then my best friend died in a bombing raid.

We were closer than sisters, my second half. For years, I couldn't mention her name without melting into a puddle." Her eyes fill with tears as she continues. "We were so young and innocent back then, but we had to grow up fast. Hunger and bombing raids will do that to you."

Gerti pulls out three cloth-wrapped journals from the bottom of the box. "I wrote these journals during that time to keep me sane and connected to my family. I still look back at those years and think about the heavy loss we all had."

Danuta reaches for the stack of journals and pauses before touching them. "Would you mind if I read them? I didn't bring anything fun to read and they will be good company in the evenings before I fall asleep. That is, if you don't mind?"

"No, not at all." Says Gerti. "But do keep in mind, you are reading the thoughts of a young girl inexperienced in the world.

How little I knew back then." Gerti picks up the stack and hands them to her. "I hope you can read my handwriting.

The rest of the material she placed back in the box. "What am I going to do with this stuff? Maybe my niece will want them?"

Her voice trails off as she turns out the light and heads up the stairs for bed after Danuta.

A week later Danuta comes home late from work and finds Gerti sitting in the dining room with more photographs spread around her. The room is illuminated by soft light from the television in the corner. Long shadows spread across the table.

Gerti's War

Scrapbooks and photo albums are stacked on the seat nearby. A lifetime of family pictures, trips from all over the world, Italy, Egypt, Israel, and the United States, cover the surface and spill down onto the seat cushions.

Startled, Gerti rises and starts for the kitchen. "Would you like something to eat? I could warm up some leftovers."

"No, sit, sit – I ate at work." Danuta says. She laughs as she picks up a black and white photograph of Gerti in an alpine hiking outfit complete with boots and spikes. "Wow, you really got around? Those spikes look lethal."

"Yes, we were part of a hiking group and Hugo loved to go to the mountains in the south. The air was so crisp and clean there." She pulls a pressed flower out of an open album and shows it to Danuta. The star pattern is easily distinguishable, like white velvet. "I picked this Edelweiss on one of our last trips down there before Hugo got sick."

Danuta sniffs it, but the scent disappeared long ago.

"Hugo liked to hike to the very top, pose for a photograph and then yodel a message down into the valley. Sometimes he could be a bit of a clown. He always made me laugh."

"I'm sorry I didn't get to meet him. He sounds very nice."

Danuta scrutinizes a photograph of Hugo before placing it back in Gerti's pile of images.

"He was. Most of the time he worked several jobs, he just couldn't bear to be idle. Sitting and watching a football game on television was an effort for him. In person he would be standing up and yelling for his team, but at home he felt awkward cheering without the team in front of him." Gerti holds a few of the photographs to her chest and sighs."

Danuta puts her hand on Gerti's shoulder and pats her briefly. "I'm going to make some coffee. Would you like a cup? Tea perhaps?"

"Tea would be wonderful." Gerti replies.

"How long have you been writing to pen-pals like me?"

"After working with the displaced persons office, I knew people scattered all over and it helps me keep up with my languages. During the past forty years, I've visited people in

Jerusalem, Egypt, France, Spain and the United States. Hugo and I traveled to the states before he was diagnosed with lung cancer. We visited two pen-pals and their families, some distant cousins, and even saw New York City. These photographs were taken on that trip." Gerti reaches for a small stack of photographs and hands them to Danuta. "We went to New Jersey, Florida, New Mexico, and California. Now it seems so long ago."

Danuta flips through the shots and notices a photograph on the table. "Is that you sitting on top of a camel?"

"Yes. Can you see the pyramids in the background?"

"Faintly. I've always wanted to go to Egypt, but that will have to wait until Eva has finished her schooling. She wants to be a doctor like me."

"Did you bring any new photographs of Eva with you? Or, photographs of your town?"

"Yes, I have a photograph of Eva in my room. I'll go get it." Gerti hears her pounding up the spiral stairway off the dining room and listens to her footsteps creak across the room to Gerti's old bedroom upstairs.

I know every nook and cranny. All my life I've lived in this house. She remembers how it looked when she and Hugo set up housekeeping right after they were married. Now it's more functional, but the items purchased during their forty years together still decorated the room. The faint smell of the small thin cigars Hugo loved so much is still recognizable when sitting on the sofa upstairs. *The house feels alive again with Danuta here.* She thinks. *I like hearing the floor creak occasionally and knowing I'm not alone.*

Danuta returns and hands Gerti a small photograph. "This was taken last year when she entered the skinny teenager years. She's thirteen but looks older for her age. I'm sorry, but I don't have any other photos with me. You must come and visit us when I get back home. Poland is still a beautiful country, flat and very green." Danuta holds Gerti's hand between hers and looks deep into her eyes. "Please say you'll come."

Gerti's War

"Yes, I'd like that. The year before Hugo died; we went on a train trip through Poland with the men's choral group. It was very beautiful. During the war, I heard many nice stories about it and always planned to visit it someday. I even thought about writing to a young man I met during the war, but somehow, I never mailed the letter. He was from Grudziadz. Is that city close to yours?"

"No, Grudziadz is about two hours by bus, but everything in Poland is by bus. Trains are too expensive. Are you talking about your first love from the journal, Sigmund?"

"Yes, Sigmund. I thought of him when we were traveling through the countryside." She pauses, "Hugo and I had a very good life filled with laughter and love. I don't regret a moment of it." Gerti stands and stuffs some of the photos them into the front of a photo album. "Someday I'll organize this better."

"How was your day at work?" Gerti blows on her tea to cool it.

"Some people don't think working with elderly patients can be rewarding, but I love it. There are so many things to check on when your patients can't tell you what is wrong. My life is filled with tests and more tests. You look a little tired and your color isn't good. Gerti, how are you feeling today? Sit here and let me get my bag. I want to check your pulse. Have you taken your heart medicine today?"

"Yes, this morning, but not yet this evening." She takes a deep breath before continuing. "Hugo's brother came by to visit this afternoon. He always upsets me to some degree." She lays her hand on her chest.

Danuta gets her blood pressure cuff and puts it on Gerti's arm slowly pumping up the wide band. "Your pulse is a little erratic and elevated. I want you to take it easy tomorrow. Rest all day. No shopping or walking through town. Let me know what you need, and I'll get it for you. And, if Hugo's brother returns, tell him you aren't taking visitors today." She leaves the room and returns with a glass of water and her medication.

"That wouldn't do much good. He never listens to me. All he wants now is to get his hands on my financial records. He thinks

I'm wealthy and wants to manage my accounts for me. Can you imagine? I spent forty years working as a bookkeeper, and he thinks I can't manage my finances! Ever since Hugo died, he shows up with that sickening smile on his face and expects me to give all my records to him." Her face turns a darker pink in frustration.

"Here take this." Danuta says as she hands her the water and two white pills.

"Helmut wants me to sell my home and move into a retirement center. Yes, we lived frugally and lived with my parents, but I'm not rich. Comfortable, yes. My friends here..."

"No more talk of money. Put your feet up and take your medication. I'm going to make you another cup of tea. You can tell me of your travels. I want to hear some funny stories."

Danuta walks into the kitchen and Gerti can hear her puttering around in the cabinets and firing up the Aga stove.

It's nice to be the one on the receiving end. Mutti would enjoy talking to her. She has the same no-nonsense way about her. Gerti's neck cramps up and she reaches to knead the side of her neck lightly.

Returning to the room, Danuta finds Gerti holding a photograph of her mother. Danuta clears a spot for the teacup and teapot to the side of the stack of photographs. She picks up a photo of a woman surrounded by flowers.

"Did your mother like flowers?" Danuta asked.

"Yes, that photo was taken on her eighty-seventh birthday. The room was filled with flowers. She died about three weeks afterwards."

Danuta handed her a cup of tea and sat down beside her.

"Her diabetes was very hard to control. Those last two years she was home bound. We had to amputate her legs just above the knees, but Mutti never complained. She was forever patient and gave me hand-kisses every time I had to help her move. It was a hard year for me."

She carefully laid the photograph of her mother back on the table and picked up another photo. "She died in February, the Berlin Wall fell in September, and then Hugo died in November.

Gerti's War

We didn't have much time from when Hugo was diagnosed until he passed. Those damn cigars took his life. I've been alone since then. This house is too quiet." She says in a low voice. Gerti pushes the photographs around until she stops at a black and white photograph of her father.

"What about your father? Did he survive the war?"

"Yes, Papa lived until 1983. During the war, he worked for the Red Cross. He received a gunshot wound to the stomach while he was moving some dead soldiers. Someone didn't check a firearm correctly and it discharged by accident. He wouldn't join Hitler's party." Rubbing her fingers along the edge of a family snapshot, she handed it to Danuta.

"A dead soldier shot your father?" Danuta asks while leaning a little closer to her.

"Sort of, papa was part of a small unit that stopped to bury dead along the train route. As they were moving the dead, a soldier's rifle fell to the ground and shot him in the stomach.

They never did get his stomach system right. He had many surgeries and was always in pain. After his fourth surgery, he said, 'Enough!' And didn't go back for further treatments." Gerti's voice starts to falter.

Danuta picks up a photograph of Gerti and Hugo beside a camel. "Tell me the story of this trip. Did you ride the camel?"

"Well, I tried, but when I sat on his back before he lifted me, the camel turned and tried to bite me. Hugo decided to be my champion and show me how to ride. He was in such good spirits.

He purchased a long white headscarf that day and spent a good deal of his energy trying to imitate Rudolph Valentino or Omar Sharif. As soon as he got on top, the camel lifted his back legs and Hugo fell forward. Then, the camel shook a little and before we knew it, Hugo was face first in the sand. I should have taken that photo instead!" She laughed remembering the incident. "He forgot to close his mouth and came up with a mouth full of sand."

"Yes, that's a good story. Tell me another one." Rifling through the stack, she stopped at a colorful photograph and asked, "Is this the Grand Canyon?"

"Yes, it is. There is a funny car story that goes with this photo..."

A few weeks later when Gerti was feeling better, Danuta finds her busy in the backyard garden. Chattering with a neighbor friend and leaning against a hoe, her hands move in wild animation as she tells a story. A large bucket filled with weeds sits beside her feet. Her faded summer apron hangs down past her skirt.

"Gerti, can I help you?" Danuta asks as she takes the bucket from her hand.

Gerti invites her over and introduces her to her neighbor, Frau Trlica. They exchanged greetings. Frau Trlica speaks a little Polish and the conversation switches to Polish-German.

"Agatha, please join us for cake this evening. I'll make something spec-i-al," Gerti says and winks at Danuta. "Maybe a custard, or sweet bread, you will just have to come over to see."

It didn't take much solicitation before Agatha agrees to join them as she leaves to answer a ringing phone.

Danuta reaches for the garden hose and begins to water the tomato and pepper plants. "Frau Trlica seems very friendly. Has she been a neighbor long?"

"Yes, she is a darling, but always loves my desserts. I've never seen someone with a sweet tooth as bad as hers. I've tried to teach her some of my recipes over the years, but they don't work for her. She is widowed too. We've been neighbors for about twenty years, but like me, she's lived all her married life in this town."

Gerti spills the weed bucket on the top of the compost pile. She stirs the bin with a large pitchfork. "It's still a small town. Everyone wants to know who you are and how we met. Some things have changed after the war, but for the most part, people are still leery about accepting strangers into their homes.

Every time I go to the market down the street, people ask if you are still here and what you are doing here."

"Don't you get many visitors?" Danuta asked.

Gerti's War

"Yes, I get a few, but I don't drive anymore, and if I have to pick someone up at the airport, I must ask a friend or two to drive me there. Rumors started as soon as you arrived. It's hard to keep a secret in this town. Do you think you can help me cut the asparagus?" Gerti asks as she points to the tall willowy plants growing against the potting shed.

Danuta rinses out the bucket, picks up a sharp knife and crouches into a bent 'warrior' pose. "Yes, I am ready. Come to me, my sweet white asparagus, and you will die quickly." She says in a deep masculine voice.

Gerti laughs. "Okay, Samurai warrior, I'll hold back the foliage if you'll dig into the mound, and we'll have steamed asparagus for dinner. This won't be too hard on your knees will it?"

"For my favorite vegetable dish, I will climb mountains." Danuta says as she carefully places a few of the stalks into the bucket. "How many of these do you want me to cut? Do you want me to chase you around the garden a little bit, so the neighbors can see? That would give them something to talk about!"

Gerti giggles. "Just a few more stalks will be plenty. I haven't laughed his much in years. Thank you for coming, Danuta.

My neighbors don't know what they are missing." They finish up in the garden and walk into the house to clean up.

Later in the kitchen while preparing the asparagus, Gerti tells Danuta more about her neighbors. "After the war we had many problems with the Displaced Persons who lived around us. We have a lot of pride in the way we do things and don't like to see our way of life changed. You should have heard the uproar caused by some immigrants from Turkey who hung their underwear on their balcony where everyone could see it. Then they cooked smelly foods with the windows open! It almost caused a riot outside the mayor's office. Everything around here has to be 'just so', neat and tidy."

"It certainly is a beautiful little town and so clean. I saw a gentleman sweeping the street with a dustpan on my way home from the clinic yesterday. You would not see such a detail to cleanliness at home. It's clean, but not THAT clean."

Gerti asks, "Have the people in the clinic been accepting of you?"

"Some are, but some are not. They ask me a lot of questions about Poland. Sometimes I can't tell if they like my responses.

People in their thirties seem to be more accepting, but the young people now don't talk to me much. I've heard a few older patients refer to me as the 'Pole.' Maybe it's because I'm 45. Do you think I'm too old?"

"You are asking the wrong person." Gerti chuckles softly.

"Help me prepare a feast for a king! How about snout pockets for dinner?"

"What are snout pockets, or shouldn't I ask? Everything you fix is perfection!"

After supper, Gerti and Danuta relax, sitting outside in the shade under the kitchen window. "There is a nice breeze today." Danuta says as she leans back against the house. "Would you like to go for a walk and digest our pork rolls? Err, I mean snout pockets."

"Yes, let me put away a few things in the kitchen and we'll walk to the outskirts of town, out to the cherry orchard.

I think we may still get a few cherries." She gently takes Danuta's hand and gives her a kiss on the back of her hand. "Thank you for helping me in the garden."

Pointing to the large cherry tree off the driveway, Gerti says, "I remember planting that tree when I was about ten years old. We used to have several fruit trees on this property, but now everything is in my extra garden plot up there." Gerti points to the edge of the woods to the north. "I have too much work to keep up with these days. Another family pays me to use the plot now. It's better this way."

Pushing against her knees, Gerti gets up and walks back into the kitchen. Danuta can hear her pulling out mixing bowls and soon afterwards the cracking of an egg into it.

"Gerti, what are you doing in there? I thought we finished in the kitchen."

"Yes, we were, but I'm going to make a cake for this evening."

Gerti's War

"Mmmmm. What kind of cake?" She asks with her mouthwatering. Danuta stretches her legs out from underneath the wooden bench and pats her stomach.

"A chocolate kirsch cake with whipped cream topping." She says in a French pastry-chef accent. "It will drive Agatha crazy."

Danuta walks into the small kitchen, comes up behind her, and gives her a warm hug. "Do you think you could adopt me? I could stay here forever!"

Gerti walks into her old room and finds the journals neatly stacked on the table beside the bed. Pulling the feather duvet off the bed, opening the window and laying the thick blanket over the windowsill to air out, Gerti takes a deep breath and looks out into the garden. It is a beautiful autumn day and the air smells like pine needles and damp earth.

Danuta has been gone a week and the house is quiet and lonely again. She picks up the journals and notices a small note falling from one of the books. *What is this?* She says to herself as she turns the paper over and sees the name "Sigmund Rhinehart" and his address in Grudziadz. *It was such a long time ago.* She puts the address back into the journal, and places it in a bookcase across the room.

Every day Gerti walks to the woods and spends a few quiet moments at the shrine before stopping at the cemetery to water the plants on Hugo's and Mutti's grave. The plots for Rolf and Marta are no longer there. The thirty-year lease expired years ago, but Hugo's grave stands out with a colorful spray of burgundy mums planted around the edges. Mutti and Papa share a common grave near Hugo's. She brings fresh flowers for Mutti with each visit, usually from the garden. People socialize with her as she tends the gravesites. It has been this way all her life.

Celebrating life in the cemetery, and knowing loved ones are watching you and looking out for you occupy her thoughts.

It is no longer forbidden to walk on the beautiful velvet grass surrounding the cemetery, and the urge hits every so often to lie down on it and pretend Marta is beside her again. Sitting on their special bench, she can hear Marta's soft laughter as if time stood still. *What kind of life would we have had Marta? No one has ever taken your place in my heart. Wait for me. I don't think it will be long now.* She says her prayers and walks slowly back to the house.

Gerti sits at the kitchen table wrapping Christmas presents for her niece and her children. Fogged windows in the kitchen make it difficult to see the heavy snowflakes falling outside.

The telephone ringing in the den disturbed her quiet revere.

"Danuta! How wonderful to hear your voice. How are you and Eva doing?" She says excitedly. "Everything all right?"

"Gerti, we are fine, but Gerti, I have found him." She says in a hushed tone.

Chapter 16 – December 1992

"Who have you found? It's so good to hear your voice." Gerti says under her breath.

"Gerti, I have found your Sigi-le." She whispers into the phone. "I wanted to do something nice for you, and I hope you don't mind, but I have talked to your Sigi-le."

"Oh my." Gerti sits back down at the table. Her knees feel like putty and her chest tightens. "What did he say?" Her hand goes to her chest to steady her heart.

"I didn't know if I could find him, but I took the bus to Grudziadz, and with a little detective work I found him living with his son in a small apartment in town. He answered the door and then I asked him if he remembered a Gertrud Zimmermann from the war. He told me he didn't know anyone with that name, but when I changed the name to your maiden name of Leicht, he just stood there looking at me. Gerti, his eyes puddled with tears. He invited me inside as he cried tears of happiness. Are you okay, do you want me to continue?"

"Yes, tell me all of it." Her voice is soft and shaking ever so gently.

"He has been a widower for ten years. He has a daughter who is married and lives nearby. He and his son live in the apartment. I think I already told you that." She says. "Anyway, he wanted to know all about you, and how you were. I didn't go into too much detail because I hadn't asked you beforehand. Gerti, he would like to know if it would be okay for him to write you. Oh Gerti." She pleads, "Please tell me you are happy with this news and that I've done something good for you."

"Yes, it is good. Thank you, Danuta. You can tell him it would be okay for him to write to me here."

"And you'll come visit us in the spring, as we talked about before?"

"Yes, I'll come. Have you received the Christmas present I sent for Eva?" As she hangs up from talking with Danuta, Gerti sits at the table and smiles nervously. *Sigi, my Sigmund. He remembers. He remembers me.*

December 1992

Dear Gerti:

I am so pleased that your friend Danuta came by to see me last week. How do we catch up after so many years? First, let me say that I must apologize for the last letter you received from me. It has been on my mind often these last forty-six years.

    I don't have a recent photograph of myself, but this photo was taken two years ago with my son, Edmund. He is a Science teacher at the 5th level in town. I think that, perhaps, you will still be able to see the young man hidden in the older body standing next to him.

    I married Anna in 1952. She died of breast cancer ten years ago. We have two children, Edmund, and my daughter Christina. She is married and lives in the town next to mine. I am recently retired and live with my son.

    This sounds so formal and awkward to me, but what I really want to say is that I would very much like for us to meet again. Would you agree? There is so much to say, and the words aren't coming to me easily as I sit here writing. Please tell me about yourself and let me know if a meeting can be arranged.

Always, Sigmund

Gerti struggled to find the right words to respond. Nervously she drops the letter into the mailbox.

Gerti's War

January 1993

Dear Sigmund:

Thank you for writing the letter. After so many years, the past keeps flashing before my eyes. I didn't ask Danuta to find you. She recently stayed with me and while here, she read my old journals from the war. This was her idea, but maybe it's a good one. True friends should be cherished.

I've been widowed for four years. My husband Hugo died from lung cancer. I'm a retired bookkeeper.

Thank you for sending the photograph. You son looks very much like you. I can see your smiling eyes haven't lost their sparkle. Hugo and I never had children, but I have several young people I am very fond of, and they help keep me busy.

I travel a little bit, keep my garden, and see friends in town. In fact, I will be attending a conference in Stuttgart on February 13 with some of my comrades from the war. Would this be a good place to meet? I will be there from February 13-15. I will be staying at the hotel near the Oberer Schlossgarten.

If you can meet me, let me know what time your train arrives and I will wait for you at the train station.

Here is an old photograph of me so that you will be able to recognize the "young girl with the nice legs."

Fondly, Gerti

Gerti sits on the cold iron bench with her coat wrapped tightly around her. The train is due to arrive any moment. She clutches the old black and white photograph of Sigi that he gave her so long ago. A steady wind blows around her and she can feel her feet tingling. They are falling asleep. *My stomach is doing flip-flops and my feet are asleep*, she thinks to herself as she looks at her watch for the tenth time. She stomps her feet to bring the feeling back into them. *How much has he changed? Will he like what he sees?*

Finally, the train pulls into the station. She watches the faces on the train with care, looking for his smile. Reviewing the image in the photograph, she checks the faces in the crowd again. People scurry past carrying luggage, and the noise of the passengers can barely be heard over the howling wind. Her heart pounds. *What should I say to him*? Nothing sounds right. She tries to think of a cleaver statement.

The crowd starts to clear and a slim well-dressed man wearing a long camel coat stands out. He holds a suitcase in one hand and a blue handkerchief in the other. His silver-white hair is neatly combed, and he has a broad smile on his face. "Gerti?" He asks.

"Sigmund?" He drops his suitcase and embraces her. "I never thought I'd live to see you again." He murmurs into her ear. He kisses her on the cheek and stands back to take another look. "You look incredible! Just like you did the last time we met. Here, let's sit down for a moment." He says as he leads her back to the bench. "Have you been waiting long?"

It's like touching an electrical current. Gerti thinks as she tries to answer Sigmund in a normal sounding voice. "No, I haven't been waiting long—just a few minutes. Sigmund, it's good to see you too. Why don't we go to a coffee shop and get out of this wind?" She suggests her voice crackling.

"Lead the way, my Queen, I will follow you anywhere." He says with a wave of his hand and a deep bow. His smile hasn't broken since he first saw her. He picks up his suitcase and lightly holds onto Gerti's arm.

"Sigmund is that the handkerchief I made for you?"

"Yes, it's one of my most cherished possessions. You didn't think I would come without it did you?"

"I am pleased you still like it." She feels a sudden rush of warmth all over.

Gerti's War

They enter a small café on the corner and Sigi helps her off with her coat and into her chair. They order drinks and sit across from each other.

"Where do we start?" Sigmund says as he looks at her with wide eyes.

"I don't know. I had prepared many items in my mind. I guess I should have written down a list. I'm a little nervous." She says as she played with her spoon.

Sigmund reaches across the table and lays his hand over the top of hers. "You never have to be nervous with me, Gerti. We will take this at whatever speed you need. How about if I start?" He stirs his coffee slowly, and after patting the top of her hand, pulls his hand back into his lap.

"Let's see, when did we last see each other? I was captured at the airbase by an American squadron. I remember we were hurrying to destroy the planes left on the field, so the Allies wouldn't be able to use them against us. We had no fuel to fly the planes off the base and our ammunition was in short supply.

Only two members of my unit were injured when the Americans arrested us. We were marched to an internment camp for processing. While waiting for my turn in line, a farmwoman handed me a bundle of civilian men's clothing through the fence. She returned a few times and gave two other soldiers clothing. We were able to walk right out the front gate of the camp without being stopped. I couldn't believe our luck!

I had no water or food, but traveling by night, I walked home to Grudziadz. It took four months. When I got home, I was devastated to find our farm in the hands of the Russians. I kept waiting in the woods by the farm, hoping to see someone I knew.

Thank goodness, it wasn't winter, or I probably wouldn't have survived. I didn't have anything with me other than the clothes I walked in wearing. I destroyed all my personal identification papers during my walk, in case the Russians stopped me. After walking to neighboring farms, I found my brothers working in a field.

Foolishly, I thought the American forces had notified the Russians to be on the look-out for an escaped prisoner."

Gerti watches the gracefulness of his hands as he spoke. She listens intently. His eyes flash hatred when he mentioned the loss of the farm, but otherwise he remained calm.

"Gerti, do you want to hear all the details, or should I just skip to the present?"

"No, go on, it's fascinating. What did you do when you saw your brothers?"

"My brothers told me about what happened to the farm. The Russians took everything. All our livestock was given to the Army. Anything of value they could get their hands on, they took.

My mother was put out of the house without a thing, only the clothes on her back."

"Did they touch her Sigi? I've heard so many horrible stories."

Sigi smiled as he looked at her. "You called me Sigi? Am I Sigi, no longer Sigmund?"

Gerti blushes. She gives him a bashful smile and his face lights up with her response.

"No, they didn't touch her in that way. She was thrown to the ground and kicked out the door." He crumbled the napkin beside him into a ball as he retells the story. "I'm sorry, it still makes my blood boil—treating that kind and gentle woman like a dog!"

Now it is Gerti's turn to reach across the table and pat Sigi's hand. "That must have been awful for her and your young brothers."

"Yes. My brothers arrived as she walked down the street. They could see the soldiers breaking my father's sundial and throwing furniture out of the door. My mother had to hold on to them, so they didn't do anything foolish. Somehow the Russians found the title and deed to the house, and we were never allowed to get the property back." He took a few deep breaths before continuing. "After all these years, I still feel the loss of my home."

"How did you survive on the road and when you got back to home?"

Gerti's War

"I ate a lot of grass. I sucked on the grass blades to keep my mouth moist. No one had food or water back then. Do you remember how dry that summer was?"

"Yes, it was bad everywhere." Gerti picks up her teacup to take a sip and notices it is empty. Sigi pushes her hand aside, fills the cup, and puts the correct amount of sugar and milk in it before placing it back in front of her. "Thank you." She says.

"My pleasure." He gently takes her fingertip and kisses it.

With her other hand, Gerti places it to her chest. Her heart is pounding hard enough for her to hear it in her ears. She reaches into her bag and takes one of her heart tablets. "You always did make my heart pound."

"Gerti, are you okay? I mean, is your health good?"

"My blood pressure gives me problems sometimes; but the medication usually controls it, unless a handsome man kisses me.

I guess there are worse ways to get your blood moving." They both smile.

"Would you like something to eat? Would you join me for dinner this evening?"

"Sigi, I would love to have dinner with you."

"Good. It's a date! Do you want me to go on or would you prefer to tell me some of your story?" He raises one of his eyebrows.

"Please go on Sigi. I'll tell you my story over dinner. How's that?"

"I can't wait." He winks at her. "Well, I was pretty miserable in the woods and practically skin and bones. We were all thin, but no one had food or money. My brothers were able to get me new papers, and eventually I found a job working in a printing company. My whole family crammed into a small one-room apartment, and we didn't have enough food between us to make one meal. It was that way until the summer of '47."

"My father came home shortly after the war ended, but weak and sick, he died three weeks later. When he died, I lost all hope. I'm sorry Gerti, but it was very bad back then. I held your handkerchief so many times trying to keep going, but I saw no end to our misery and I wasn't going to pull you down with us. Can you forgive me?"

Gerti smiles. "Yes, Sigi. There is nothing to forgive. We were young and so confused. My mother helped me a lot during that time too. You will always be my first love."

"But not the last, I hope."

Gerti blushes again. "You always say the nicest things to me, Sigi. I need to take a little break and move a bit. Do you feel like doing a little walking after sitting so long on the train?" She says as she rises from the chair.

"Yes, that would be lovely." He says. She excuses herself to use the facilities.

When she returns, Sigi has already paid the check and holds her coat out for her. "Look what I found by your coat." There in his hand the photograph he sent her. "Who is this handsome rascal?" He holds up the photograph next to his face and tries to compose the same smile.

"Sigi, I have missed you terribly." She takes his arm as they leave.

"I can't believe we've been talking for two hours. Where would you like to go?" He asks.

"We aren't far from the Castle Square. We could walk around and look at some of the shops." Gerti says as she buttons her coat and pulls on her gloves.

"Lead the way, my lady."

During the next two hours, they slowly walked through the shops along the square. Sigi tells her of his internship with the printing company. During those years, in the evenings he taught football skills to young boys and took classes at the university.

He received certification in accounting and taught the craftsmanship of bookbinding for several years. Eventually, a large female prison complex hired him to be their accountant.

"Gerti, I've had a hard life. I've always worked hard, and my children have been a joy. I'm very close to my son. We practically live on top of each other. My daughter has been married for the last few years, but I don't get to see her very often. When I retired from the prison, she took over my job."

Gerti's War

"I have a small pension to keep me going, but not much else to my name." He says in a low voice. "Can you tell me about you? I want to hear everything, and I can't wait much longer." He stops walking and rubs his hands together to warm them up.

"Yes, I'll tell you about myself. I was in Berlin when the war ended. Do you remember my friend Leni?"

"I remember Louise, and yes, now I remember you talking about her. By the way, thank you for writing as often as you did. Your letters gave me much joy." He gently places her hand on his arm as they continue walking. She can feel the electricity shooting up her arm even with gloves on. He holds her hand in place.

"Leni and my friend Paul were able to get me out of Berlin just as the Russians moved in. In fact, we saw them down the street. We made it to the American zone, and after going through processing at several locations, I was sent to a Prisoner of War camp. They didn't like my authorization papers and my 'top secret clearance'. It took months before they released me and I had to walk home too. Now, I don't remember much about that journey. I just wanted to get home in one piece."

"Did they treat you well in the camp?"

"Yes, better than at some camps, but once I returned home, I dug my heels in and didn't want to leave again for years. I worked for six years with the Center for Displaced Persons and then worked as a bookkeeper for forty years. Strange, how we are both accountants." She said as she stops to admire a dress in a shop window.

"I met Hugo at a football game and we courted for over two years before we married. It took forever to get all my trousseau items together. Remember how hard supplies were to get back then?"

"I remember. I bet you were a beautiful bride. Are you hungry yet or too cold? How about we stop at that little restaurant over there for dinner?" He points to a quaint shop with heavy rough timber beams and stone arched windows.

"That would be fine. Sigi, do you have any photographs of your family with you?"

"Yes, they are old, but I have some in my suitcase."

"Aren't you tired of carrying your bag around? Would you like to check into your hotel before we eat?"

"No, I'd rather talk to you some more. Don't give my suitcase another thought."

They entered the restaurant. He helped her remove her coat and held the chair out for her. "Danke." She says again as her face flushes a deep crimson. They quickly order entrees before the conversation starts up again.

"So, you married Hugo. Tell me about him."

"Hugo was my rock." She smiles and looks up at the gray clouds outside the window. He was a kind-hearted man who loved to smoke cigars. He loved to keep busy and worked as an engraver for years." She pulls out a set of keys from her bag. "See this keychain and fob? Hugo made it for me. The detail is quite good."

Sigi examined it and agreed to the craftsmanship. "Hugo was in the infantry, captured in Belgium, and sent to a Prisoner of War camp in Scotland. I was lucky to meet him when I did. Not many young men came home from the war in our district. We lived on the upper floors of my parents' house during our married life. We had a small kitchen up there, living room, bath and bedroom. On Sundays, we would have dinner with my parent's downstairs. Everyone got along well. My father died in the early 80's and my mother died the year Hugo did. Now, my house is too quiet. What else do you want to know?"

"Have you traveled much? What do you do for fun?" He says as his eyes dance.

"Yes, Hugo and I traveled quite a bit. We went to Turkey, Israel, Spain, France, the United States, and England. I have pen pals all over the world and I write to them and visit when I can. I speak a little English, some Spanish, and a little Hebrew, and I am good with French. For fun, I work in the garden. My little raised beds are just so." She motions with her hands into small rectangular partitions.

"Gravel walkways beside the house?" He says as he leans in closer to her.

Gerti's War

"Yes, it's very neat and practical."

"What vegetables will you grow this spring?"

"Maybe you have some suggestions for me." She says, flirting back with a big smile.

He reached across the table and caressed the side of her face. "Oh Gerti, you don't know how much meeting you has meant to me. I feel like a young man of twenty again."

"Yes Sigi, it is a good thing for both of us, but it's getting late; do you think we could spend more time together tomorrow?"

"As you wish." He says as he lifts her hand from the table and kisses her palm in a long deep kiss.

It takes a few moments for Gerti to compose herself. Her eyes opened wide. She places her hand into her lap so that he cannot see the uncontrolled shaking they are now making. Grabbing her leg doesn't do much good as her leg begins to shake as well.

"Please allow me to escort you to your hotel. What was the address again?"

Gerti softly names the hotel and address before he helps her out of the chair and into her coat. "Sigi please let me pay for dinner. You paid for lunch."

"I invited you to dinner remember, it's my treat." He leaves the table for a moment and pays the bill before they leave the restaurant.

"Sigi let me take care of everything tomorrow as my treat. I have many things I want to show you."

He frowns and quickly looks away. "Gerti, maybe the young people today pass along the expenses between themselves, but it's something I've never done before. It makes me uncomfortable."

She smiles as she holds on to his hand and gives it a little squeeze. "Trust me, you'll love it. It will be my pleasure."

Walking the few blocks to the hotel, they enter the lobby with their hair blown into wild array. Quickly, they both try to arrange their hair into some order while Gerti nervously moves her purse from hand to hand. "Sigi, this evening has been a dream. What time would you like to meet tomorrow? Where are you staying by the way?"

Sigi stands in front of her and gently lifts her chin to look right into his eyes. "Gerti, would you mind if our evening didn't end quite yet? Please let me walk you to your door."

"When you look at me like that, I can't remember a thing." She says with a giggle. "Wait a minute while I get my key and look at the room number." She fumbles with the contents of her purse before holding up a brass key with the hotel tag attached.

"Allow me." He says as he leads her to the elevator and pushes the button for the third floor. The elevator door opens, and he walks her to the door as he put his suitcase on the floor.

With a quick turn of the knob, he opens the door for her. For the first time this evening, there is a long moment of silence between them.

Sigi picks up his bag and places it inside as the door closes. Gerti walks across the room and turns on the light, illuminating the small chintz decorated room with a full-size bed and heavily carved wooden furniture. A small bathroom is visible adjacent in the back of the room. She turns to say something to him, but he cuts her off before she can get out the first word.

"Gerti, I know this is awkward for us, but I have something very important to ask you." He walks across the room, takes off his coat, and drapes it into the chair before taking her hands in his. "It has been ten years since I've held a woman in my arms. Would you mind, I mean-could you let me hold you for a while? What I miss most these ten years is the long agonizing emptiness of the night. I promise to be a gentleman." He says lowering his eyes and holding his arms out ever so lightly.

Gerti takes off her coat and gloves placing them on the chair next to his coat. She keeps her back to him as she takes off her shoes and walks over to the bed. "Sigi, why don't you join me here for a while?" She says patting the bed. "It may be a tight fit, but I'm tired of hugging a flat pillow."

"Are you sure?"

Gerti's War

"Yes. Funny how you miss the little things the most, isn't it? I miss Hugo's shaving gear in the bathroom and his slippers out on the porch."

From behind Sigi pulls her into his arms. "I miss the smell of her shampoo on the pillow beside me and the way she would say 'you never know…'." He takes a deep breath against her neck.

"Gerti, you smell like a fresh rain storm on a summer's day." He snuggles his chin in against her neck taking long deep breaths.

Gerti takes one of his hands and holds it out for inspection. "When we were younger I was captivated by your hands. They still hold my attention." She turns them over many times. "Hands have never affected me with anyone but you." Her breathing slows and gets deeper. She closes her eyes for a moment and whispers to Sigi, "Tomorrow would you like to meet some of my friends and go to the car museum?"

"As you wish, my Queen." Are the last words she hears as she falls into a deep sleep.

Gerti awakes with a jolt, her whole body awakening in an instant. She is lying on the bed in a hotel room with a man spooned against her back. It takes a few blinks for the past evening to come back to her. After a several deep breaths, she slowly turns her head and gazes at the still sleeping Sigi beside her, his mouth turned in a very slight smile. A beam of filtered light from the window illuminates him. Gerti leans over and kisses him lightly on the cheek.

It isn't until she is in the bathroom with the door closed that she realizes she had just spent the night with another man! *Heavens! What will her friends say if they see Sigi coming out of her room so early in the morning?* She holds on to the edge of the sink and looks into the mirror. Turning on the water, splashing her face and combing her hair into waves does nothing to settle her nervous stomach.

She pulls her shoulders back and gazes into the mirror again. *I've done nothing wrong and I won't let them judge my actions. I'm lucky to have time with Sigi and I plan on enjoying myself.* After a quick brushing of her teeth, she says out loud to her reflection, "He's mine for the day."

She quietly turns the handle of the door and peeks into the bedroom. He is still sleeping in the same position. Walking softly across the room she gathers clean clothes and after a quick change in the bathroom she kneels beside the bed. "Sigi….Sigi, wake up sweetheart." She whispers into his ear.

His smile broadens wider, but his eyes remained closed. "Say that again." He murmurs.

As she leans in to whisper again, he grabs her shoulders and kisses her hard and long on the lips.

The world melts away for both as a deep hunger takes over. Electricity shoots out of her hands and feet and the room spins off its axis.

"Now, THAT'S the way to wake up in the morning." Sigi says as he holds her against his chest. "You make my whole body come alive, Gerti."

"Yes, you certainly made me feel alive. My limbs have been tingling in a new and wonderful way. I can feel you touching me before you do. It's as if your body was sending little sparks out caressing me."

His eyes pool with tears as he responds. "Gerti, that's one of the nicest things anyone has ever said to me. We do have some sort of connection, don't we?"

She kisses him on the cheek and says, "I'll go downstairs and get you some coffee while you change and get ready. Okay?"

"My lady, I can be ready in five minutes."

Gerti returns to the room with two cups of coffee in her hands. Sigi sits on the bed and tying his shoes. Next to him are a few snapshots lying on the made-up bed. She joins him as she hands him a cup. "Would you mind if I look at these?"

"I brought them for you." He shows her photographs of his son and a wedding photograph of his daughter and her husband.

"You and Ana?"

Gerti's War

"Yes. This was taken before her diagnosis, breast cancer. She looks healthy and happy in this shot. All her dark curly hair fell out with the treatments. She managed a small wholesale business until she got too sick to work. Her illness lasted five years. My daughter had a hard time dealing with it."

"You have beautiful children, Sigi."

"*Danke.* I told my son about visiting you, but I haven't said anything to my daughter. She's been trying to set me up with dates for years. This is the first time I've been interested, and Gerti, I am VERY interested." He drops the photos into his suitcase.

Gerti quickly changes the subject and reaches for her pocketbook. "Let's go down and have a little breakfast. They have some hard rolls and jelly and maybe a little fruit, and we can plan our day."

At breakfast, they decide to visit the automotive museums of Mercedes and Porsche before taking the train down to Boblingen to re-visit the neighborhood where they met. Memories come flooding back as they try to capture the past. Landmarks are few and a new business encompasses the old Communication building site.

Everything is modernized. The narrow brick streets are now wide avenues with sidewalks. The character of the city has lost its touch of history.

Arriving back at the hotel later in the day, they meet a few of Gerti's friends in the lobby and join them for a drink. She explained to her friends she is going to take Sigi to old Strasbourg the next day and would miss the big dinner with all the girls. Quickly, they leave the women before too many questions come their way. Gerti didn't miss the expression on Helga's face as she nodded her approval.

They dine in a small Italian restaurant a few blocks away and celebrate with two bottles of Riesling white wine. Leaving the restaurant, they walk back to the hotel.

"Gerti, this has been one of the best days of my life. Thank you." He says as he lifts her hand and places it on his shoulder. He spins her around and softly sings a waltz melody in her ear.

"How long can you stay? Sigi, do you have to get back home?"

He stops the waltz at the entrance of the hotel. "I had to get a visa and it isn't an easy process. I spent an entire day at the visa office waiting for processing and they made me come back the next day to pick it up. I have a three-month allowance. Right now, I don't see any reason to return. Do you?"

Gerti looks at her watch and says quickly, "I checked the train schedule and we can take the 8:00 o'clock train, spend the day in Strasbourg, and then take the bus to Arnbach." She pauses before adding, "Sigi, would you come back home with me?"

His eyes flood with emotion. He kisses her hand again and says, "Your most humble servant."

Chapter 17 – February 1993

The wind died during the night and when they step off the train in Strasbourg, the weather is cool and clear. The spires of the Cathedral of Notre Dame can be seen far in the distance, standing like a majestic pink angel hovering over the city.

Closer inspection reveals dark black renovation scaffolding covering parts of the lower gothic tower sections. Many of the buildings they pass are undergoing some sort of renovation.

The older buildings are easy to recognize, as their rooflines consist of a series of bumps, holes, and creative wood patching. A few large stork nests are stuffed into some of the tallest chimneys. The ancient buildings displayed charm and character as the buildings themselves resembled faces; some with eyes shut (windows missing), wrinkles (curved roofs) and leaning doors (lopsided grins). Gerti points to a block of old homes, leans towards Sigi and whispers, "I think that roof is beyond repair."

"Nothing is impossible, Gerti. I'm here right now with you."

As they get closer to the Cathedral, gargoyles and waterspouts reveal themselves as they decorate the ragged corners. They stop to have a cup of coffee at a street café at the edge of the cobblestone section known as Old Town.

"I always dreamed of coming here with you, Gerti. Please let's take a boat ride on the canal over there." He says as he points to the walled partition. "I know it will be cold, but they have protective plastic sides up on the boats. What do you say, feel like a boat ride?"

"Sure, maybe we could do that after lunch. Let's stop at the hotel over there and see if we can store our luggage for the day so we don't have to carry them. I want to buy a disposable camera too. Let me know if you see one for sale around here."

After finishing tea and coffee and securing their luggage, they head for the cathedral. The massive stone courtyard surrounding the building is completely enclosed with restaurants and shops looking as though they hadn't changed in four hundred years. Many original signs and historical markers swing in the breeze.

"Sigi, close your eyes and take a deep breath. Now, imagine its 1820 and the courtyard is filled with peasants and merchants from all over France. The noise around the church is loud with vendors of all types. Can you see their faces? Hear the horses' hooves on the stones? What do you think people thought of this church the first time they saw it? Look at the rose window... oh, I can't wait to get inside."

"Yes, I can see and smell it! I've never done this before—stepping back into history in my mind. I can smell horses, pigs and chickens, and the peasants. Wow! They stink too. Ha! This is a pleasure."

Absorbed in the details of its history, he stops to read a large plaque on the building. "They don't open for a few more minutes, let's walk around the church. Started in 1015..." He says lightly as he tries to keep up with her.

"After we tour the cathedral, what else would you like to do, besides the canal?"

"When I visited during the war, it had a different atmosphere here. Not many people were out on the streets and the square was filled with many soldiers. Of course, when the weather is warm, I bet this courtyard gets crowded. Let's find that camera. I'd like to get several pictures of us together and just spend the day with you, Gerti. Let's get food for a picnic lunch."

Gerti and Sigi walk for hours before taking the canal ride.

The tour of the cathedral takes a while as they waited to see the astrological clock inside strike noon. Strolling along the shop avenue, Gerti purchases a gift for his son and daughter. Sigi is entranced at the selection at a food specialty store and fills his basket with many different items including a small red checked tablecloth and a tiny hand-painted plate for them to share.

Wrapping in the blankets provided by the water taxi, they snuggle together to keep warm. They are alone except for the boat operator. Geri's cheeks are flushed, but as much from the cold as from Sigi's presence. Leaning over to him, she whispers into his ear, "Sigi, my cheeks hurt from smiling so much." The

Gerti's War

ride passes quickly. They hurry to get their bags from the hotel and meet the bus at the central station.

The bus is crowded and Gerti points out places of interest to Sigi along the way. Pockets of deep Edel pine forests begin to cover the landscape as they get closer to Arnbach. Gerti identifies sections of the woods that are beginning to die from acid rain pollutants. Sigi sits quietly, fidgeting in his seat as they near the city. He holds her hand and listens closely to her stories.

She tells him about Helmut and the problems that they might encounter with Hugo's side of the family. The words spill out faster and faster.

"I am having trouble keeping up with who is who." Sigi says.

"I am sorry, I must be rattling on a bit."

"Gerti, it will be all right." He pats her hand.

Dusk is falling as they pull into the small station in Arnbach. The neighborhood grocery store illuminates the street.

Gerti nods her head in the direction of her home and they begin to walk. The streets have long shadows stretching across their way. The pavement has a recent light dusting of snow on it. Sigi holds onto her arm as she leads him to the house. They pass a few of Geri's friends near the grocery store.

"Welcome to my home, Sigi." She says, fumbling with the keys as she stops on the corner in front of a large two-story house.

Their footsteps mark the otherwise pristine snow on the driveway. She pauses for a moment at the bottom of the porch steps and Sigi gently takes the keys from her. "Allow me." He says as he leads her to the front door. She checks the mailbox as he puts the key into the lock. The heavy wooden door opens and they both enter, put down their suitcases and Gerti reaches for the light switch.

"Gerti, it's so big, it's beautiful." He says with awe.

She points to the brass rack by the door and tells him, "Put your coat, and wet shoes here." She leaves him for a moment and returns with a pair of Hugo's slippers in her hands. "I hope these will fit." She says as she places the shoes on the floor.

She turns, walks into the kitchen, and puts water in the kettle to boil. "Would you care for some tea? How about I give you a quick tour of my home while the water is boiling?"

Sigi enters the kitchen wearing a tight pair of slippers and a big smile on his face. "They fit perfectly." He says as he points his toes. The fabric is stretched to the limits. His long thin foot pushes against the shoe that is a size too small.

Geri's home tour is delayed as she begins showing him everything in the kitchen and pantry. Windows line one wall of the pantry and the sill is packed with potted plants of all kinds. A selection of Geri's shoes lines the hallway on the floor out to the garden. They are on their second cup of tea before they leave the room. An hour later, the home tour and history lesson are complete, and they are back in the kitchen. Out of breath, Gerti sits down at the kitchen table.

"Ahhh, I didn't know I could talk so much. I'm sorry Sigi; you probably didn't want to know so much detail about my past. I over-did it when I showed you all those knickknacks. Are you hungry? Let me check to see what is in the refrigerator." She says as she gets up and opens the refrigerator. Sigi comes up behind her, pulls her back up, and turns her around.

"Gerti, you don't have to worry about that right now." He says as he leans in toward her and takes her in a deep embrace.

"Thank you. Thank you for inviting me and making me feel so welcome." He pulls back slightly and kisses her. "I'd rather have you for dinner." He says as he kisses her again.

"Sigi, you make me all light headed. It has been such a wonderful day. I don't want it to end." She walks over to the table and sits down again. "Having you here—seeing you standing in this room… I, I must be dreaming." She shakes her head and rubs her eyes as she smiles.

Gerti manages to keep Sigi's visit quiet for a few days, and they only venture out of the house a few times. On the fifth day, word of her visitor reaches her family and they have company.

Gerti's War

Gerti and Sigi have just finished a large dinner and are sitting in the dining room. The dishes are still on the table in front of them and they are quietly talking when there is a knock at the door. Sigi gets up to answer the door for her, but she motions him to sit back down. She takes a deep breath before opening the door.

"Helmut and Gudrun, what a pleasant surprise! Please come in. There is someone I'd like for you to meet." She says trying to sound light-hearted. They enter the foyer and keep their coats buttoned. Pursed lips and woolen scarves are tightly wrapped around their necks making their heads look small compared to the thick coats bundled around them.

"Afternoon, Gerti." Says Helmut as his eyes fix on Sigi.

His voice is pitched, and she can tell he is agitated. "Helmut and Gudrun Zimmermann." He says without taking Sigi's outstretched hand. He moves to stand in front of Gerti and says, "Gerti, can we have a word ALONE with you?"

"Helmut, first you must shake hands with Sigmund Rhinehart, an old friend of mine from the war." She steps back and Sigi extends his hand in greeting again.

Reluctantly, Helmut takes Sigi's hand and gives it a short shake before withdrawing it quickly. "Gerti, we have some urgent business to discuss with you. Herr Rhinehart, would you excuse us for a moment?"

Sigi starts to leave the room, but Gerti stops him. She grabs Sigi by the arm and weaves her arm around his. "Sigi, don't mind Helmut, everything is urgent with him. I'd appreciate you staying right here."

Gudrun, who hasn't said a word, is shocked by Gerti's response and lets her mouth hang open. *Her opinions always echo those of her husband.* Gerti thinks to herself as she looks at Gudrun. *She hasn't had an original thought of her own since she married that narrow-minded man!*

"Helmut, would you like to sit down? We've just finished dinner, but there is some wine open. Would you care for a glass?"

She moves to the cabinet in the living room to get two more fluted stems.

"Harrumph!" Says Helmut as he fans his coat and stomps a few clumps of snow off his shoes. "Now Gerti, this is a family matter. Surely, you don't want to discuss family matters with a stranger? No, Gudrun and I do not want anything to drink."

Keeping her back to him, she fumbled with the glasses in the cabinet. "Helmut, I have known Sigi longer than I have known you.

He is no stranger to me. Now, tell me what you need to talk about so urgently?" She turns and places the empty wineglasses on the corner of the cabinet and sits down in a chair in the living room. Sigi walks over next to her. Gudrun still has her mouth hanging open as she stands in the doorway. Gerti notices Helmut's fists are clenched by his side and his face has turned a slight shade of red.

"Gerti, it has come to my attention and as head of this family, I have come here asking what ARE his intentions (pointing to Sigi) and how can YOU dishonor the memory of Hugo by having a man stay in your home? I forbid it! It is unthinkable! Have you lost your mind or are you under the influence of an unsavory character?!" His face turns a deep shade of purple by the time he finishes the last sentence and bits of spittle sit at the edges of his mouth.

Gerti feels Sigi's hand tense in response to the outburst, but before he could say anything, she rises out of the chair and stands directly in front of Helmut. "Helmut, YOU are not head of this family? What family? The family who stood by me for thirty years of my life with Hugo, never once welcoming me and making me feel a part of your family. I was always Hugo's wife, nothing more in your eyes. Every year I extend overtures of welcome to you and your brother and get nothing in return." She takes a step towards him as he retreats. "Where were you when I needed compassion and family after Hugo died?" She pauses, steps forward and takes another deep breath. "Hugo was ten times the man you will ever be. This MAN is my business and my business alone. He is a wonderful man, and I will not stand here

Gerti's War

in MY house and listen to you make insinuations regarding his character! Please leave!" She takes another step toward him as she steps around the coffee table.

"Now Gerti, I am only trying to look out for you. After all, you are a married woman--."

"Widowed, Helmut – widowed four years and counting every lonely night!" She continues to make her way toward him, leading them to the door.

Helmut grabs Gudrun arm as he opens the door and pushes her outside. "Gerti..."

"Helmut, until you can apologize to Herr Rhinehart and me, you are no longer welcome in my home. Do I make myself clear?" She shuts the door in his face before she can hear his answer.

Sigi comes up behind her and embraces her. She turns and hugs him back. "Sigi, could you get me a glass of water and my medication off the counter in the kitchen? I think it's time for another pill." She says as she walks back into the living room and plops down on the sofa.

Before she knows it, he is kneeling beside her with the water and medicine in hand. "Gerti, I don't want to be the cause of trouble with your family. Maybe I should leave?" He says.

She takes the tablet and swallows it. "Sigi, you've brought more life into me than I have felt in the last four years combined. I want you to stay."

She reaches out and puts her hand on his shoulder. "I've never stood up to that nasty little man before and it feels good!

Did you see the look on Gudrun's face? Her mouth was still hanging open when I shut the door! It's the first time I've gotten the last word in on him in my life and it is glorious!"

She closes her eyes and replays the speech in her mind. "Of course, I shouldn't have said that he isn't the head of the family, but it's how I really feel. For once, I said what I wanted to say right to his face! The family will probably shut me out of gatherings for a while and gossip is going to run rampant, but we'll live through it. "Quiet little Gerti Zimmermann is now a wanton woman!" She sighs and pauses before saying, "Sigi, would you mind holding me for a while?"

During the next two months Gerti and Sigi, use the time to get to know each other. They travel and do a little sightseeing, plan on what to plant in the garden, visit with friends in town, but most of all they enjoy staying at home and preparing delicious meals for each other. Helmut didn't apologize and most of the family stayed away from Gerti during his visit.

By the end of his stay, the gossip died down and people were talking about someone else in town. Many women pulled Gerti aside and commented on how handsome and attentive he was. *Frau* Trlica asked if he had any brothers who were single. They are greeted with smiles from many of the women in town. The men, however, rarely smiled back.

Sigi's has a heavy heart as he said "Good-bye," now that his Visa was close to expiring. They both cried at the station.

Promising to be together next month after her visit with Danuta, she gives him one last kiss.

The next day Helmut confronts her outside a friend's house as she walked down the sidewalk. "Gerti, the whole town has been talking about your behavior and how disrespectful you have been to Hugo's memory." His tirade continues as he spouts off his unrealistic views of the world around him. By the time he finishes, she can feel her heart tightening and her body begins to shake all over.

She slowly backs up and makes her way to the porch steps. Her friend, Pamela, who heard Helmut's outburst, runs to her aid and helps her into the house. After a few minutes inside, she says, "Gerti, we've got to get you to the clinic. Do you think you can walk to the car?" Gerti is hospitalized at the clinic for a few days while they check her heart rate and medications.

Agatha Trlica helps her around the house when she is discharged. They are sitting in the kitchen drinking tea and discussing Helmut. "I just don't like the man, never have. Do you know that he sent me a letter last week advising me to turn over my financial accounts to him while I was in the hospital? He doesn't come to see me, nor did anyone else in his family, but they did invite me to Horst's birthday party this weekend. He is just as bad as Helmut. How in the world did Hugo come out of that family?" She says as she blows on her tea.

"Gerti, I think you should talk to a lawyer or something. Make it perfectly clear by the law that you want nothing to do with Helmut or his brother in case you should have more health problems." Says Agatha as she cut a piece of butter cake. "This cake is really good. Why don't you try some?"

"No thanks Agatha. I haven't had much appetite lately. My energy reserves ran out when Sigi left. I'm going to eat healthy and start my walking again. Want to join me on my two-week renovation program? I can use the company." Gerti rises and drinks a tall glass of water.

"I'll try, but usually my hip starts to bother me when I walk too much. Why don't we start slow and see how it goes?" She says as she cuts another small piece of cake for herself. "Who gave you this cake?"

"I don't know. There were two cakes and some preserves on the shelf in there when I got back." She says as she points to the pantry door. "Maybe I should see a lawyer."

"It must be comforting to have a man around the house again. I don't want an argumentative man, just a helpmate, like Sigmund. If you get tired of him, I'll be glad to keep him company." Agatha says finishing off the last piece of cake. Crumbs cover the tablecloth in front of her, leaving a trail from the plate to her lap.

"Things are so different with Sigi than they were with Hugo. Maybe I didn't appreciate Hugo enough, but at my age, time without a life-partner has been misery. Hugo and I had planned to travel and do some projects together once Mutti passed, but we only had a few good months." Gerti reaches for a tissue and holds it in her hand. "Don't put your life on hold, Agatha. I'll never do it again. Sigi makes me feel strong and I look at life totally differently when he is around." Putting the cake dishes into a pile, she walks over to the sink. "Okay, Agatha, grab your walking shoes, I need to get some exercise, and you're coming with me."

Visiting Danuta and her daughter couldn't go by fast enough for Gerti. All she could think of was Sigi and how close she is to seeing him again. She watches her diet and continues her daily walks. She admits to Danuta how much better she is feeling now away from extended family. Danuta keeps a close eye on her during her visit and reviews her medications and heart rate during the week. Gerti feels younger and happier by the time she arrives in Grudziadz.

Sigi and a small crowd of people are waiting for her at the bus station. After a short embrace, he introduces his brothers Heinrich, Viktor, and wife Rosa. Sigi whispers to her that Edmund and Christina will be meeting them for dinner in a few hours. Conversing is difficult as Viktor is the only one who speaks a little German. They welcome Gerti with smiles and open arms.

Her reception group flows down the street and into a small restaurant. She takes in the incredible panoramic view from the side of the hill overlooking the Vistula River. Several bottles of wine are passed around as Heinrich stands, and gives a little welcoming speech. Sigi quietly translates a rough version into her ear. His warm breath on her neck gives her goosebumps.

Gerti is even welcomed by the other customers in the restaurant with toasts and greetings. She is overwhelmed to see such an outpouring of open hospitality among so many. "Sigi, everyone is so happy here. I am very touched by this reception." She says as she wipes a tear from the edge of her eye. "Do they do this for everyone?"

"Well, lots of my friends are here and we always are ready to celebrate. I'm bursting with pride having you by my side again." He says puffing out his chest and smiling to his brother again. "Everyone has been very curious about meeting you. I've done

Gerti's War

nothing but talk about you since I got back. How was your visit with Danuta and how are you feeling?"

"I feel absolutely fantastic!" She says as she raises her glass. "Please tell everyone I've looked forward to meeting them all and I'm working on learning Polish as soon as possible." She drains the glass. "To good friends, Slavic hospitality, and hope." She says as Sigi refills her glass.

Sigi's son, Edmund, gives them privacy and moves in with a friend during her visit. Sigi's apartment is small with two bedrooms, one bath, and a combination kitchen-living room area.

They are in the southern part of town near a complex of large industrial buildings. It is not very scenic in this area, but convenient in location to transportation. It only takes a short bus ride to get to the prison complex where Christina now works. Edmund's school is five blocks away.

They visit Edmunds' class and Gerti takes questions from a group of children regarding life in Germany. Sigi enjoys being the translator. The classroom has many posters on the walls, but textbooks and electronic equipment items are old and worn. The modern world has yet to catch up in this classroom. Sigi tells her, "They haven't had a budget increase in years. Edmund has been saving for three years to buy a computer."

The next day is clear and temperatures have warmed. Sigi carefully packs a picnic lunch for them. Gerti sits at the small table in the kitchen finishing her second cup of tea.

"I'm really excited about our trip today. How long will it take to get to the farm?"

"Oh, I haven't been in years. I guess we should be there in about an hour. They've made some changes to the house and split some of the acreage, but it should be beautiful this time of year." He says as he puts sandwiches into a rucksack.

"Before we get on the bus I want to buy you a hat of some kind. With all the walking we've done, you're getting a little pink on the tip of your nose." He kisses her nose. Would you like to go into the Old Town center first? There are lots of shops there and you can look until you find something you like."

"That's sounds great. Do you think we could find an electronic store in the area? One that carries calculators and computers?"

"Yes, but if you need to add figures, I'm a wiz." He turns and picks up a pad of paper and a pencil.

Gerti puts on her shoes and straightens her hair. "I'd like to buy a few calculators for Edmund's classroom. How can a teacher teach without good tools? I noticed several ancient versions around the room. Would he accept a gift like that?"

"Yes, he would be speechless and very appreciative. He spends a lot of time with those kids. My time was always focused on the sports field, but Edmund has been more studious." Sigi picks up the basket. "Ready?"

After spending a little longer than planned in Old Town buying a large floppy straw hat and pricing calculators, they catch the bus and head out of town. They pass several different monuments around town as they weave through narrow streets and onto the secondary roadway system. Sigi points to the castle that remains on a hillock and mentions he'd like for them to hike up there before she leaves. "It has a great view of the city; the whole valley is laid out for you."

"I'd like that. Sigi, when can you come visit again? Can we go to the Visa office while I'm here and get the paperwork started? It's quite unbearable for me to stay in Arnbach without you. Our garden is waiting." She says batting her eyelashes.

"Tomorrow, yes, tomorrow we will look into that." He says as he points out another special landmark for her. He has a faraway look in his eyes as talk about the history of the town.

They spend days in and out of the Visa office checking the status of his request. There is one delay after another and even paying a large bribe to the clerk doesn't move things along very well. Just before Gerti is scheduled to leave, Sigi receives word his visa has come through, but it is only for two weeks instead of three months. Disappointed, they can think only of the two days left of her visit.

Gerti's War

Sigi's daughter, Christina, has them over for dinner on Gerti's last night for a little celebration. After the meal, Christina's husband, Peter, stands and offers a toast to Gerti's safe journey. Their hospitality has been wonderful. Christina offers Gerti a beautiful lace tablecloth runner to take home with her.

"Christina, this has all been too much. I, I don't know what to say." Says Gerti.

"I made this years ago. I made it for Momma when she was going through her treatments. She died before I finished it. I want someone special in my father's life to have it. You've made him so happy." She says holding back the tears.

"Thank you. I will take good care of it." She gives her a hug and smiles at Peter.

"Before we leave tonight there is something I'd like to say to all of you." Sigi says as he looks at his family. Edmund glances quickly at Christina and smiles. "Gerti." He says as he helps her sit back down on the sofa. His knee popped with a definite bang as he put his weight on it. He takes her hands in his. "You've brought hope and love back into my life. Once I let you go, but never again. Time is too precious, family too rare." There is a slight pause before he says, "Gerti, will you marry me?" He looks up hopefully into her face.

"Oh Sigmund, yes, yes I will marry you." She says as tears run down her cheeks. She kisses him as Christina and Peter embrace and Edmund rushes in to hug his father. Everyone is hugging, kissing and laughing. Peter announces that he is going to open another bottle of wine and everyone raises their glasses.

"A family, I've got a family again." She says against Sigi's neck. "And, children..."

Sigi holds her against his chest and murmurs against her cheek, "If my last words are not 'I love you' you'll know it is on the tip of my tongue. I truly love you, Gerti, and I'm going to spend every minute showing you just how much I do."

"Sigi, you make me so happy, but should we live here or in Germany?" She looks up at him, questioning this big decision.

"Where would you like to live? I will follow you anywhere." He says still smiling.

Lois Buchter

"Sigi, we have so much room in Germany, and the garden, we could travel, and..."

"As you wish, my Queen." He says as he kisses her hand lovingly.

The End

About the Author

Lois has been an active storyteller for the last fifteen years. Gerti's War is her first non-fiction novel and the reason she started writing. Lois' life changed when she was visiting Gerti and extended family in Germany and a photo album fell out and onto her foot. That photograph showed Gerti's father wearing a WWII German uniform with another German officer in a wagon. Lois casually asked her cousin, "What did you do in the war?" However, she was not prepared for Gerti's answer. Gerti told Lois that she had been in the Hitler Youth and was fourteen when the war started. Lois literally dropped to her knees. The kindest woman she had ever known, couldn't be a "Nazi"? *Gerti's War* covers the years 1938-47 showing what life was like in Germany during the war and afterwards as taken from Gerti's journals from the time and the stories she told.

Lois lives in California with the best dog in the world who happily sits at her feet while she writes. Occasionally she walks said dog, sculpts in marble, clay and stone; paints, cuts glass and works in fiber arts. Lois sees the world differently and pursues her love of a good story in novels and screenplays. She has previously self-published a children's fairytale, *Legend of Cinnamon Valley*, under the pen name Lois Frazier. Lois has written two other books; and is a screenwriter with several screenplays, teleplays, and shorts in her portfolio. She also works with children teaching classes…

www.ingramcontent.com/pod-product-compliance
Lightning Source LLC
Chambersburg PA
CBHW070421010526
44118CB00014B/1845